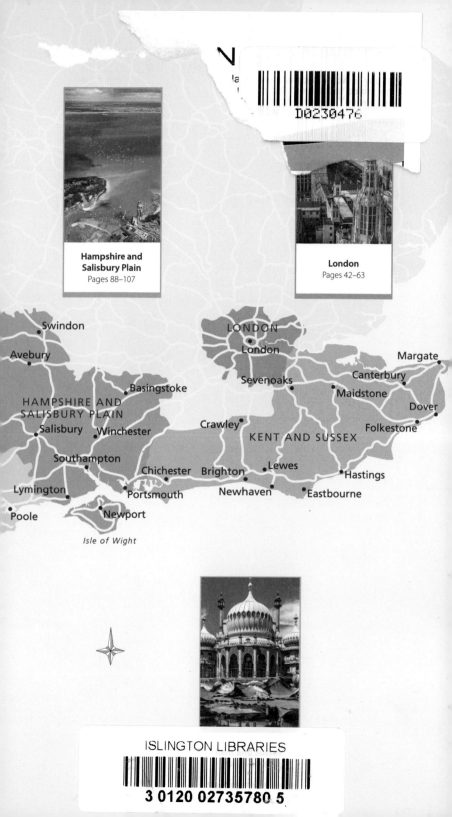

Hampshire and Salisbury Plain
Pages 88–107

London
Pages 42–63

Swindon

Avebury

LONDON

London

Sevenoaks

Margate

Canterbury

Basingstoke

Maidstone

HAMPSHIRE AND
SALISBURY PLAIN

Dover

Salisbury   Winchester

Crawley

Folkestone

KENT AND SUSSEX

Southampton

Chichester   Brighton   Lewes

Hastings

Lymington

Portsmouth

Newhaven   Eastbourne

Poole   Newport

Isle of Wight

EYEWITNESS TRAVEL

England's South Coast

DK EYEWITNESS TRAVEL

England's South Coast

Main Contributors **Ros Belford, Leonie Glass, Matthew Hancock, Nick Rider, Joe Staines, Amanda Tomlin**

Managing Editor MadhuMadhavi Singh
Editorial Manager Shikha Kulkarni
Senior Manager Design and Cartography
Priyanka Thakur
Project Editor Beverly Smart
Editor Parnika Bagla
Project Designer Stuti Tiwari Bhatia
Designer Bhavika Mathur
Cartography Manager Suresh Kumar
Senior Cartographer Subhashree Bharati
Senior DTP Designer Azeem Siddiqui
DTP Designer Tanveer Zaidi
Picture Researcher Susie Peachey

Main Contributors
Ros Belford, Leonie Glass, Matthew Hancock,
Nick Rider, Joe Staines, Amanda Tomlin

Illustrators
Peter Bull Art Studio, Arun Pottirayil

Printed in China

First published in Great Britain in 2017
by Dorling Kindersley Limited
80 Strand, London WC2R 0RL

17 18 19 20 10 9 8 7 6 5 4 3 2 1

Copyright © 2017 Dorling Kindersley
Limited, London
A Penguin Random House Company

A CIP catalogue record is available
from the British Library.

ISBN 978-0-24129-031-6

MIX
Paper from
responsible sources
FSC™ C018179
www.fsc.org

The iconic Houses of Parliament and
Big Ben clock tower, London

Introducing England's South Coast

Colourful terraced houses lining the harbourfront at the resort of Weymouth, Dorset

◀ **Title page** Spectacular Durdle Door, Dorset   **Front cover image** Ilfracombe Harbour and St Nicholas Chapel, Devon
Back cover image Stonehenge, England's most famous prehistoric monument

Contents

Church of St Michael de Rupe in Dartmoor National Park, Devon

Mountain biking along the stunning coastline of the Isle of Wight

Illustration of the open-air Great Bath at the Roman Baths complex in Bath, Somerset

HOW TO USE THIS GUIDE

This guide helps you to get the most from your visit to England's South Coast. It provides detailed practical information and expert recommendations. *Introducing England's South Coast* maps the region, sets it in its historical and cultural context, and describes events through the entire year. *England's South Coast Region by Region* is the main sightseeing section, which covers all the important sights with maps, photographs and illustrations. Information on hotels, restaurants, shopping, entertainment and outdoor activities is found in *Travellers' Needs*. The *Survival Guide* has advice on everything from visas, personal security and health to getting around, money and communications.

ENGLAND'S
SOUTH COAST
REGION BY
REGION

England's South Coast at a Glance	40–41
London	42–63
Kent and Sussex	64–87
Hampshire and Salisbury Plain	88–107
Dorset and Somerset	108–131
Devon	132–151
Cornwall	152–169

England's South Coast Region by Region

England's South Coast has been divided into six regions, each with a separate chapter. The most interesting places to visit have been numbered on a *Regional Map* at the beginning of each chapter.

1 Introduction
The landscape, history and character of each region is described here, showing how the area has developed over the centuries and what it offers the visitor today.

2 Regional Map
This shows the road network and airports and gives an overview of the entire region. All the sights are numbered here and there are also useful tips on getting around.

Sights at a Glance lists all the chapter's sights, following the numbering on the *Regional Map*.

A suggested route for a walk is shown with a dotted red line.

Stars indicate the sights that no visitor should miss.

3 Street-by-Street Map
This gives a bird's-eye view of a key area covered in the chapter. The numbered sights have fuller descriptions on the pages that follow.

4 Detailed information

All the important towns and other places to visit are described individually. They are listed in order, following the numbering on the *Regional Map*.

Each region of England's South Coast can be quickly identified by its colour coding.

Story boxes highlight a special feature or interesting story about the town or sight.

A tour suggests the best route covering all the sights in an area of natural beauty or historical interest.

5 Town Map

Major towns have a map showing the main sights, each of which is described in detail. The map also shows the town's transport hubs.

The Visitors' Checklist provides all the practical information needed to plan your visit.

6 Top Sights in England's South Coast

These are given two full pages. Places of interest are shown from a bird's-eye view, with specific sights and features picked out and described, and accompanied by images.

Numbered circles point out major features of the sight listed in the key.

Directories contain contact details for all the organizations and companies mentioned in the text.

7 Practical Information

The *Travellers' Needs* and *Survival Guide* sections offer information on practical aspects such as visas and paperwork, responsible travel, health, money, hotels, restaurants, entertainment, activities and shops.

INTRODUCING ENGLAND'S SOUTH COAST

DISCOVERING ENGLAND'S SOUTH COAST

The itineraries on the following pages have been designed to cover many of the South Coast's finest sights, while keeping long-distance travel to a minimum. First comes a week-long exploration of the South East, beginning in London, before heading to Kent and then travelling westwards across the chalk downs of Sussex and Hampshire. A week spent in the South West takes in the golden sands of Poole, the windswept landscape of Dartmoor and the elegance of Georgian Bath. The spectacular coastline itself is a major feature of both tours, with trips to the magnificent Seven Sisters cliffs in Sussex, the naval stronghold of Portsmouth and the fossil-rich beaches of Dorset. Each itinerary offers some additional suggestions for those wishing to extend their stay. Select and combine the tours that most appeal, or simply dip in and out for inspiration.

Dartmoor
With its rugged moorland scenery and dramatic waterfalls, Dartmoor has much to offer lovers of the great outdoors. The moor covers a massive quantity of granite, which has been used as a building material since the Bronze Age.

Key
— A Week in the South East
— A Week in the South West

Lynmouth
Barnstaple
Exm
Clovelly
Bude
Boscastle
Tintagel
Dartmo
St Austell
Plymouth
St Ives
Land's End

A Week in the South West

- Get in touch with nature in the **New Forest**, where England's Norman kings hunted deer.

- Scour the sandy beach at **Lyme Regis** for fossils, evidence of the prehistoric past of Dorset's coastline.

- Experience the dark and brooding landscape of **Dartmoor**, the setting for Arthur Conan Doyle's famous Sherlock Holmes mystery novel *The Hound of the Baskervilles*.

- Soak up the enchanting atmosphere of pretty **Tintagel**, the legendary home of King Arthur and the Knights of the Round Table.

- Climb to the top of **Glastonbury Tor** for fabulous long-distance views across the unique watery landscape of the Somerset Levels.

- Learn how the Romans in Britain relaxed with a visit to the baths they built in the city of **Bath**.

Bath
The baths and temple, built around a natural hot spring, were the centre of civic life in Roman Bath.

◄ *Hastings* (1810), an unfinished sketch by Joseph Mallord William Turner

Portsmouth
This city is home to HMS *Warrior*, the Royal Navy's first iron-hulled warship. Launched in 1860, it was turned into a museum in 1987.

A Week in the South East

- Marvel at the splendour of **Westminster Abbey**, the location for royal coronations since 1066.

- View the majestic **Seven Sisters** white cliffs, one of England's most spectacular sights.

- Enjoy the sea air in lively **Brighton**, home to attractive Regency-era buildings, George IV's Royal Pavilion and the fun-filled Brighton Pier.

- Discover how England ruled the waves by visiting some of the navy's most historic ships in **Portsmouth**.

- See the house in **Chawton** where Jane Austen spent her final years and completed her most famous novels.

- Explore the beautiful city of **Winchester**, King Alfred the Great's ancient capital.

Bristol
Bath
Newbury
Windsor
London
Chatham
Somerset Levels
Guildford
Royal Tunbridge Wells
Dunster
Glastonbury Tor
Chawton
Crawley
Glastonbury
Winchester
Taunton
Southampton
Lewes
Battle
Rye
Cerne Abbas
Lyndhurst
New Forest
Chichester
Brighton
Poole
Portsmouth
Seaford
Seven Sisters
eter
Lyme Regis
Dorchester
Abbotsbury
Alum Bay
Isle of Wight
Sidmouth

0 kilometres 40
0 miles 40

Brighton
A thriving seaside town, Brighton has had three piers since it became a fashionable resort in the late 18th century. Only one, Brighton Pier, built in 1899, is still intact and open to the public.

A Week in the South East

- **Airports** Heathrow is 22 km (14 miles) west of central London, and Gatwick 48 km (30 miles) south of central London. Both have express trains that link with London's Underground network.

- **Transport** A car is necessary to cover most of this tour, but is not recommended for travel in London. Main cities and towns are linked by rail.

Tower Bridge, a flamboyant piece of Victorian engineering that opened in 1894

Day 1: London

Start your day at the **Tower of London** *(see p61)* and enjoy a tour with a Beefeater. Then walk west to the Monument, Sir Christopher Wren's column commemorating the Great Fire of London. Cross London Bridge for a view of **Tower Bridge** *(see p61)*, and forage for lunch at the food stalls of **Borough Market** *(see p193)*. Spend the afternoon admiring modern art at **Tate Modern** *(see p60)*. Cross the stunning Millennium Bridge to see **St Paul's Cathedral** *(see pp58–9)*, and have dinner in the City before watching a play at **Shakespeare's Globe** *(see p60)*.

Day 2: London

Take a self-guided tour around **Westminster Abbey** *(see pp50–51)*, and stroll through Parliament Square into serene St James's Park. Skirt the lakeside to reach **Horse Guards Parade** *(see p49)*, where mounted sentries trot in at 11am for the **Changing of**

the Guard *(see p46)*. Then wander through **Trafalgar Square** *(see p52)* into Chinatown. After a dim sum lunch here, visit the **National Gallery** *(see pp52–3)*, packed with masterpieces. End the day with supper at the Piazza in **Covent Garden** *(see p53)*.

Day 3: Royal Tunbridge Wells

Pretty **Royal Tunbridge Wells** *(see p70)* has been a fashionable spa town since the early 17th century. Visit the town's famous spring before exploring the upmarket shops housed in the elegant Pantiles promenade. Stop for lunch at **Thackeray's** *(see p186)*, and then head off on a drive to the lovely Scotney Castle, with its picturesque moat. Return to Tunbridge Wells in the evening.

Day 4: Rye and Seven Sisters

Head south through the High Weald, an ancient landscape of woodland, to **Rye** *(see pp78–9)*, once an important medieval fortified port. Travel west to the site of the Battle of Hastings, close to **Battle Abbey** *(see p80)*. Next, continue along the coast road to Seaford, gateway to one of the South Coast's most stunning viewpoints: along the chalk cliffs of the **Seven Sisters** *(see p81)*. Finish your day at the market town of **Lewes** *(see p81)*.

Day 5: Brighton and Chichester

Popularized two centuries ago by the Prince Regent, **Brighton** *(see pp82–3)* was one of Britain's first sea-bathing resorts and retains a stylish glamour. Tour the exotic **Royal Pavilion** *(see pp84–5)*, and then stroll along the Victorian

pier before enjoying a lunch of fish and chips on the seafront. In the afternoon, head along the coast road to **Chichester** *(see p87)*, a city dominated by its medieval cathedral. Round off the day with a show at the Chichester Festival Theatre (advance booking required).

Day 6: Portsmouth

A few miles outside Chichester is **Fishbourne Roman Palace** *(see p87)*. The largest surviving Roman villa in Britain, it contains exquisite mosaics. From here, continue along the coast to **Portsmouth** *(see p94)* and explore some of the city's famous ships, such as HMS *Victory* and HMS *Warrior*. For a fantastic view of the harbour, visit the 170-m (558-ft) **Spinnaker Tower** *(see p94)* on the waterfront.

> **To extend your trip...**
> From Portsmouth, take a car ferry to the **Isle of Wight** *(see p95)*. Visit Osborne House, the retreat of Queen Victoria, and admire the multicoloured sands of Alum Bay.

Day 7: Winchester

Jane Austen wrote most of her novels at her home in **Chawton** *(see p92)*, 45 km (28 miles) north of Portsmouth. The house is now a museum, filled with plenty of memorabilia, including a lovely patchwork quilt Austen made herself. From here it is a short drive to **Winchester** *(see pp92–3)*. Step into the Great Hall to see King Arthur's (alleged) Round Table, then tour the Norman cathedral and find Austen's grave.

The Seven Sisters, dramatic chalk cliffs at the mouth of the River Cuckmere, East Sussex

Pretty thatched cottages at Swan Green, on the outskirts of Lyndhurst, in Hampshire

A Week in the South West

- **Airports** International visitors to southwest England will usually arrive at Heathrow or Gatwick, but there are also airports at Bristol and Exeter.
- **Transport** A car is needed to cover the places on this tour.

Day 1: New Forest
The **New Forest** (see p97) has a name that is rather misleading; claimed as a new royal hunting ground by the Normans, it is one of the oldest areas of woodland in the South. Start your day at **Lyndhurst** (see p97), a village with many pubs. There are great walks from here and plenty of wildlife to see, including the wild New Forest ponies. Leave the forest at Ringwood for the seaside town of **Poole** (see pp112–13). Enjoy a dip at Sandbanks beach followed by supper at **Rick Stein** (see p189) restaurant.

Day 2: Dorset
Head southwest for the historic market town of **Dorchester** (see p118), immortalized by Thomas Hardy as the setting for The Mayor of Casterbridge and surrounded by picturesque villages. Essential stops nearby include the famous **Cerne Abbas Giant** (see p119) and Hardy's childhood home at Higher Bockhampton. Head west to **Abbotsbury** (see p115), with its medieval Swannery and lovely gardens, then follow the coast to **Lyme Regis** (see p117) to look for fossils along the beach.

Day 3: Exeter
After a morning walk on the Cobb, Lyme Regis's famous harbour wall, continue west to **Exeter** (see pp136–7), stopping off at the Regency seaside resort of **Sidmouth** (see p137) for a mid-morning coffee. In Exeter, start by visiting the 14th-century cathedral, before braving the **Underground Passages** (see p137), the city's medieval water-supply system. Finish with an evening meal at the **Jack in the Green** (see p190) pub.

Magnificent 14th-century vaulting in the nave of Exeter Cathedral, Devon

Day 4: Dartmoor, Boscastle and Tintagel
From Exeter it is a short drive to **Dartmoor** (see pp142–3), a landscape of brooding hills and granite tors. The Rock Inn at Haytor Vale is well placed for lunch after a hike on **Haytor**

Rocks (see p142). Next, drive west to **Boscastle** (see pp156–7) and spend the afternoon admiring the Cornish coast. It is a 6-km (4-mile) hike along the South West Coast Path to the ruins of **Tintagel Castle** (see p156), said to be the birthplace of King Arthur. Spend the evening in Boscastle.

> **To extend your trip...**
> Head south from Boscastle to **Land's End** (see p169), the westernmost point of England. En route visit pretty **St Ives** (see p168), home to Tate St Ives and the Barbara Hepworth Museum.

Day 5: The Atlantic Highway
The scenic Atlantic Highway runs along the north coast of Cornwall and Devon. The first stop is **Bude** (see p156). Once a bustling port, this town is now a magnet for families drawn to its beaches. At **Clovelly** (see p151), work up an appetite for a cream tea with a walk along Hobby Drive before heading to the busy market town of **Barnstaple** (see p149).

Day 6: Exmoor and Glastonbury
Dartmoor's softer sister, **Exmoor** (see pp122–3) is where heathery hills tumble to meet the sea in a succession of pretty villages. Trundle up the steep cliffs on the water-powered funicular railway in the fishing village of **Lynmouth** (see p148) and walk the ramparts at **Dunster Castle** (see p122). Next, head eastwards, across the wild heathland of the Quantock Hills to **Glastonbury** (see pp124–5). As the legendary site of the Holy Grail, the town has drawn visitors since the Middle Ages. It is now best known for its music festival.

Day 7: Bath
Charismatic **Bath** (see pp128–31) is an irresistibly beautiful city. Founded by the Romans, the immaculately restored open-air baths provide a glimpse of life in Roman Britain in the 1st century. There are guided tours of the city's Palladian terraces and crescents, which remain much as they did when Austen lived here over 200 years ago.

Putting England's South Coast on the Map

The region covered in this guide comprises the coastal counties of Kent, East Sussex, West Sussex, Hampshire, the Isle of Wight, Dorset, Somerset, Devon and Cornwall, as well as London and the landlocked county of Wiltshire. Bounded to the south by the English Channel, a narrow stretch of sea separating England from France, the region covers about 35,000 sq km (13,500 sq miles) and has a population of around 19.5 million. The southeast counties are largely defined by chalk downland, while the landscape to the west is more varied, ranging from the limestone cliffs of Cheddar Gorge in Somerset to the granite coast around Land's End in Cornwall – England's westernmost point. The biggest city after London is Bristol, built near the mouth of England's longest river, the Severn.

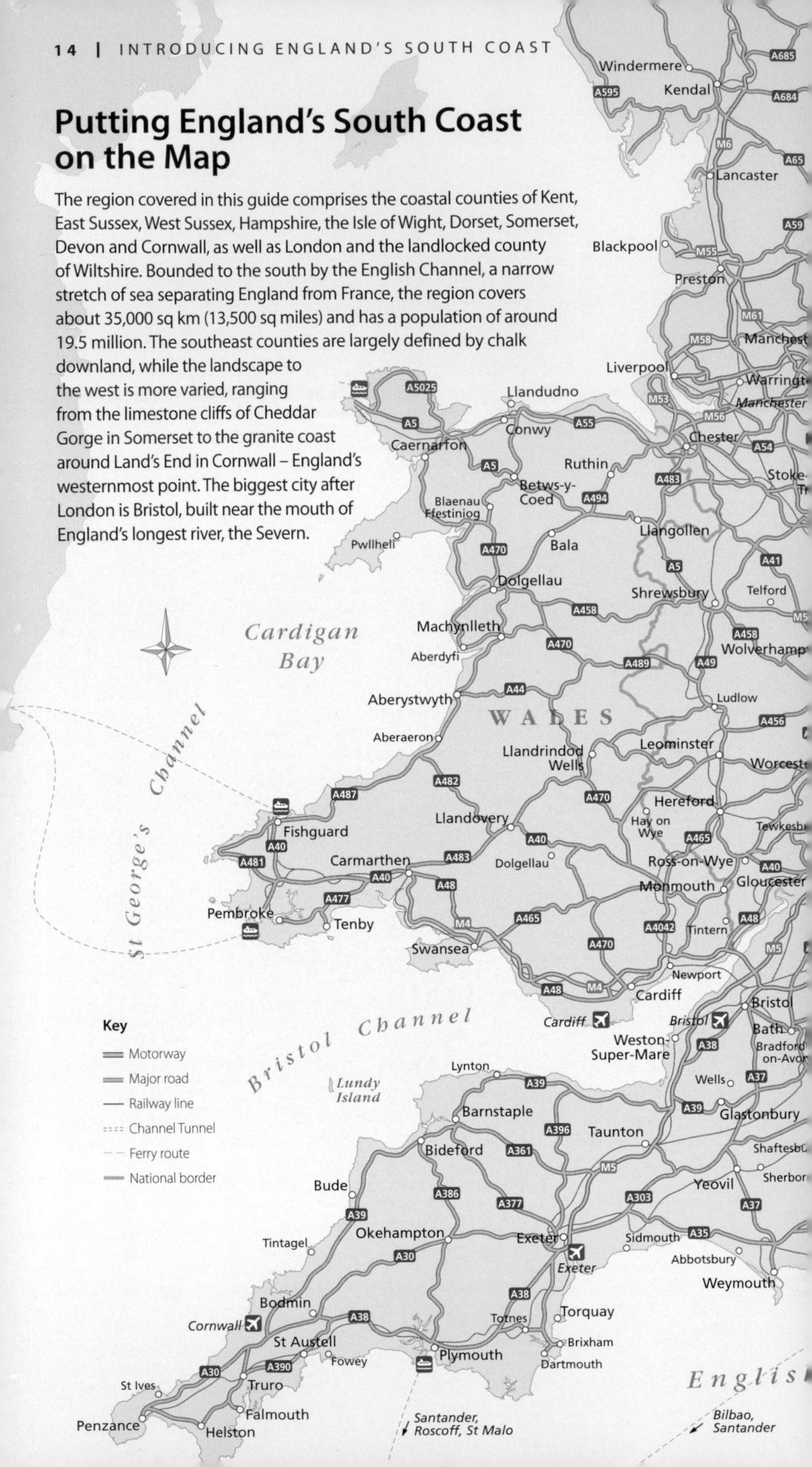

Key

- ▬ Motorway
- ▬ Major road
- — Railway line
- ⋯⋯ Channel Tunnel
- – – Ferry route
- — National border

Cardigan Bay

St George's Channel

Bristol Channel

Englis...

Windermere
Kendal
Lancaster
Blackpool
Preston
Liverpool
Warringt
Manchester
Manchest
Chester
Stoke-
Ti
Llandudno
Conwy
Ruthin
Betws-y-Coed
Llangollen
Shrewsbury
Telford
Caernarfon
Blaenau Ffestiniog
Bala
Dolgellau
Machynlleth
Wolverhamp
Aberdyfi
Pwllheli
Ludlow
Aberystwyth
WALES
Leominster
Worcest
Aberaeron
Llandrindod Wells
Hereford
Hay on Wye
Tewkesb
Fishguard
Llandovery
Ross-on-Wye
Carmarthen
Dolgellau
Monmouth
Gloucester
Pembroke
Tenby
Tintern
Swansea
Newport
Cardiff
Bristol
Bath
Cardiff ✈
Bristol ✈
Weston-Super-Mare
Bradford on-Avon
Wells
Lundy Island
Lynton
Glastonbury
Barnstaple
Taunton
Shaftesbu
Bideford
Sherbor
Bude
Yeovil
Okehampton
Exeter
Sidmouth
Tintagel
Exeter ✈
Abbotsbury
Weymouth
Bodmin
Totnes
Torquay
Cornwall ✈
St Austell
Brixham
St Ives
Fowey
Plymouth
Dartmouth
Truro
Penzance
Falmouth
Helston
Santander, Roscoff, St Malo
Bilbao, Santander

A685, A595, A684, M6, A65, A59, M55, M61, M58, M53, M56, A54, A5025, A5, A55, A483, A494, A5, A41, A470, A458, A458, M5, A470, A489, A49, A44, A456, A470, A482, A487, A40, A481, A483, A48, A477, M4, A465, A4042, A48, A470, A48, M4, M5, A38, A37, A39, A396, A39, A361, M5, A386, A377, A303, A37, A35, A39, A30, A38, A30, A390

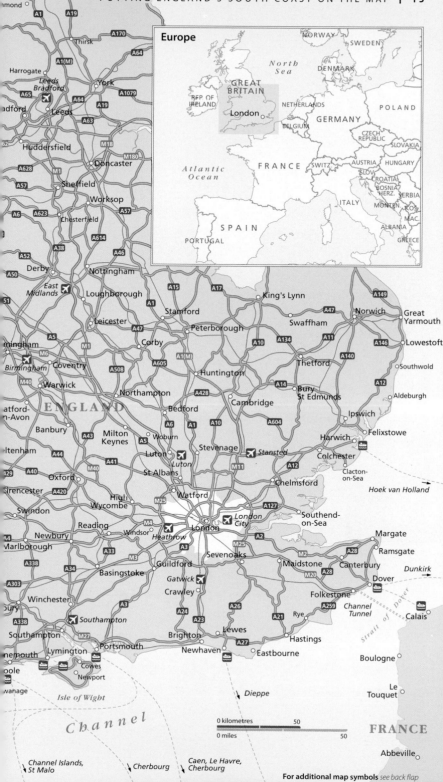

For additional map symbols *see back flap*

A PORTRAIT OF ENGLAND'S SOUTH COAST

Much of Britain's most stunning scenery stretches along England's South Coast – from the gently rolling downland of Sussex and Hampshire to the dramatic rugged terrain of Cornwall. It is an outstandingly beautiful area at the heart of the country's history, with a wealth of grand houses, sturdy castles and striking cathedrals enhancing the spectacular landscape.

Although the English often talk of a North-South divide, it is difficult to pin down the characteristics of a typical "southerner", not least because there is a surprising variety across the nine counties that stretch along England's southern coast. The South East – Kent, East Sussex, West Sussex and Hampshire – is the most populous and prosperous area of Britain by a sizeable margin. West of Bournemouth it is a different story. The West Country, Cornwall in particular, has a wilder, more primitive landscape, and is a harder place to earn a living.

What both the southwest and southeast parts of the South Coast have in common is their longstanding connection to the Royal Navy; the cities of Portsmouth and Plymouth have long been important naval bases. The region also boasts the best weather in Britain, and holiday-makers have been flocking to resorts such as Brighton, Bournemouth and Torquay since the 19th century.

The Industrial Revolution of the late 18th century, which contributed so much to the wealth of Britain, bypassed large areas of the south of England. Although towns and cities grew, the land continued to be mostly used for farming. Today, country life is still rooted in agriculture with many rural communities based around small market towns or picturesque villages, usually with a medieval church at their centre and a pub or village hall functioning as their social hub. Ancient customs, such as celebrating the arrival of spring, are still observed – with many interesting local variants – across much of the South Coast.

Sheep grazing on the picturesque South Downs near the village of Ditchling in East Sussex

◀ Colourful fishing boats docked in the harbour of Coverack, a Cornish fishing village

Customers outside Mol's Coffee House in Exeter, Devon

Politics and Society

England was divided into administrative counties in the 11th century, and despite some boundary alterations those in the South have remained roughly unchanged since that time. Big cities are run by unitary authorities, and counties by a county council supported by a district council, with elections taking place every four years. When it comes to party politics, the South Coast is overwhelmingly Conservative, with especially strong support in rural areas. In the 2016 referendum, while most of London wished to remain in the European Union, there was more variation along the South Coast: relatively affluent cities, such as Brighton and Bristol, were keen to remain, while those in poorer rural districts, such as North Devon and North Kent, tended to favour leaving.

The region is as divided by class as the rest of Britain, and social mobility is extremely static. Wealth and background are contributory factors, as is the education system: only 7 per cent of Britons are privately educated, but they account for over 50 per cent of the country's elite professionals. Affordable housing is a problem for many residents: South East property is more expensive than anywhere in the country apart from London, while the South West is the region where the most second houses are owned in the country.

The big cities in the South, such as Bristol, are thriving centres of multiculturalism, but prejudice still exists and racial tensions can arise, especially in poorer areas. Of the region's 19.5 million population, 6 per cent are from non-white ethnic groups, though the number is greater in cities and less in rural areas. Regional accents have almost disappeared from the South East, but can still be heard in the South West, where the West Country "burr" is still much in evidence.

Art and Culture

Much of the regional character of the stunning South Coast has been captured in the works of its many writers and artists. Jane Austen's novels vividly reflect her life among the gentry of Regency Hampshire and Bath. A hundred years later, Thomas Hardy created an unforgettable picture of rural Dorset in novels such as *Tess of the D'Urbervilles*. The beauty of particular areas has been a magnet for many painters. The great landscape artist Joseph Mallord William Turner regularly visited the popular seaside town of Margate in Kent and had a studio at Petworth House in Sussex, the home of his patron Lord Egremont. Since the 19th century, St Ives has been home to a colony of like-minded artists, attracted by the light and Cornwall's primal

Performance of the opera *Eugene Onegin* at Glyndebourne, Sussex

Vineyards and traditional oast houses at the spectacular 14th-century Bodiam Castle in East Sussex

landscape. Every major city along the South Coast has a municipal art gallery, usually focusing on local artists.

In more recent times, inspired by the success of Glastonbury and the Isle of Wight festivals, there has been an explosion of popular music festivals across the South Coast. A lot of these are family friendly, offering many other types of entertainment than just music. Classical music is equally well represented, with a world-renowned orchestra based in Bournemouth, full-scale country-house operas at Glyndebourne and Grange Park, and popular cultural festivals in Brighton and Bath, among others. Theatre-lovers have plenty to choose from, including the longest continuously running theatre in England, the Bristol Old Vic, and the imaginative Chichester Festival Theatre, which transfers many of its productions to London's West End.

Rock oysters, a popular South Coast delicacy

Economy

With around 78 per cent employment, the South Coast is well above the national average. Farming remains an important, if economically small, activity: the South Downs have been nibbled smooth by sheep over the centuries; Kent is famed for its hop gardens; and the West Country is abundant in cider orchards. The last 30 years have seen a boom in wine production, especially sparkling wine, with vineyards thriving from Kent to Cornwall. Fishing is another traditional industry, but one that has declined substantially in the last 20 years. Small Devon and Cornish fleets are all that survive of a once major enterprise. The service industry accounts for most employment, but there's a lot of variation: the South East is particularly strong in high-tech innovation, as is Bristol and London, whereas the South West relies more on travel and rural activities. Tourism makes a significant contribution to the region's economy. The tourist industry supports more than 25 per cent of employment in Cornwall and around 10 per cent of employment in Devon, with these counties boasting the largest hotel and restaurant sector in the country. The region as a whole attracts around 21 million visitors every year, who come to admire the stunning countryside, outstanding architecture, unspoiled beaches and picturesque towns and villages around England's spectacular South Coast.

Medieval Church Architecture

Romanesque architecture existed in England prior to 1066, but it was the Normans who consolidated it with a major programme of church building, from modest parish churches to grandiose cathedrals. The heavy solidity of Romanesque, with its rounded arches, gave way to the lighter, pointed-arch style of Gothic architecture introduced from France at the end of the 12th century. The Gothic style developed through several phases, its structures growing ever-more daring and its decoration more ornate and fanciful.

Canterbury Cathedral, showing the Perpendicular cloisters and crossing tower

Norman c.1066–c.1190

The Romanesque style is derived from Roman architecture. The Norman version was bigger than late Anglo-Saxon architecture and characterized by massive walls, rounded arches and solid supporting piers. Ceilings were barrel-vaulted (semicircular in section) or groin-vaulted (two intersecting barrel vaults).

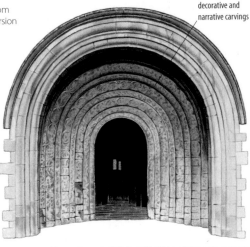

Elaborate decorative and narrative carvings

The South Portal of Malmesbury Abbey
The magnificent arched entrance to this church opens onto an equally beautiful porch. Both are decorated with carvings of saints and mythological creatures.

Early English c.1190–c.1250

The use of the pointed arch, or lancet, marked the earliest phase of Gothic architecture in England. Windows became taller and more slender, vaulting was divided into sections supported by arched diagonal ribs, and capitals became increasingly ornate.

Statues of the 12 apostles adorn the second tier of the gable.

The towers were originally meant to be topped by spires.

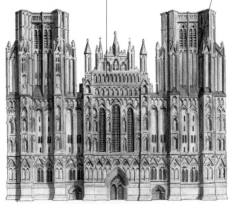

The West Front of Wells Cathedral
This beautiful façade features decorative sculptures, which would originally have been painted in bright colours.

Salisbury Cathedral's rib-vaulted cloisters

Decorated c.1250–c.1350

This style is characterized by the use of tracery: ornamental patterns within the top section of a window or opening. Patterning also became more elaborate in vaulting, with ribs being employed for aesthetic as well as structural purposes.

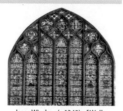

Jesse Window (c.1340) of Wells Cathedral, with its elegant tracery

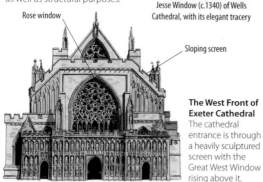

Rose window

Sloping screen

The West Front of Exeter Cathedral

The cathedral entrance is through a heavily sculptured screen with the Great West Window rising above it.

Perpendicular c.1350–c.1530

This is an English, late Gothic style in which the emphasis is on vertical lines; windows were larger, their arches flatter and lower, and the glass divided into elaborate panels. Vaulting became more intricate and included fan vaulting, named after the ornate fan-shaped semicones that radiate out from the top of a pier or pillar.

Vertical lines dominating Bath Abbey's exterior

Ornamental boss

Trefoil-headed panel

The Nave Roof of Sherborne Abbey

There are fans on the sides of the ceiling, lozenges at its centre and circular bosses at the intersection of the ribs on the nave roof. This exquisitely ornate roof dates from the late 14th century.

Terms Used in the Guide

Cathedral: a church containing a cathedra, or bishop's throne. It is the principal church of an administrative area, or diocese.
Basilica: a church with a nave higher and wider than its two aisles, nominally built on an east-west axis.
Nave: the main, central section of a church or cathedral.
Aisle: lateral section of a church, on one or both sides of the nave.
Chancel: eastern section of a church containing the altar and choir. It is usually separated from the nave by a screen.

Apse: the semicircular termination of a church or chapel.
Ambulatory: the aisle running round the east end of the church, behind the altar.
Arcade: a set of arches with supporting piers or columns.

Capital: carved top of a pier or column.
Clerestory: a row of windows that light the nave from above the aisle roof.
Triforium: the arcaded passageway located just below the clerestory.
Transept: the transverse section of a cruciform church.
Crossing: the centre of a cruciform church where the transept crosses the nave.

Vault: an arched stone ceiling.
Rib vault: a vault supported by projecting ribs of stone.
Buttress: a mass of masonry built to support or strengthen a wall.
Flying buttress: an arched support transmitting the thrust of a vault downwards.

Gargoyle: a carved grotesque figure, often a waterspout.
Rose: a large, circular window. Also known as a Catherine window.
Tracery: an ornamental carved stone pattern within a Gothic window.

Portal: monumental entrance to a church, often decorated.

Rural Architecture

Until the middle of the 19th century, most people lived and worked in the country, with communities forming in or around a village. The pattern of British villages dates back some 1,500 years, when the Saxons established settlements that were usually centred on a communal green or pond. Most of today's villages existed at the time of the Domesday Book in 1086, though few buildings survive from then. Settlements evolved organically around a church or manor, with buildings created from local materials. Today, a typical village contains structures of various dates, from the Middle Ages onwards. The church is usually the oldest, followed perhaps by a barn, a manor house or cottages.

Abbotsbury in Dorset, a typical rural village built up around a church

Timber-Framed House

These structures can be found throughout southeast England, and often have a tall central open hall flanked by two-storey bays with the upper floor "jettied", or overhanging the ground floor.

A steep-pitched roof covers the whole house.

The eaves are supported by curved braces.

The timbers that frame the house are usually made of oak.

Medieval Barn

Barns in the medieval period were constructed from wood or stone and built on a massive scale. Roofs were usually supported by crucks, curved timbers extending from the walls. The largest barns belonged to the great monastic estates and were used to store crops. Some were used for tithes: one tenth of a farmer's harvest, which he was obliged to donate to the clergy as a form of tax.

An old tithe barn with a timber cruck roof in the village of Lacock

A tiled roof keeps the crops dry.

The entrance is big enough for large wagons.

Openings in the walls aid ventilation.

The walls and doors are weatherboarded.

Thatched Cob Cottage

Popular in the West Country, these cottages have walls of cob covering a timber frame. Cob is a mixture of wet earth, lime, dung, reed, straw, gravel, sand and stones.

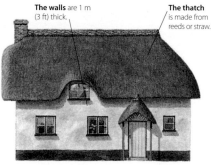

The walls are 1 m (3 ft) thick.

The thatch is made from reeds or straw.

Building Materials

The choice of materials depended on local availability. A stone cottage in Sussex county might be made from flint, or in the Cotswolds, limestone. Timber for beams was usually oak. Flint and pebble were popular in the chalky southeast. Slate is still quarried in Cornwall and brick has been widely used since Tudor times.

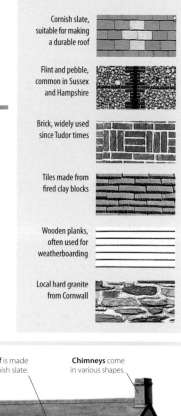

Cornish slate, suitable for making a durable roof

Flint and pebble, common in Sussex and Hampshire

Brick, widely used since Tudor times

Tiles made from fired clay blocks

Wooden planks, often used for weatherboarding

Local hard granite from Cornwall

Weatherboard House

These were built chiefly in southeast England in the 18th and 19th centuries. The timber boarding acted as cladding to keep out the cold and rain.

Bay windows add light and space.

The roof is surfaced with tiles.

Stone Cottage

Structures like this 19th-century Cornish farmhouse were built from local materials. Granite walls and slate roof tiles give protection from the harsh Atlantic storms.

The roof is made from Cornish slate.

Chimneys come in various shapes.

Windows are often small in cold areas.

The walls are made of tough local granite.

Gardens Through the Ages

Gardens were an integral part of the villas and palaces of Roman Britain, establishing a pattern of enclosed formal gardens that continued with the monastic gardens of the Middle Ages. The Elizabethan knot garden became more elaborate in Jacobean times, as the range of plants greatly increased. The 18th century brought a taste for large-scale "natural" landscapes with lakes, woods and meadows, creating a distinctively English style. Since then, debate has raged between supporters of natural and formal gardens, developing into the eclecticism of the 20th century when "garden rooms" in differing styles became popular.

Grottoes
Small artificial caves, usually with an elaborate interior, were used to add a touch of romance and mystery to 18th-century gardens.

Blackthorn

Classical temples were a feature of many 18th-century gardens and were often exact replicas of buildings that the designers had seen in Greece.

Elaborate Parterres
A feature of the aristocratic gardens of the 17th century, these formal gardens divided by ornamental flower beds were revived in Victorian times. Examples include this one at Lanhydrock, Cornwall.

Maple

Ideal Landscape Garden
Classical Greece and Rome inspired the gardens of the early 18th century, such as Stourhead. Clumps of trees played a critical part in the serene landscapes.

Winding paths were carefully planned to allow changing vistas to open out as visitors strolled around the garden.

Design and Formality

A flower garden is a work of artifice, an attempt to tame nature rather than to copy it. Growing plants in rows or regular patterns, interspersed with statues and ornaments, imposes a sense of order. Designs change to reflect the fashion of the time and the introduction of new plants.

Medieval gardens usually had a herber (a turfed sitting area) and a vine arbour. A good reconstruction is Queen Eleanor's Garden in Winchester.

Tudor gardens featured edged borders, knot gardens and mazes. The Tudor House and Garden in Southampton also has beehives and heraldic statues.

Herbaceous Borders
Gertrude Jekyll (1843–1932) was the high priestess of the mixed border. Her eye for pretty colour combinations can be seen in the flower beds of the garden at Hestercombe in Somerset.

"Capability" Brown (1715–83)
Britain's most influential landscape designer, Lancelot Brown (known to all his employers as "Capability" Brown) moved away from traditional formal gardens in favour of a more naturalistic approach. Popular with the aristocracy, he enhanced the parkland of country houses with picturesque vistas of serpentine artificial lakes and groups of trees.

Landscape architect Lancelot Brown

Yew

Cedar of Lebanon

The Palladian bridge was a favourite feature, often decorative rather than practical.

Rhododendron

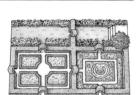

Knot Gardens
These formal gardens were in vogue in the 1500s. Intersecting lines of lavender or box hedges were often filled with flowers, herbs or vegetables. This one is at Avebury Manor in Wiltshire.

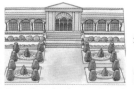

Orangeries such as the one at Bowood House, Wiltshire, were built for growing exotic plants like oranges. They were highly fashionable in the 18th century.

Victorian gardens, their formal beds a mass of colour, were a reaction to the landscapes of "Capability" Brown. Tyntesfield, Somerset, is an example.

20th-century gardens were often divided into themed sections or "rooms", as at Sissinghurst, Kent. Growing wild flowers was a popular choice.

Coastal Wildlife

England's long and varied southern coastline – ranging from the stark granite cliffs of Land's End to the coastal marshes of North Kent – is matched by an equally diverse range of wildlife. Beaches are covered with the colourful shells of molluscs, while rock pools form miniature marine habitats teeming with life. Caves are used by larger creatures, such as grey seals, and cliffs provide nesting sites for birds. In the spring and early summer, an astonishing variety of plants grow on the foreshore and cliffs, seen at their best from one of the National Trails, such as the South West Coast Path. The plants in turn attract many moths and butterflies.

A colony of nesting Kittiwakes on a cliff ledge at Seaford Head in Sussex

Chesil Beach
This beach *(see p117)* has an unusual ridge of pebbles stretching 29 km (18 miles) along the Dorset coast. The pebbles increase in size from northwest to southeast due to the varying strengths of coastal currents. The beach encloses a lagoon called the Fleet, a habitat for the Abbotsbury swans *(see p115)* and a large number of wildfowl.

The Painted Lady
Often seen on clifftop coastal plants, this butterfly migrates to Britain in spring.

High tides wash up driftwood and shells.

Clifftop turf contains many species of wild flowers.

Thrift
Found in hummocks of honey-scented flowers, thrift is a familiar sight on cliff ledges in spring.

Peregrine Falcon
These birds sometimes breed in rocky coastal areas.

Marram grass roots
help hold back sand against wind erosion.

Grey Seals
Spotted on remote beaches, grey seals come on land to give birth to their young.

A Beachcomber's Guide
The best time to observe the natural life of the seashore is when the tide begins to roll back, before the scavenging seagulls pick up the stranded crabs, fish and sandhoppers, and the seaweed dries up. Much plant and marine life can be found in the secure habitat provided by rock pools.

The Swale Estuary
In North Kent, the Swale Estuary has a rich variety of flora and fauna; many different seabirds can be seen feeding on the mudflats.

Collecting Shells

Most of the edible molluscs, such as scallops and cockles, are classed as bivalves. Others, such as whelks and limpets, are classed as gastropods.

Great scallop

Common cockle

Common whelk

Common limpet

Seaweed
Bladder wrack is a type of seaweed that resembles coral or lichen when in water.

Rocks are colonized by clusters of barnacles, mussels and limpets.

Oystercatchers
These birds have a very distinctive orange beak. They usually hunt along the shore, feeding on all kinds of shellfish.

Starfish
Also known as sea stars, starfish are aggressive predators of shellfish. The light-sensitive tips of their tentacles help them to "see".

Mussels
Widespread and plentiful, mussels can be harvested for food.

Rock pools teem with crabs, mussels, shrimps and plant life.

Velvet Crab
Often found hiding in seaweed, the shell of the velvet crab is covered in fine downy hair.

Grey Mullet
Newly hatched grey mullets can be seen in rock pools.

ENGLAND'S SOUTH COAST THROUGH THE YEAR

Every British season has its particular charm. Southern England is more temperate than the rest of the country, but the weather is always variable and visitors are almost as likely to experience a crisp, sunny February day as to be caught in a heavy shower in July. With four national parks along the South Coast, there is plenty of opportunity to enjoy the rich variety of flora and fauna across the seasons, from the stunning springtime bluebells of Cornish woodland to the vivid blaze of autumnal colours in the New Forest. A number of annual events and ceremonies, such as the summer and winter solstice celebrations at Stonehenge, help to mark the passage of the year.

Vibrant bluebells during spring in a woodland near Redruth, Cornwall

Spring

As the days get longer and warmer, the countryside starts to come alive. At Easter, many stately homes and gardens open their gates to visitors for the first time. The season is the focal point of the gardening year, with bright, colourful blooms inspiring gardeners to start working on their summer displays. The first of the music and arts festivals of the year begin during springtime.

March

St Piran's Day (5 Mar), various venues, Cornwall. Parades in honour of a local Cornish saint.
Bristol International Jazz & Blues Festival (mid-Mar), various venues in the city. Top acts celebrate Bristol's long association with jazz music.

April

Cornwall Spring Flower Show (first weekend), Boconnoc House, Lostwithiel. A showcase for the best of Cornish horticulture.

St George's Day (23 Apr), nationwide. Celebrations are held in honour of England's patron saint and William Shakespeare's birthday.

May

Beltain (1 May), Butser Ancient Farm, near Waterlooville, Hampshire. This festival marks the start of summer with the burning of a 9-m- (30-ft-) high Wicker Man at sunset.
Obby Oss Festival (1 May), Padstow, Cornwall. Crowds follow a Hobby Horse in a May Day celebration (see p157).
Furry Dance (8 May), Helston, Cornwall. A celebration with dancing and a mummers' play, a traditional English folk production (see p165).
Brighton Festival (last 3 weeks), Sussex. One of England's largest annual performing arts festivals.

Straw Wicker Man at the Beltain festival

Glyndebourne Festival Opera Season (mid-May–end Aug), near Lewes, Sussex. The renowned Glyndebourne opera house stages world-class productions throughout the summer.
Ageas Salisbury International Arts Festival (late May–early Jun), various venues. Performing arts and family programmes.
Bath Festival (late May), various venues, Somerset. A ten-day multiarts festival featuring classical, jazz, and folk musicians, as well as contemporary writers.
Chelsea Flower Show (late May), Royal Hospital, London. One of the world's most prestigious flower shows.
Chippenham Folk Festival (last week), Wiltshire. Performances of traditional folk music and dances.
English Wine Week (week beginning Spring Bank Holiday), all over southern England. A celebration of wine at vineyards and restaurants.

A performance of George Frideric Handel's *Saul* directed by Barrie Kosky at Glyndebourne

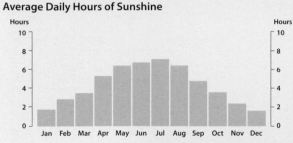

Average Daily Hours of Sunshine

Hours

| | | | | | | | | | | | |
|Jan|Feb|Mar|Apr|May|Jun|Jul|Aug|Sep|Oct|Nov|Dec|

Sunshine Chart
The South has markedly more sunshine than the rest of the country, with the sunniest spots found along the southeast coast. July is the best month, with a daily average of around 6.7 hours per day, rising to over 8 hours per day in resorts such as Bognor and Eastbourne.

Summer

Life moves outdoors in the summer months. Cafés and restaurants place tables on the pavements and pub customers take their drinks outside. Village fêtes – which include traditional games and local stalls – are organized. Swimming pools and beaches start to get crowded, and coastal resorts such as Margate, Brighton and Torquay come into their own. The rose, England's national flower, bursts into bloom in millions of gardens. Cultural treats include open-air theatre performances, outdoor concerts and film screenings.

June

Royal Bath and West Show *(first week)*, Shepton Mallet, Somerset. One of the oldest surviving agricultural shows in England.
The Grange Festival *(mid-Jun–mid-Jul)*, Grange Park, near Alresford, Hampshire. An annual opera festival at a country house.
Royal Academy of Arts Summer Exhibition *(mid-Jun–late Aug)*, London. A varied art show featuring the work of professional and amateur artists.
Summer Solstice at Stonehenge *(21 Jun)*, Wiltshire. A celebration of the year's shortest day at England's most mysterious monument.
The Championships, Wimbledon *(late Jun–early Jul)*, London. The most prestigious tennis tournament in the world.
Glastonbury Festival *(late Jun)*, Somerset. A legendary five-day long festival of contemporary music and performing arts *(see p125)*.

A reveller in a flamboyant costume performing at the Notting Hill Carnival

July

Love Supreme *(early Jul)*, near Lewes, Sussex. A three-day greenfield jazz festival.
Pommery Dorset Seafood Festival *(early Jul)*, Weymouth. One of the largest seafood festivals in the country.
Henry Wood Promenade Concerts *(mid-Jul–mid-Sep)*, Royal Albert Hall, London. Famous concert series popularly known as the Proms.
Bestival *(late Jul)*, Lulworth Castle, Dorset. A four-day family-friendly music festival.
Port Eliot Festival *(late Jul)*, St Germans, Cornwall. A creative arts festival, with performing arts, music, fashion, comedy and food.

Families watching an acrobat show at the Port Eliot Festival, Cornwall

Sidmouth Folk Week *(late Jul–early Aug)*, Devon. A festival of traditional music, dance and craft *(see p137)*.
Whitstable Oyster Festival *(late Jul)*, Kent. A celebration of the landing of the oysters, with music, food stalls and parades.
WOMAD *(late Jul)*, Charlton Park, near Malmbesbury, Wiltshire. Popular world music and dance festival.

August

Cowes Week *(early Aug)*, Isle of Wight. The UK's premier sailing regatta.
Airbourne International Airshow *(mid-Aug)*, Eastbourne, Sussex. Free airshow with vintage and modern planes.
Purbeck Valley Folk Festival *(late Aug)*, near Swanage, Dorset. Set on a farm on the Jurassic Coast, this festival features young folk, roots and world music.
Rye International Jazz & Blues Festival *(late Aug)*, Sussex. World-class jazz musicians perform at different venues across Rye.
Notting Hill Carnival *(last weekend)*, London. A West Indian street carnival featuring floats, bands, Caribbean food and stalls.

Average Monthly Rainfall

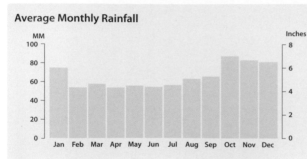

Rainfall Chart
The West Country's oceanic climate produces an average of 83 mm (3.25 in) of rain per month, compared to the rest of the South's 62.5 mm (2.5 in). Upland areas, such as Dartmoor or the South Downs, usually receive higher rainfall.

Participants in the Bonhams London to Brighton Veteran Car Run

Falmouth Oyster Festival (*mid-Oct*), Cornwall. This festival celebrates the start of the oyster-dredging season.
Canterbury Festival (*third and fourth weeks*), Kent. Music, drama and the arts.
Apple Day (*21 Oct*), nationwide, especially in Kent, Devon and Somerset. A celebration of apples and orchards, with tastings and cider-drinking events.

Autumn

All over England on 5 November, bonfires are lit and fireworks let off to celebrate the foiling of an attempt to blow up the Houses of Parliament by Guy Fawkes and his co-conspirators in 1605 (*see p36*). Cornfields become golden, trees turn fiery yellow through to russet, and orchards are heavy with apples and other autumn fruits. In churches throughout the country, thanksgiving festivals mark the harvest. The shops stock up for the run-up to Christmas, their busiest time of the year.

September
End of the Road Festival
(*early Sep*), Larmer Tree Gardens, near Blandford, Dorset. This music festival focuses on alternative music, mostly folk, and Americana.
Agatha Christie Festival
(*mid-Sep*), Torquay, Devon. Special events are held in honour of the famous crime book author at her birthplace of Torquay (*see p138*).
Jane Austen Festival (*mid-Sep*), Bath, Somerset. This ten-day-long festival hosts parades,

readings and discussions in the town where Austen lived for five years (*see p92*).

October
Harvest Festivals
(*whole month*), nationwide, especially in farming areas. Gifts of fruit and vegetables are made in church and school ceremonies to give thanks for the harvest.
Winchester Poetry Festival
(*early Oct*), Hampshire. Readings, workshops and literary discussions.

Flowers and produce adorning a church font for the Harvest Festival

November
Bonhams London to Brighton Veteran Car Run (*first Sun*). Pre-1905 cars make up the entrants at this annual motoring event, with drivers and passengers dressed in period costumes.
Lewes Bonfire (*5 Nov*), Sussex. The biggest and wildest celebration of Guy Fawkes Night with parades, bonfires and firework displays.
Christmas Market at Winchester Cathedral (*mid-Nov–mid-Dec*), Hampshire. German-style Christmas market with a large open-air ice rink.

A parade at the Bonfire Night celebrations in Lewes, East Sussex

Average Monthly Temperatures

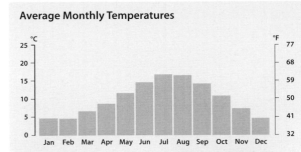

Temperature Chart
The warm sea around Cornwall gives it the highest average annual UK temperature of 11–12° C (52–4° F), although the hottest summer days can be over 30° C (96° F). London and the South East are only marginally cooler, while both areas experience their coldest spells in February.

Choirboys singing carols at Westminster Abbey, London

Public Holidays

New Year's Day (1 Jan).
Easter weekend (Mar or Apr) begins on Good Friday and ends on Easter Monday.
May Day (usually first Mon in May).
Late Spring Bank Holiday (last Mon in May).
August Bank Holiday (last Mon in Aug).
Christmas and **Boxing Day** (25 and 26 Dec).

Winter

Brightly coloured fairy lights and Christmas trees decorate town centres across southern England as shoppers rush to buy their seasonal gifts. Carol services are held in churches and cathedrals across the region, and pantomime, a traditional entertainment for children deriving from the Victorian music hall, fills theatres in major towns.

In some coastal towns, hardy swimmers brave the sea for a Christmas Day swim, while many sporting events, notably horse racing and football, take place on Boxing Day. Most offices close between Christmas and the New Year, but many shops reopen for the January sales on 26 December – a paradise for bargain-hunters.

A costumed couple at Rochester's Dickensian Christmas

December
Rochester's Dickensian Christmas (first weekend), Kent. The town where Charles Dickens spent his last years hosts costumed processions, carol singing and readings in honour of the author.
Burning of the Clocks (21 Dec), Brighton, Sussex. Beautiful lantern parades and spectacular fireworks celebrate the winter solstice.

January
London New Year's Day Parade (1 Jan), central London. A grand midday parade through central London, beginning at Piccadilly Circus.
Apple Wassailing (early Jan), mainly Devon, Somerset and Kent. The ancient custom of singing to apple trees and drinking their health is meant to ensure a good harvest.

February
Chinese New Year (late Jan or early Feb), Chinatown, London. Colourful parades, performances and fireworks mark the start of the Chinese New Year.
Purbeck Literary Festival (mid-Feb), Wareham, Dorset. Workshops, readings, talks and other events celebrate the region's literary heritage.
Hurling the Silver Ball (Shrove Tue and the second Sat after), St Columb Major, Cornwall. An ancient game in which two teams attempt to carry a silver ball to goals 3 km (2 miles) apart.

Traditional lanterns decorating the streets in Chinatown during Chinese New Year

THE HISTORY OF ENGLAND'S SOUTH COAST

A mere 32 km (20 miles) from France at its closest point, the South Coast has acted as England's defensive bulwark ever since the last successful invasion in 1066. Southern shipbuilding and maritime expertise were crucial in helping establish the country as a great imperial power, making ports such as Bristol and London, and the great naval bases of Portsmouth and Southampton, incredibly wealthy. In more recent times, the South Coast's proximity to London and Europe, its dramatic history and its sheer beauty have made it a magnet for tourists from across the globe.

In the distant past, England's South Coast was joined to continental Europe by a chalk ridge running between the Weald in southern England and Artois in northeastern France. The first human settlers are thought to have arrived in Britain via the ridge around 900,000 years ago, during an interglacial period. They were probably hunter-gatherers, and have been classified as *Homo antecessor*. Subsequent ice ages either wiped them out, or sent them heading back south to escape the extreme cold. Sometime between 450,000 and 200,000 years ago, a huge glacial lake to the north of the Weald–Artois ridge overflowed, gouging a deep channel through it and into the Atlantic. When sea levels rose between the ice ages, the channel formed a permanent barrier between Britain and the Continent.

The South Coast, especially the South West, abounds in prehistoric sites. The oldest complete skeleton of a modern human was found in caves at Cheddar Gorge in Somerset and dates from about 9,000 years

Celtic Battersea Shield from the Iron Age

ago, around the start of the Mesolithic period. Mesolithic, or Stone Age, settlers were hunter-gatherers who used flint-tipped spears and arrows to hunt wild animals. Important Mesolithic sites include the Mendip Hills in Somerset and Bouldnor Cliff on the Isle of Wight. The next wave of arrivals introduced farming to Britain in around 4000 BC, clearing away woodland for domesticated animals and plants in what would become known as the Neolithic period. They constructed defendable causewayed camps, made long barrows to bury their dead and built mysterious henges, the most famous being Stonehenge and Avebury, both in Wiltshire.

During the Bronze and Iron Ages, beginning around 2300 BC, the creation of tools and artifacts became more sophisticated. Some of the most beautiful objects were made by the various warlike tribes who arrived in Britain around 550 BC. Loosely described as Celts, they were not a unified people, but their cultures and languages overlapped.

c. 450,000–200,000 BC Glacial lake gouges a channel between Britain and the Continent		*Stonehenge, a prehistoric temple aligned with the sun*		**c. 2500 BC** Stonehenge is built	**55–4 BC** Julius Caesar invades Britain but does not conquer any territory
500,000 BC	100,000	15000	10000	5000	1000	500

7000–6000 BC As the last Ice Age ends, rising sea levels submerge the land link between Britain and Europe

4000 BC Farming is introduced to Britain

550–350 BC Migration of Celtic people from southern Europe

◀ Lithograph by Joseph Ratcliffe Skelton illustrating Julius Caesar's army landing in Britain in 54 BC

Roman Rule

In AD 43, Emperor Claudius sent a Roman fleet carrying 40,000 troops to Richborough, in Kent, on the pretext of intervening in a dispute between two warring tribes. The Catuvellauni, under their leader Caratacus, resisted but were defeated near the River Medway in Kent. The Roman general Vespasian then headed west, only encountering any real opposition from the Durotriges tribe at Maiden Castle in Dorset. The Romans established Londinium as an important commercial centre on the north side of the Thames, making it their capital by the end of the 1st century.

The Roman general Vespasian

The Roman occupiers could be brutal – they persecuted the Druids (the Celtic religious and professional elite) to extinction – but generally treated the indigenous tribes as client states. By the beginning of the 3rd century all inhabitants, except slaves, were granted Roman citizenship. Around the same time, Christianity was also introduced to Britain. The Romans' legacy in military and civil construction can be seen in the buildings that still stand across the South Coast, including at the palatial villa at Fishbourne, the coastal fort at Portchester and, most impressive of all, the beautiful baths at Bath.

The Anglo-Saxons

By AD 410, the Roman occupation had ended and Roman Britain began to break up into separate kingdoms. Before long, another set of invaders arrived: these were Germanic tribes from Western Europe, collectively known as Anglo-Saxons. Jutes occupied Kent and the Isle of Wight and Saxons controlled Sussex before spreading westwards.

The Anglo-Saxons were pagans but gradually a succession of kings converted to Christianity. In 597, Pope Gregory sent monks to Kent, led by St Augustine, who established a cathedral at Canterbury and became its first Archbishop. Wessex, with Winchester as its de facto capital, was the greatest of the southern Anglo-Saxon kingdoms. By the end of the 9th century it included almost all of southern England, save for a small, powerless Cornish kingdom. Wessex was invaded by the Vikings in 871, but fought back and won

St Augustine preaching to Ethelbert, the Anglo-Saxon king of Kent

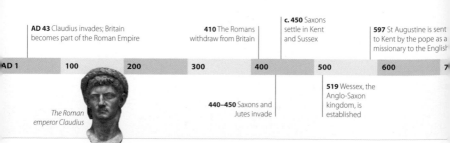

AD 43 Claudius invades; Britain becomes part of the Roman Empire

410 The Romans withdraw from Britain

c. 450 Saxons settle in Kent and Sussex

597 St Augustine is sent to Kent by the pope as a missionary to the English

AD 1   100   200   300   400   500   600   7

The Roman emperor Claudius

440–450 Saxons and Jutes invade

519 Wessex, the Anglo-Saxon kingdom, is established

the decisive Battle of Edington in Wiltshire under its most celebrated king, Alfred the Great. Alfred's grandson, Athelstan, became the first king of a united England in 937.

Norman Invaders

Harold II was the last Anglo-Saxon king of England, but his claim to the throne was disputed by William of Normandy, who in 1066 landed with an invasion fleet at Pevensey in Sussex. Harold was defeated and killed at the Battle of Hastings. To consolidate their victory, the Normans built a series of castles, including those at Arundel, Pevensey, Dover and Rochester. Many of those who fought alongside William were rewarded with titles and large expanses of land. The new Norman aristocracy treated native Anglo-Saxons as serfs, and French remained the language of the ruling elite until the 13th century.

The Norman monarchs had close ties to the Church. They embarked on a programme to build more cathedrals, expand existing religious buildings and increase the number of monasteries. The Cistercian order, which arrived in England in the early 12th century, played a very important role in the agricultural economy. They introduced improved farming techniques and organized methods for selling produce. Forde Abbey in Dorset was an important Cistercian foundation.

The Middle Ages

The Plantagenet family from Anjou in France was the dynasty that succeeded William's descendants. Henry II was the first Plantagenet king, infamous for falling out

The death of Wat Tyler at Smithfield during the Peasants' Revolt

with his former friend Thomas Becket, the Archbishop of Canterbury, who he had murdered in 1170. Becket was canonized in 1173 and Canterbury became an important pilgrimage site. Henry II's son King John was equally disputatious, regularly clashing with the barons, then the most powerful noblemen in the land. In 1215, John was forced to sign Magna Carta at Runnymede near Windsor. This agreement limited royal power and enshrined certain fundamental rights in law. Fifty years later the barons, led by Simon de Montfort, rebelled against John's son King Henry III and defeated him at the Battle of Lewes.

The first outbreak of the plague known as the Black Death appeared at Melcombe Regis in Dorset in 1348. Spreading along the southern coast of England and then inland, it is thought to have wiped out around one third of the entire population. The resulting labour shortage, combined with restrictions on wages and heavy taxation, provoked the Peasants' Revolt of 1381. Led by Wat Tyler, Kentish rebels occupied the Tower of London, but were defeated and the concessions promised by Richard II were rescinded.

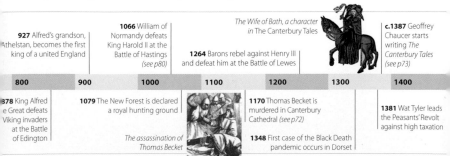

927 Alfred's grandson, Athelstan, becomes the first king of a united England

1066 William of Normandy defeats King Harold II at the Battle of Hastings *(see p80)*

The Wife of Bath, a character in The Canterbury Tales

1264 Barons rebel against Henry III and defeat him at the Battle of Lewes

c.1387 Geoffrey Chaucer starts writing *The Canterbury Tales (see p73)*

| 800 | 900 | 1000 | 1100 | 1200 | 1300 | 1400 |

878 King Alfred the Great defeats Viking invaders at the Battle of Edington

1079 The New Forest is declared a royal hunting ground

The assassination of Thomas Becket

1170 Thomas Becket is murdered in Canterbury Cathedral *(see p72)*

1348 First case of the Black Death pandemic occurs in Dorset

1381 Wat Tyler leads the Peasants' Revolt against high taxation

A painting depicting the Royal Navy, on the right, using fire ships to attack the Spanish Armada at the Battle of Gravelines in 1588

The Tudors

Henry Tudor defeated the last Plantagenet king, Richard III, in 1485, ending a 30-year dynastic struggle known as the Wars of the Roses. Henry's son, Henry VIII, is considered to be England's most notorious king. In 1533 he divorced his wife, Catherine of Aragon, without papal consent, in order to marry Anne Boleyn, thus precipitating the Reformation in England. This included the Dissolution of the Monasteries, whereby Henry VIII closed down all monasteries and appropriated their assets. His daughter Mary I tried to re-establish Catholicism and executed many Protestants. Mary's half-sister Elizabeth I returned the country to Protestantism, but in 1588 was faced with a Spanish invasion force, the Armada. After engaging with the Royal Navy off Plymouth, the Spanish fleet was dispersed following the Battle of Gravelines.

England owed its naval prowess to Henry VIII, who built heavily armed ships, such as the *Mary Rose*, and established important dockyards at Portsmouth and Chatham. Prior to that, England's maritime protection was largely the responsibility of the Cinque Ports, five coastal towns in Kent and Sussex that provided a fleet in return for exemption from certain taxes.

The Stuarts

Elizabeth I named James VI of Scotland as her heir and he was crowned James I of England in 1603. Two years later, a group of dissident Catholics planned but failed to blow up Parliament and kill the king in the Gunpowder Plot. There were deep divisions over religion: the Church of England was the official faith, but some Protestants wished to reform it, and many worshippers remained loyal to Catholicism. In 1620 a group of fundamental Protestants, or Puritans, left Plymouth on board the *Mayflower* to start a new life in America. Eventually things came to a head in a standoff between Parliament and King Charles I, who believed he ruled by divine right. In the ensuing seven-year Civil War, most of the South supported Parliament. Charles I was executed at London's Whitehall Palace in 1649. Though the monarchy was restored in 1660 under Charles II, it suffered

King Henry VIII

1497 John Cabot leaves Bristol for his first voyage to North America

1536–41 Following the English Reformation, Henry VIII dissolves England's monasteries

1555–8 Execution of Protestants during the reign of Mary I

1588 Spanish invasion fleet, the Armada, is defeated by the English fleet

1620 Pilgrim Fathers set off from Plymouth for the New World

1642 Civil War breaks out; the Parliamentarians control much of the South

1660 Restoration of the monarchy under Charles II

1647 Charles I executed at London's Whitehall Palace

1703 The Great Storm devastates central and southern England

| 1450 | 1500 | 1550 | 1600 | 1650 | 1700 | 17 |

another reversal when James II was ousted from power for his Catholic leanings. His daughter Mary II and son-in-law William of Orange became the new, staunchly Protestant, joint monarchs in 1689.

The Georgians

The expansion of the British Empire in the 18th century meant increased trade, much of it facilitated by slavery, but also several expensive wars. The resultant high taxation, especially on imported luxuries, led to smuggling along the entire length of the South Coast. As wealth increased, so leisure became more sophisticated. Spa towns, such as Royal Tunbridge Wells and Bath, became increasingly fashionable and seaside resorts began to proliferate. The quiet Sussex village of Brighthelmstone developed into the popular seaside resort of Brighton after the Prince Regent built his exotic Royal Pavilion there in 1787.

The historic iron-hulled steamship, SS *Great Britain*, designed by Brunel

The threat of French invasion loomed throughout the 18th century and, following the French Revolution, Britain was at war with France from 1792 to 1815. Invasion plans ended in 1805, when Lord Nelson's fleet defeated Napoleon's navy at the Battle of Trafalgar.

The Victorian Era

The invention of the steam train and the railway boom of the 1840s caused an infrastructure revolution as raw materials could now be transported more quickly across the country. By 1850, it was possible to travel from London to Dover, Brighton, Portsmouth, Bristol and Exeter by train. The era's greatest engineer, Isambard Kingdom Brunel, was the chief designer for the Great Western Railway. He also created spectacular ships, including the SS *Great Britain*, the world's first iron-hulled steamship, launched from Bristol in 1843.

Modern Times

Shipbuilding was still a major industry at the start of the 20th century, and many British battleships were built in Portsmouth and Devonport. When the British Army was stranded in France in 1940, during World War II, naval vessels and other private boats evacuated over 300,000 soldiers from the beaches of Dunkirk. Four years later, some 5,000 naval vessels set off from ports across the entire South Coast as part of the Allied D-Day invasion of France. After the war, traditional industries, such as fishing and agriculture, declined. The economy became more diverse, with leisure pursuits and tourism playing a big role. The opening of the Channel Tunnel in 1994 provided a physical link to mainland Europe, but Britain's close ties to the Continent suffered a setback in 2016 when the electorate voted for withdrawal from the European Union (EU) following 43 years of membership. Despite this, the South Coast is likely to remain an increasingly attractive prospect for the millions of visitors who flock here every year.

1805 The Royal Navy, led by Nelson, defeats Napoleon at Trafalgar

Statue of Admiral Nelson

1944 A combined British, American and Canadian force invades occupied Normandy; troops are transported in ships from across the South Coast

| 1800 | 1850 | 1900 | 1950 | 2000 | 2050 |

1836–8 London linked to the South Coast by railway

1864 Opening of the Clifton Suspension Bridge across the Avon Gorge

1994 The Channel Tunnel opens

2016 The UK votes to leave the European Union in a national referendum

1940 Hundreds of private ships set off from Ramsgate to help evacuate the British Army from Dunkirk

ENGLAND'S SOUTH COAST REGION BY REGION

England's South Coast at a Glance

The Normans established the counties of England for administrative purposes; those along the South Coast roughly tally with the earlier kingdoms of the Anglo-Saxons. While each county has retained an identity of its own, there is a noticeable difference between the gently undulating landscape of the South East and the wilder countryside of the South West, with its long, rugged peninsula tapering down to Land's End. Whether visitors wish to discover the medieval architecture of the great cathedrals and castles, explore the stunning variety of the countryside, or simply enjoy the beauty of the miles of coastline, this region offers a huge array of attractions throughout the year.

Stourhead *(see pp106–7)*
This Wiltshire stately home is renowned for its exquisite 18th-century landscaped garden.

Exmoor *(see pp122–3)*
Stretching across north Devon and west Somerset, this wild moorland is home to the rare Exmoor pony, Britain's oldest breed of horse.

0 kilometres 50
0 miles 50

Bristol
Bath
Cheddar
Wells
Glastonbury
Shaftesbu
Lundy Island
Barnstaple
Bridgwater
Clovelly
Bideford
Taunton
DORSET AN
SOMERSE
(see pp108–3
Bude
DEVON
(see pp132–51)
Exeter
Boscastle
Sidmouth
Okehampton
Weymouth
CORNWALL
(see pp152–69)
Torquay
Newquay
Bodmin
Plymouth
St Austell
Looe
Brixham
St Ives
Truro
Penzance
Falmouth
Helston

Dartmoor *(see pp142–3)*
A national park since 1951, Dartmoor's bleak but beautiful landscape is dotted with huge outcrops of granite called tors (an Old English word meaning high rocky hill).

Land's End *(see p169)*
This is mainland Britain's westernmost point. It features the arch of Enys Dodnan, beyond which are the rocks collectively known as the Armed Knight.

◄ The picturesque harbour at Looe, a fishing village in Cornwall

Stonehenge *(see pp102–3)*
This vast, awe-inspiring stone circle was built in the Neolithic period, around 2500 BC. Its function remains a mystery, but the position of the stones suggests a connection with the sun and the passing of the seasons.

Tower of London *(see p61)*
Built after the Norman conquest of 1066, this fortress was intended both to protect London from invasion and to deter the native population from insurrection.

LONDON
(see pp42–63)

London

Margate

Marlborough

Sevenoaks
Canterbury
Ramsgate

**HAMPSHIRE AND
SALISBURY PLAIN**
(see pp88–107)

Maidstone
Dover

Crawley

Royal
Tunbridge Wells

Salisbury
Chawton

Winchester
KENT AND SUSSEX
(see pp64–87)

uthampton

Chichester

Hastings

ngton
Portsmouth

Eastbourne

le
Cowes

nage
Isle of Wight

Rye *(see pp78–9)*
A major port in the Middle Ages, Rye retains many of its medieval buildings and fortifications.

The New Forest *(see p97)*
Covering 570 sq km (220 sq miles), this spectacular area in Hampshire is a unique mix of pasture, heathland, ancient woodland and river valleys.

Brighton *(see pp82–5)*
This bustling town's busy promenade features the i360 Viewing Tower and the Brighton Pier, which opened in 1899.

LONDON

One of the most vibrant and exciting cities in the world, London is astonishingly rich in history, with many of its most famous buildings, such as Buckingham Palace, the Tower of London, Westminster Abbey and St Paul's Cathedral, reflecting its royal past. With world-class theatres, some of the world's best museums and art galleries, elegant parks and beautiful gardens, and endless opportunities for shopping and dining, there's a huge amount on offer all year round for visitors to the UK's capital.

Around AD 43, the Romans founded a settlement by the River Thames, which grew into a major administrative and communications centre and port during the 1st and 2nd centuries. They called it Londinium. Nine hundred years later, a separate city of Westminster emerged when Edward the Confessor decided to build himself a palace close to the new abbey church of St Peter. This became the political and ceremonial heart of the kingdom and has remained so to this day, with Westminster Abbey and the Houses of Parliament standing just a few yards away from each other. Gradually, as houses were built on the land in between, the two cities merged.

Today the City of London functions as the capital's business and financial hub, while the West End, the city's social and cultural centre, is home to many of London's most popular sights, including the renowned theatres of Shaftesbury Avenue and Charing Cross Road, the busy shopping thoroughfares of Oxford Street and Regent Street, and the cultural treasures of the British Museum and the National Gallery.

The southern shore of the river is no less rich in attractions: the Southbank Centre is home to the National Theatre, the Hayward Gallery and a cluster of concert venues. Further east is the converted power station that is now Tate Modern, while nearby Shakespeare's Globe, opened in 1997, is a faithful reconstruction of an Elizabethan theatre. For such a bustling metropolis, London also boasts plenty of green oases, whether it is the open spaces of Regent's Park – the home of the famous ZSL London Zoo – or the more intimate tranquillity of St James's Park in the heart of Westminster.

Panoramic view of the skyline of Canary Wharf and the City of London, seen from One Tree Hill in Greenwich Park

◀ London's iconic Big Ben clock tower, one of the world's most recognizable landmarks

Exploring London

London and its adjacent suburbs, known as Greater London, cover an area of some 1,570 sq km (606 sq miles). The West End, where many of the most famous sights are found, sits on the north side of the River Thames and stretches from the edge of Hyde Park to Covent Garden, while the main business and financial district lies further east in the ancient City of London. Exclusive Kensington, known for its high-end shops and residences, is home to three of London's finest museums.

Buckingham Palace with the pretty Memorial Gardens in full bloom

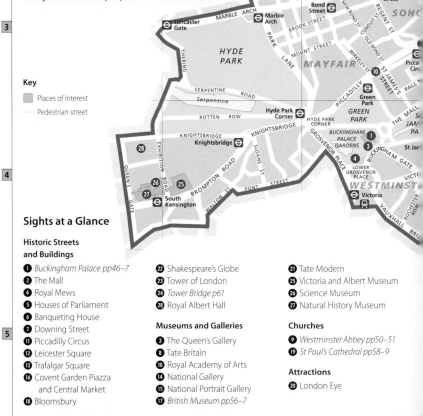

Key

- Places of interest
- Pedestrian street

Sights at a Glance

Historic Streets and Buildings

- ❶ *Buckingham Palace pp46–7*
- ❷ The Mall
- ❹ Royal Mews
- ❺ Houses of Parliament
- ❻ Banqueting House
- ❼ Downing Street
- ⑪ Piccadilly Circus
- ⑫ Leicester Square
- ⑬ Trafalgar Square
- ⑯ Covent Garden Piazza and Central Market
- ⑱ Bloomsbury

- ㉒ Shakespeare's Globe
- ㉓ Tower of London
- ㉔ *Tower Bridge p61*
- ㉘ Royal Albert Hall

Museums and Galleries

- ❸ The Queen's Gallery
- ❽ Tate Britain
- ⑩ Royal Academy of Arts
- ⑭ National Gallery
- ⑮ National Portrait Gallery
- ⑰ *British Museum pp56–7*

- ㉑ Tate Modern
- ㉕ Victoria and Albert Museum
- ㉖ Science Museum
- ㉗ Natural History Museum

Churches

- ❾ *Westminster Abbey pp50–51*
- ⑲ *St Paul's Cathedral pp58–9*

Attractions

- ⑳ London Eye

1

The skyline of the City of London seen from across the Thames, showing the Leadenhall Building, the Gherkin and the Tower of London

Nike, winged goddess of victory, atop the Wellington Arch in Hyde Park

Getting Around

The quickest way to get around the capital is via the London Underground (the Tube) or by bus (see pp212–13), but keep in mind that both forms of transport can get crowded and the roads become very busy, especially at peak times, so it is often easier and more pleasant to walk. A number of bridges cross the Thames in central London and there is also a river bus with stops on both sides of the river.

❶ Buckingham Palace

The Queen's official London home and office is an extremely popular attraction. Architect John Nash began converting the 18th-century Buckingham House into a palace for George IV in 1826 but was dismissed in 1831 for overspending his budget. The first monarch to live in the palace was Queen Victoria, after she came to the throne in 1837. The palace tour takes visitors through the State Rooms, but not into the Royal Family's apartments.

The Music Room
is where state guests are presented and royal babies are christened.

Blue Drawing Room

Grand Staircase

State Dining Room

The Changing of the Guard

Soldiers taking part in the traditional Changing of the Guard ceremony

Dressed in brilliant scarlet tunics and furry hats called bearskins, the palace guards stand in sentry boxes outside the palace. Crowds gather to watch the colourful military ceremony as the guards march from Wellington Barracks to Buckingham Palace, parading while the palace keys are handed by the old guard to the new.

The Queen's Gallery features masterpieces from the Queen's priceless collection of art.

❷ The Mall

SW1. **Map** C4. ⊖ Charing Cross, Green Park.

This impressive broad triumphal approach from Trafalgar Square to Buckingham Palace was created by Aston Webb when he redesigned the front of the palace and the wonderful Victoria Monument in 1911.

The spacious tree-lined avenue follows the course of an old path at the edge of St James's Park. The path was laid out in the reign of Charles II, when it became London's most fashionable and cosmopolitan promenade. The Mall is used for royal processions on special occasions. Flagpoles down both sides fly the national flags of foreign heads of state during official visits. The Mall is closed to traffic on Sundays.

❸ The Queen's Gallery

Buckingham Palace Rd, SW1. **Map** C4. **Tel** 0303 123 7300. ⊖ St James's Park, Victoria. **Open** 10am–5:30pm daily (last adm: 4:15pm). **Closed** 25 & 26 Dec; check website for details. 🖼 📷 ♿ 🖼 🅦 royalcollection.org.uk

The Royal Family possesses one of the finest and most valuable art collections in the world, rich in the works of old masters such as Rembrandt, Vermeer, Holbein and Leonardo da Vinci. The Queen's Gallery hosts a rotating programme of exhibitions, and displays royal portraits by Sir Thomas Lawrence, Anthony van Dyck and Sir Joshua Reynolds.

The Mall leading to Buckingham Palace, lined with Union Jacks, the national flag of the UK

The East Wing
The façade was added by Aston Webb in 1913.

White Drawing Room

Green Drawing Room

Throne Room is where the Queen carries out many formal ceremonial duties, under the richly gilded ceiling.

The Royal Standard flies while the Queen is in residence.

Royal Balcony
On special occasions the Royal Family waves to crowds from here. The Duke and Duchess of Cambridge shared a kiss here after their wedding in 2011.

The Changing of the Guard takes place on the palace forecourt.

---

❹ Royal Mews

Buckingham Palace Rd, SW1.
Map C4. **Tel** 0303 123 7300.
🚇 Victoria. **Open** Feb & Mar, Nov & Dec: 10am–4pm Mon–Sat (last adm: 3:15pm); Apr–Oct: 10am–5pm daily (last adm: 4:15pm); subject to closure at short notice (call ahead).
Closed 25 & 26 Dec. 🔲 🔲 🔲
🔲 🔲 9:30am–5pm daily.
🔲 **royalcollection.org.uk**

The Mews is worth visiting for all lovers of horses and royal pomp. Designed by John Nash in 1825, the stables and coach house contain the horses and coaches used by the Royal Family on official occasions. Star exhibits include the Glass Coach used for royal weddings, the Gold State Coach, in use for all coronations since 1821, and the Diamond Jubilee State Coach built for the Queen in 2012.

❺ Houses of Parliament

SW1. **Map** D4. **Tel** 020 7219 4114. 🚇 Westminster. **Open** Visitors' Galleries: check website for details. Access to the galleries is by a queuing system. **Closed** during parliamentary recesses. 🔲 Sat and during parliamentary recesses; book in advance. 🔲 🔲 🔲
🔲 **parliament.uk/visiting**

There has been a Palace of Westminster here since the 11th century, though only Westminster Hall remains from that time. The present Neo-Gothic structure was built after the old palace was destroyed by fire in 1834. Sir Charles Barry was the principal architect, while his assistant Augustus Pugin designed the Gothic detailing. Since the 16th century, the site has been home to the two Houses of Parliament: the Commons and the Lords. The

Equestrian statue of Richard the Lionheart in front of the Neo-Gothic Houses of Parliament

House of Commons consists of elected Members of Parliament (MPs). The House of Lords comprises mainly appointed life peers, but also hereditary peers and Church of England bishops.

Street-by-Street: Whitehall and Westminster

The broad avenues of Whitehall and Westminster are lined with imposing buildings that serve as the historic seat of both government and the established church. On weekdays the streets are crowded with civil servants who work in the area, while at weekends they take on a different atmosphere with a steady flow of tourists.

❼ Downing Street
Sir Robert Walpole was the first Prime Minister to live here in 1732.

❾ ★ Westminster Abbey
The abbey is London's oldest and most important church.

The Cabinet War Rooms and Churchill Museum served as Winston Churchill's World War II headquarters.

St Margaret's Church is the parish church for MPs.

Central Hall
(1911) was built for the Methodist Church in 1911.

Richard I's Statue
Marochetti's bronze statue was erected in 1860.

Dean's Yard
An arch near the west door of the abbey leads into this grassy square, surrounded by picturesque buildings from different periods.

The Burghers of Calais
is a cast of Auguste Rodin's 1886 sculpture.

KING CHARLES STREET

STOREY'S GATE

GREAT GEORGE STREET

BROAD SANCTUARY

PARLIAMENT SQUARE

ST MARGARET STREET

GREAT COLLEGE STREET

ABINGDON STREET

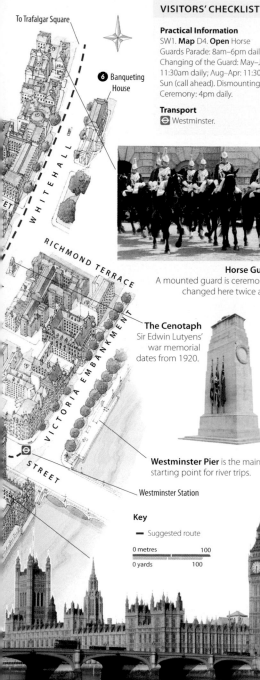

6 Banqueting House

VISITORS' CHECKLIST

Practical Information
SW1. **Map** D4. **Open** Horse Guards Parade: 8am–6pm daily. Changing of the Guard: May–Jul: 11:30am daily; Aug–Apr: 11:30am Sun (call ahead). Dismounting Ceremony: 4pm daily.

Transport
Westminster.

Horse Guards
A mounted guard is ceremonially changed here twice a day.

The Cenotaph
Sir Edwin Lutyens' war memorial dates from 1920.

Westminster Pier is the main starting point for river trips.

Westminster Station

Key
— Suggested route

0 metres 100
0 yards 100

★ Houses of Parliament
...e seat of government is dominated by a clock tower holding the 14-tonne ...ll Big Ben, hung in 1858. Its deep chimes are broadcast daily on BBC radio.

6 Banqueting House

Whitehall, SW1. **Map** D3. **Tel** 020 3166 6154. Charing Cross. Charing Cross. **Open** 10am–5pm daily. **Closed** public hols & functions (call ahead). limited. **w** hrp.org.uk

Completed by Inigo Jones in 1622, this was the first building in central London to embody the Palladian style of Renaissance Italy. In 1629 Charles I commissioned Rubens to paint the ceiling with scenes exalting the reign of his father, James I. The paintings symbolize the divine right of kings, disputed by the Parliamentarians, who executed Charles I outside the building in 1649.

7 Downing Street

SW1. **Map** D4. Westminster. **Closed** to the public.

Number 10 Downing Street has been the official residence of the British Prime Minister since 1732. It contains the Cabinet Room, the State Dining Room and a private apartment. Next door, Number 11 is the residence of the Chancellor of the Exchequer. For security reasons, members of the public cannot visit Downing Street without authorized access.

8 Tate Britain

Millbank, SW1. **Map** D4. **Tel** 020 7887 8888. Victoria, Vauxhall. Pimlico. to Tate Modern (every 40 mins). **Open** 10am–6pm daily (to 10pm on select Fridays). **Closed** 24–26 Dec. for major exhibitions. Atterbury St. **w** tate.org.uk

Founded in 1897, Tate Britain has the world's largest collection of British art from the 16th to the 21st century. Highlights include John Constable's *Flatford Mill* (1816–17), John Everett Millais' *Ophelia* (1851–2) and Francis Bacon's *Three Studies for Figures at the Base of a Crucifixion* (c.1944). The Clore Gallery contains the Turner Bequest, some 300 oil paintings and 200 works on paper that were left to the nation by the great Romantic landscape painter J M W Turner *(see p76)*.

❾ Westminster Abbey

Westminster Abbey has been the burial place of Britain's monarchs since the 11th century and the setting for many coronations and royal weddings. Half national church, half national museum, it is one of the most beautiful buildings in London, with an exceptionally diverse array of architectural styles, ranging from the austere French Gothic of the nave to the complexity of Henry VII's Chapel. The abbey's aisles and transepts are crammed with an extraordinary collection of tombs and monuments honouring a number of Britain's greatest public figures, ranging from politicians to poets.

North Entrance
The mock-medieval stonework is Victorian.

★ Nave
At a height of 31 m (102 ft), the nave is the highest in England. The ratio of height to width is 3:1.

Coronation Chair
Constructed in 1301, this chair has been used at every coronation since 1308.

KEY

① **Statesmen's Aisle**

② **Flying buttresses** are external supports that help redistribute the great weight of the roof.

③ **The Sanctuary** was built by Henry III. It contains the relics of Edward the Confessor and has been the scene of 38 coronations.

④ **Pyx Chamber** is where newly minted coins were tested.

Coronation of Queen Elizabeth II

Coronation

The coronation ceremony is over 1,000 years old and the abbey has been its fittingly sumptuous setting since 1066, when William the Conqueror was crowned on Christmas Day. The coronation ceremony of the present monarch Queen Elizabeth II, in 1953, was the first to be televised.

★ **Henry VII's Chapel**
Also known as the Lady Chapel, it was built between 1503 and 1519. It features superb late Perpendicular vaulting and choir stalls dating from 1512, as well as two stained-glass windows installed in 2013.

WILLIAM SHAKESPEARE 1564-1616

Poets' Corner
A host of great poets are honoured here, including Shakespeare, Geoffrey Chaucer and T S Eliot.

VISITORS' CHECKLIST

Practical Information
Broad Sanctuary, SW1. **Map** D4.
Tel 020 7222 5152. **Open** Abbey (Royal Chapels, Poets' Corner, Choir, Statesmen's Aisle, Nave): 9:30am–3:30pm Mon–Fri (to 6pm Wed), 9:30am–1:30pm Sat. Chapter House, Pyx Chamber & Museum: 10am–4pm Mon–Sat. College Garden: 10am–4pm Tue–Thu. NB: Abbey museum closed for renovation until 2018. 🅿 ☕ 🏪 ♿ limited, access from the North Entrance. 🚻 Evensong: 5pm Mon–Fri (evening prayers Wed), 3pm Sat & Sun. 📷 🖥 🎧 EH W **westminster-abbey.org**

Transport
🚇 Victoria. 🚌 3, 11, 12, 24, 53, 87, 88, 148, 159, 211. Ⓣ Westminster. 🚤 Westminster Pier.

★ **Chapter House**
This beautiful octagonal structure is worth seeing for its 13th-century tiles. It is lit by six huge stained-glass windows showing scenes from the abbey's history.

Historical Plan of the Abbey

The first abbey church was established as early as the 10th century, but the present French-influenced Gothic structure was begun in 1245 at the behest of Henry III. Because of its unique role as the coronation church, the abbey escaped Henry VIII's onslaught on Britain's monastic buildings.

Key
- ☐ Built between 1055 and 1272
- ☐ Added 1376–1420
- ☐ Built between 1500 and 1512
- ☐ Completed 1745
- ☐ Restored after 1850

Cloisters
Built mainly in the 13th and 14th centuries, the cloisters link the abbey church with the other buildings in the complex.

The Annenberg Courtyard at Burlington House, home to the Royal Academy of Arts

❿ Royal Academy of Arts

Burlington House, Piccadilly, W1.
Map C3. **Tel** 020 7300 8000.
🚇 Piccadilly Circus, Green Park.
Open 10am–6pm daily (to 10pm Fri).
Summer Exhibition: Jun–Aug.
Closed Good Fri & 24–26 Dec.
🖼 🎟 by appt. 🎧 ♿ 🍴 🛍 📷
🌐 **royalacademy.org.uk**

The Royal Academy was founded in 1768 to train artists and to promote and exhibit works of art. It is best known for its Summer Exhibition, an annual event displaying works by established and unknown artists. For the rest of the year, there are exhibitions of both international and British art. The courtyard of Burlington House, one of London's few surviving mansions from the early 18th century, contains a statue of the academy's first president, Sir Joshua Reynolds.

An exceptional permanent collection (not all on display) includes one work by each current and former academician; the highlights are displayed in the Madejski Rooms.

⓫ Piccadilly Circus

W1. **Map** C3. 🚇 Piccadilly Circus.

Dominated by neon billboards, Piccadilly Circus is a hectic traffic junction surrounded by shops and restaurants. It began as an early 19th-century crossroads between Piccadilly and John Nash's Regent Street. It was briefly an elegant space, edged by stucco façades, but by 1910 the first electric advertisements had been installed. For years people have congregated at its centre, beneath the iconic winged statue of the Shaftesbury Memorial Fountain, often mistakenly called Eros, which was erected in 1892.

⓬ Leicester Square

WC1. **Map** D3. 🚇 Leicester Sq, Piccadilly Circus.

Named after the Earl of Leicester who built a grand house here in 1635, the square was first laid out in the 1670s and soon became a fashionable place to live. In the 18th century residents included scientist Sir Isaac Newton, the painter Joshua Reynolds and the surgeon John Hunter. Today it forms the heart of London's West End entertainment district and is home to cinemas, including the Empire and a large Art Deco Odeon – both are often used to screen major film premieres.

⓭ Trafalgar Square

WC2. **Map** D3. 🚌 3, 6, 9, 11, 12, 13, 15, 23, 24, 29, 53, 87, 88, 91, 139, 159, 176, 453. 🚇 Charing Cross.

Built on the former site of the Royal Mews, Trafalgar Square commemorates the famous 1805 victory of Admiral Lord Nelson over Napoleon's fleet at the Battle of Trafalgar *(see p37)*. At its centre stands a 51-m- (169-ft-) tall column topped with a bronze statue of Nelson. Trafalgar Square opened in 1844, a few years after the National Gallery, which occupies the whole of its north side. A popular meeting place, the square is also used for public rallies and events.

At the northwest corner, the Fourth Plinth features temporary artworks by leading national and international artists.

⓮ National Gallery

Trafalgar Sq, WC2. **Map** D3. **Tel** 020 7747 2885. 🚆 Charing Cross.
🚇 Charing Cross, Leicester Sq, Piccadilly Circus. **Open** 10am–6pm daily (to 9pm Fri). **Closed** 1 Jan & 24–26 Dec. 🎟 🎧 ♿ via Sainsbury Wing and Getty entrances. 🍴 🛍
📷 🌐 **nationalgallery.org.uk**

The National Gallery is London's leading art museum, with a collection of over 2,300 paintings, most on permanent display. It was established in 1824, after Parliament agreed to purchase 38 major paintings at the instigation of famous art patron Sir George Beaumont, who also donated 16 works from his own collection. These became the core of a national collection of European art that now ranges from Cimabue in the 13th century to Pablo Picasso in the 20th century.

The imposing Neo-Classical building, designed by William Wilkins, opened in 1838. Its many outstanding Renaissance paintings include Jan van Eyck's *The Arnolfini Portrait* (1434), Da Vinci's masterpiece *The Virgin of the Rocks* (1508) and Hans

The Virgin of the Rocks (1508) by Leonardo da Vinci at the National Gallery

For hotels and restaurants in this region see p174 and pp184–5

Holbein's *The Ambassadors* (1533). It is equally strong in 17th- and 18th-century works, and has a fine collection of Impressionist and Post-Impressionist paintings, including Pierre-Auguste Renoir's *At the Theatre* (1876–7) and Vincent van Gogh's *Sunflowers* (1888). The gallery recently purchased its first non-European work, *Men of the Docks* (1912), by American artist George Bellows.

A major extension, the Sainsbury Wing, was completed in 1991. It houses the Early Renaissance collection and has a special exhibition space and lecture hall in the basement.

⓯ National Portrait Gallery

2 St Martin's Pl, WC2. **Map** D3. **Tel** 020 7306 0055. 🚇 Charing Cross. 🅔 Charing Cross, Leicester Sq. **Open** 10am–6pm daily (to 9pm Thu & Fri). BP Portrait Award: Jun–Sep. Taylor Wessing Photographic Portrait Prize: Nov–Feb. **Closed** 24–26 Dec. 🅿 for special exhibitions. 🎧 🅖 Orange St entrance. ✎ 🖥 📷 🆆 **npg.org.uk**

This fascinating museum was founded in 1856 to celebrate Britain's rich history through portrait painting and sculpture; photography was added in 1932. Subjects are those who have made a significant contribution to Britain's history, for better or worse: kings, queens, artists, thinkers, scientists, heroes and villains from all periods since the late 14th century.

The oldest works are on the top floor and include a Holbein cartoon of Henry VIII and paintings of some of his wives. Other early portraits include the Ditchley portrait of Elizabeth I and the Chandos portrait of Shakespeare, which may have been painted from life.

The collection runs roughly chronologically from the top floor down, with 20th-century figures from the worlds of art, pop and politics represented on the first floor. Recent commissions are placed on the ground floor, which is also used for temporary exhibitions, such as the annual BP Portrait Award and the Taylor Wessing Photographic Portrait

The Ditchley portrait of Elizabeth I on display at the National Portrait Gallery

Prize. The gallery's rooftop restaurant provides wonderful views across Trafalgar Square.

⓰ Covent Garden Piazza and Central Market

Covent Garden, WC2. **Map** D3. 🅔 Covent Garden. 🅖 cobbled streets. 🆆 **coventgarden.london**

The 17th-century architect Inigo Jones planned the Piazza in Covent Garden as an elegant residential square, modelled on the piazza in the Tuscan town of Livorno, which he had seen during his travels in Italy. For a brief period, the Piazza became one of the most fashionable addresses in London, but it was superseded by the even grander St James's Square, which lies to the southwest. Decline accelerated when a fruit and vegetable market opened here. By the mid-18th century, the Piazza had become a haunt of prostitutes and most of its houses had turned into seedy lodgings, gambling dens, brothels and taverns.

Meanwhile, the wholesale produce market became the largest in the country and in 1828 a market hall was erected to ease congestion. The market, however, soon outgrew its new home and despite the construction of new buildings, such as the Floral and Jubilee halls, the congestion grew worse. In 1973, the market moved to a site in south London, and over the next two decades Covent Garden was redeveloped. Today only St Paul's Church remains of Inigo Jones's buildings, and Covent Garden, with its many shops, cafés, restaurants, market stalls and street entertainers, is one of London's liveliest districts.

Stalls, shops and restaurants in the 19th-century Central Market hall in Covent Garden

London's Parks and Gardens

Whether it's a tree-filled square in Bloomsbury or one of the large Royal Parks, you are never far from a green space in London. Some are ancient Crown lands and some are commons (land historically owned by the general public). Others were created from the gardens of private houses or disused land. All have their own particular charm and character, from the intimacy of the Chelsea Physic Garden to the rolling acres of Hampstead Heath. Londoners like to make the most of these open spaces: for exercise, entertainment or simply escaping the bustle of the city's streets.

Holland Park
A haven of green in busy West London, with acres of peaceful woodland, an open-air theatre and a café.

Kew Gardens
The world's premier botanic garden, Kew houses an amazing variety of plants from all over the globe. The living collections are complemented by spectacular Victorian glasshouses, a pagoda and a tree-top walk.

Historic Cemeteries

In the late 1830s, a ring of seven private cemeteries was established around London to ease the pressure on the monstrously overcrowded and unhealthy burial grounds of the inner city. Today the cemeteries, notably Highgate, Kensal Green and Abney Park, are well worth visiting for their flamboyant monuments and grandiose mausoleums.

Memorial to Robert William Siever, Kensal Green

0 km   1
0 miles   0.5

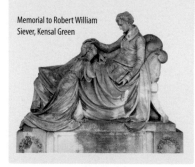

Richmond Park
London's largest Royal Park, Richmond is designated a national nature reserve, and features roaming deer and magnificent river views.

Regent's Park
Surrounded by John Nash's graceful buildings, this is one of London's most civilized retreats. It is home to a large boating lake, an open-air theatre and ZSL London Zoo.

Hampstead Heath
is a breezy open space embracing a variety of landscapes.

St James's Park
In the heart of the West End, this park is a popular escape for office workers. It is also a reserve for wildfowl.

Green Park, with its shady trees and benches, offers a cool, restful spot bordering Buckingham Palace.

...ersea Park
...leasant ...side spot ... a man-made ...ing lake.

Kensington Gardens and Hyde Park
The Albert Memorial is in Kensington Gardens, while neighbouring Hyde Park features a recreational lake.

Greenwich Park
Home to the National Maritime Museum and the Queen's House, Greenwich Park has fine views from the Old Royal Observatory on the hilltop.

London Squares

From the 17th to the late 19th century, many houses in the more exclusive areas of central London, such as Bloomsbury, were laid out as squares, with a railed-off piazza or garden in the centre, surrounded by roads and buildings. Many of these squares still exist today, and most are open to the public. Beautifully maintained, they provide small, green oases for visitors and passersby alike.

Elegant Russell Square in Bloomsbury

⓱ British Museum

The oldest national public museum in the world, the British Museum was established in 1753 to house the collections of the physician Sir Hans Sloane (1660–1753). Sloane's collection has been augmented with gifts and purchases from all over the world, and the museum now contains objects spanning thousands of years. The main part of the building (1823–50) was designed by architect Robert Smirke, but the architectural highlight is the magnificent, modern, glass-roofed Great Court, designed by Foster and Partners.

★ Egyptian Mummies
Animals such as this cat (30 BC) were preserved alongside humans by the ancient Egyptians.

Upper floors

90
91
67
95
62
61 58
59
73

34

Montague Place entrance

33

26

24

35

30

21
20
19 22
9
4
8

78 77
17
18
16 10
7

15

Turquoise Pectoral from Aztec Mexico
Snakes were sacred to the Aztecs and this double-headed serpent (c.1400–1521) was probably worn during religious ceremonies.

★ Parthenon Sculptures
These reliefs from the Parthenon in Athens were brought to London by Lord Elgin around 1802 and are housed in a special gallery.

Gallery Guide

The Greek and Roman collection, and the Middle Eastern collection are found on all three levels of the museum, predominantly on the west side. The African collection is located on the lower floor, while Asian exhibits are found on the ground and upper floors on the north side of the museum. The Americas collection is located in the northeast corner of the ground floor. Egyptian artifacts are found in the large gallery to the west of the Great Court and on the first floor.

Ground floor

Key to Floorplan

- ☐ Asian collection
- ■ Enlightenment
- ☐ Coins and medals
- ☐ Greek and Roman collection
- ☐ Egyptian collection
- ☐ Middle Eastern collection
- ☐ European collection
- ☐ Temporary exhibitions
- ☐ Non-exhibition space
- ☐ Africa, Oceania and the Americas

★ **Lindow Man**
The skin on this 2,000-year-old human body was preserved by the acids of a peat-bog in Cheshire. He was probably killed in an elaborate ritual.

VISITORS' CHECKLIST

Practical Information
Great Russell St, WC1. **Map** D2.
Tel 020 7323 8000. **Open** 10am–5:30pm daily (selected galleries until 8:30pm Fri). **Closed** 1 Jan, Good Fri & 24–26 Dec. 🖪 🕮 🖳 🖾 **W british museum.org**

Transport
🚆 Euston, King's Cross. 🚌 1, 8, 10, 14, 19, 24, 25, 29, 38, 55, 73, 134, 188. 🚇 Holborn, Russell Sq, Tottenham Court Rd.

The Great Court is London's largest covered square, with shops, cafés, a restaurant, display areas and educational facilities.

65
53
54
55
52
51
50
49
46
41
40 **39** **47**
36 **38**
37
70
68
69
69

First floor

The Reading Room was built in 1857.

Mildenhall Treasure
The Great Dish was among the 34 pieces of 4th-century AD Roman silver tableware ploughed up in Suffolk in 1942.

1
ℹ
2
3

Waddesdon Bequest Gallery

Main entrance

The Egyptian Gallery
This gallery on the ground floor houses the famous Rosetta Stone. Found in 1799, the inscription on it enabled 19th-century scholars to decipher Egyptian hieroglyphs.

Houses on Bedford Square, Bloomsbury

⑱ Bloomsbury

WC1. **Map** D3. 🚇 Russell Sq, Tottenham Court Rd.

A traditional centre of the book trade, Bloomsbury is home to numerous writers and artists. It is dominated by the British Museum and the University of London and characterized by fine Georgian squares. These include Russell Square, where the poet T S Eliot (1888–1965) worked for publisher Faber & Faber for 40 years; Queen Square, which contains a statue of Queen Charlotte, wife of George III; and Bloomsbury Square, laid out in 1661. A plaque here commemorates members of the Bloomsbury Group *(see p81)*. Several members of the group, including prominent figures such as novelists Virginia Woolf and E M Forster, lived in houses around Gordon Square. Charles Dickens lived at 48 Doughty Street during a brief but critical stage in his career, and it was here that he wrote *Oliver Twist*.
His former home is now the **Charles Dickens Museum**, which has rooms laid out as they were in Dickens's time, with objects taken from his other London homes and first editions of many of his works.

Queen Charlotte (1744–1818)

🏛 **Charles Dickens Museum**
48 Doughty St, WC1. **Tel** 020 7405 2127. **Open** 10am–5pm Tue–Sun. 🖾
🖳 🖾 **W dickensmuseum.com**

⑩ St Paul's Cathedral

The Great Fire of London in 1666 left the medieval cathedral of St Paul's in ruins. Christopher Wren was commissioned to rebuild it, but his design for a cathedral on a Greek Cross plan (where all four arms are equal in length) met with considerable resistance. The authorities insisted on a conventional Latin Cross, with a long nave and short transepts, which was believed to focus the congregation's attention on the altar. Despite the compromises, Wren created a magnificent Baroque cathedral, which was built between 1675 and 1710 and has since formed the setting for many state ceremonies.

★ West Front and Towers
Inspired by the work of Italian architect Francesco Borromini, the towers were not on Wren's original plan. He added them in 1707, when he was 75 years old. Both were designed to have clocks.

The Nave
An imposing succession of massive arches and saucer domes open out into the vast space below the main dome.

KEY

① **The west portico** consists of two storeys of coupled Corinthian columns, topped by a pediment carved with reliefs showing the Conversion of St Paul.

② **The balustrade**, designed by John James, was added in 1718 against Wren's wishes.

③ **The lantern** is made out of stone and weighs a massive 700 tonnes.

④ **The Golden Gallery** has splendid views over London.

⑤ **The oculus** is an opening through which the cathedral floor can be seen.

⑥ **Stone Gallery**

⑦ **The high altar** canopy was constructed in the 1950s, after the cathedral was bombed in World War II, and is based on designs by Wren.

⑧ **An entrance leads down to the crypt**, which lies underneath the cathedral and contains the tombs and memorials of popular heroes.

⑨ **The south portico** was inspired by the beautiful porch of Santa Maria della Pace in Rome.

Main entrance approached from Ludgate Hill

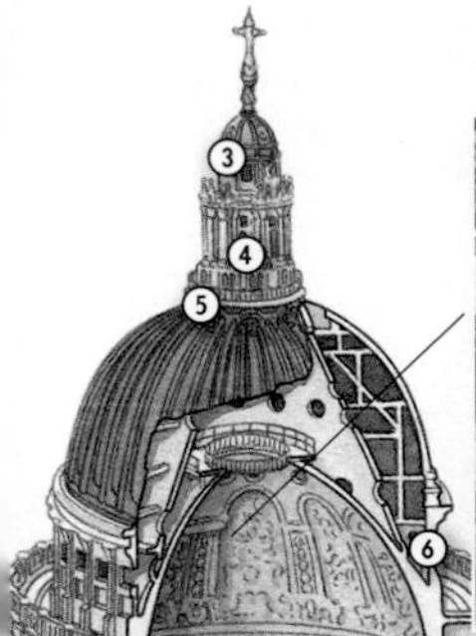

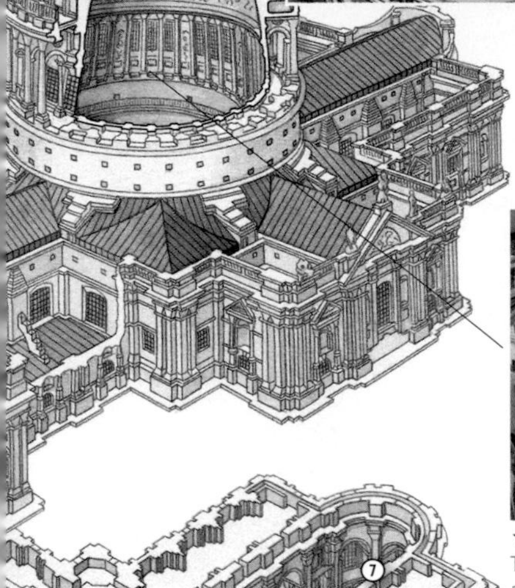

★ **Dome**
At 111 m (360 ft),
the elaborate
dome is one of
the highest in
the world.

VISITORS' CHECKLIST

Practical Information
Ludgate Hill, EC4. **Map** E3.
Tel 020 7246 8350. **Open** 8:30am–
4pm Mon–Sat. NB: check website
for closures of all or part of the
cathedral. 🎧 includes audio
guide. 📷 🎧 ♿
✝ Eucharist: 11:30am Sun.
Evensong: 3:15pm Sun. ♫
📱 🏛 🌐 stpauls.co.uk

Transport
🚇 St Paul's, Mansion House.
🚌 4, 11, 15, 17, 23, 25, 76, 172.
🚆 City Thameslink.

★ **Whispering Gallery**
The dome's unusual acoustics mean that words whispered
against the wall can be heard clearly on the opposite side.

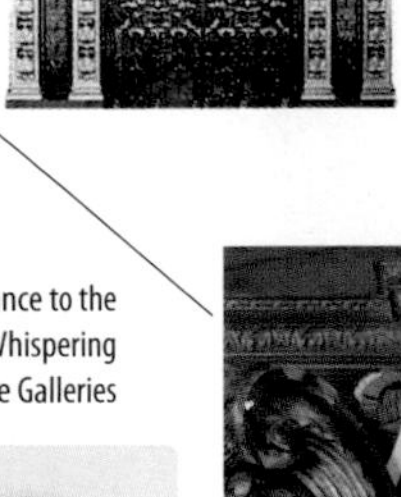

Quire
Jean Tijou, a
Huguenot refugee,
created much of
the fine wrought
ironwork in Wren's
time, including
these quire screens.

Entrance to the
Golden, Whispering
and Stone Galleries

Christopher Wren (1632–1723)

One of the most brilliant scientists of his age,
Sir Christopher Wren began his impressive
architectural career at the age of 31. A
leading figure in the rebuilding of London
after the Great Fire of 1666, he designed a
total of 52 new churches. Although Wren
never visited Italy, his work was influenced
by Roman Baroque and Renaissance
architecture, as is apparent in his famous
masterpiece, St Paul's Cathedral.

Acclaimed architect
Christopher Wren

Quire Stalls
The quire stalls and organ case
were made by Grinling Gibbons,
a wood carver from Rotterdam.
He and his team worked on the
carvings for two years.

The iconic London Eye towering over County Hall on the South Bank of the River Thames

⑳ London Eye

Jubilee Gardens, South Bank, SE1.
Map D4. 🚌 11, 24, 211. 🚇 Waterloo,
Westminster. 🚢 London Eye Pier.
Open Apr–Sep: 10am–9:30pm daily
(to 11:30pm on select days); Oct–Mar:
10am–8:30pm daily. **Closed** 2nd & 3rd
week in Jan. NB: tickets can only be
booked online or at the counter (book
well in advance in summer). 🦽 pick
up prepaid tickets at County Hall
(adjacent to Eye) 30 mins before
boarding time. 🦽 🖥 📷
Ⓦ londoneye.com

The London Eye is a 135-m
(443-ft) observation wheel that
was installed on the South Bank
to mark the millennium. Its
enclosed passenger capsules
offer a 30-minute ride as the
wheel makes a full turn, with
breathtaking views over London
and for up to 42 km (26 miles)
around. Towering over one
of the world's most familiar
riverscapes, it has understandably
captured the hearts of Londoners
and visitors, and is one of the
city's most popular attractions.
Trips on the wheel are on the
hour and every half-hour.

㉑ Tate Modern

Holland St, SE1. **Map** E3. **Tel** 020 7887
8888. 🚇 Blackfriars, Southwark. 🚢 to
Tate Britain (every 40 mins). **Open**
10am–6pm daily (to 10pm Fri & Sat).
Closed 24–26 Dec. 🦽 for major
exhibitions. 📷 🦽 🖊 🖥 📷
Ⓦ tate.org.uk/modern

Looming over the southern bank
of the Thames, Tate Modern
occupies the converted Bankside
power station, a dynamic space
for one of the world's premier

collections of modern and
contemporary art. The gallery's
west entrance leads into the
huge central Turbine Hall, which
houses a newly commissioned
installation every year. The
galleries for the permanent
collection and special exhibitions
begin on level 2 and continue
to level 4, with a bridge leading
across the Turbine Hall into the
Switch House. This striking ten-
storey building opened in 2016
and displays work from 1960 to
the present, with the basement
space, formerly occupied by the
power station's oil tanks, used
for live art, film and video.

The displays in the permanent
galleries are organized by different themes such as "Artist and
Society" and "Materials and
Objects". Tate Modern's best
known works include Picasso's
Weeping Woman (1937), Henri
Matisse's paper cut-out *The Snail*
(1953) and Louise Bourgeois'
giant spider sculpture *Maman*
(1999). The top floor of the Switch
House provides stunning views.

Environs

Once a busy commercial centre
of wharves and warehouses, the
South Bank of the Thames is now
filled with a variety of attractions,
all accessible from the Queen's
Walk riverside promenade. Some
of the highlights include the
Southbank Centre, made up
of concert venues and an art
gallery, and the nearby National
Theatre. Further east at London
Bridge is one of London's newest
landmarks, **The Shard**, a 95-storey
glass skyscraper resembling a
giant spire, with restaurants and
an observation deck.

🏛 **Southbank Centre**
Belvedere Rd, SE1. **Tel** 020 7960 4200.
Open 10am–11pm daily. NB: Queen
Elizabeth Hall, Purcell Room & Hayward
Gallery are closed for refurbishment
until 2018. 📷 🦽 🖊 🖥
Ⓦ southbankcentre.co.uk

🏙 **The Shard**
Joiner St, SE1. **Tel** 0844 499 7111.
Open Apr–Oct: 10am–10pm daily;
Nov–Mar: 10am–7pm daily (to 10pm
Thu–Sat). 🦽 🖊 🖥 Ⓦ **theview
fromtheshard.com**

㉒ Shakespeare's Globe

21 New Globe Walk, SE1. **Map** E3.
Tel 020 7902 1500; 020 7401 9919 (box
office). 🚇 Southwark, London Bridge.
🚢 Bankside Pier. **Open** Performances:
late Apr–early Oct. Exhibition: 9am–
5:30pm daily. **Closed** 24 & 25 Dec. 📷
🎞 every 30 mins. 🦽 for exhibition;
limited for performances. 🖊 🖥 📷
Ⓦ **shakespearesglobe.com**

Opened in 1997, this circular
building is a reproduction of an
Elizabethan theatre, close to the
site of the original Globe where
many of Shakespeare's plays
were first performed. It was built
using handmade bricks and oak
laths, fastened with wooden pegs,
and has the first thatched roof
allowed in London since the
Great Fire of 1666. The theatre
was erected after a heroic
campaign by American actor
and director Sam Wanamaker,
with Mark Rylance appointed as
its first artistic director in 1995.
Open to the elements (although
the seating area is covered), it
operates only in the summer.
Beneath the theatre, the Globe's
exhibition covers many aspects
of Shakespeare's work. Groups

The spectacular oak-and-thatch reproduction
of the Globe Theatre

For hotels and restaurants in this region see p174 and pp184–5

may book to see the foundations of the nearby Rose Theatre, an Elizabethan playhouse.

㉓ Tower of London

Tower Hill, EC3. **Map** F3. **Tel** 0844 482 7777. 🚆 Fenchurch St. 🚌 15, X15, 25, 42, 78, 100, D1, D9, D11, RV1. 🚇 Tower Hill; Tower Gateway (DLR). 🚢 Tower Pier. **Open** Mar–Oct: 9am–5:30pm daily; Nov–Feb: 9am–4:30pm daily. Ceremony of the Keys: 9:30pm daily (book in advance). **Closed** 1 Jan & 24–26 Dec. 🗺 🎧 ♿ limited. 📷 🖥 📷 **w** hrp.org.uk

Soon after William the Conqueror became king in 1066, he built a fortification here to guard the entrance to London from attack via the Thames Estuary. In 1097 the White Tower was completed in sturdy stone; other fine buildings have been added over the centuries. The tower has served as a royal residence, armoury, treasury and, most famously, as a prison. Prisoners escorted there entered from the river through "Traitor's Gate". Some were tortured, and among those who met their death here were Edward IV's young sons, the "Princes in the Tower", and two of Henry VIII's wives, Anne Boleyn and Catherine Howard. Today, the tower is a popular attraction, housing the Crown Jewels and other exhibits, including a display on the Peasants' Revolt of 1381, the only time the tower's walls were breached. The most celebrated residents are the ravens; legend has it that the kingdom will fall if they desert the tower. Guided tours are led by the colourful Yeoman Warders, popularly known as Beefeaters.

A Yeoman Warder at the Tower of London

㉔ Tower Bridge

SE1. **Map** F3. **Tel** 020 7403 3761. 🚇 Tower Hill. 🚢 Tower Pier. **Open** Tower Bridge Exhibition: Apr–Sep: 10am–6pm daily; Oct–Mar: 9:30am–5:30pm daily. **Closed** 24–26 Dec. 🗺 📷 ♿ access lift. **w** towerbridge.org.uk

This flamboyant piece of Victorian engineering, designed by Sir Horace Jones, was completed in 1894 and soon became a symbol of London. Its two Gothic towers contain the mechanism for raising the roadway to permit large ships to pass through. The towers are made of a steel framework clad in stone, linked by two high-level walkways which were closed between 1910 and 1982 due to their popularity with suicides and prostitutes. The bridge houses the Tower Bridge Exhibition, with interactive displays bringing its history to life. The steam engine room here powered the lifting machinery until 1976, when the system was electrified. Visitors can enjoy lovely river views from the walkways.

Displays on the bridge in one of the high-level walkways, Tower Bridge Exhibition

Walkways, open to the public, give panoramic views over the Thames and London.

Lifts and 300 steps lead to the top of the towers.

The Victorian winding machinery was originally powered by steam.

Roadway
When raised, it creates a space 40 m (135 ft) high and 60 m (200 ft) wide, big enough for large cargo ships.

Engine room

South Bank

Entrance

North Bank

㉕ Victoria and Albert Museum

Cromwell Rd, SW7. **Map** B4. **Tel** 020 7942 2000. 🚌 14, 74, 414, C1. ⊖ South Kensington. **Open** 10am–5:45pm daily (to 10pm Fri; check website for details). **Closed** 24–26 Dec. 🎫 ♿ 🚻 🖼 📷 🌐 **vam.ac.uk**

The Victoria and Albert Museum (V&A) contains one of the world's greatest collections of art and design, with an eclectic array of treasures ranging from early Christian devotional objects and the religious art of Southeast Asia to Baroque sculpture and cutting-edge furniture design. Originally founded in 1852 as the Museum of Manufactures, it was built to inspire students and improve the standard of British design. It was renamed by Queen Victoria in memory of Prince Albert in 1899, the year the current building was begun.

Over 130 galleries, covering fashion, photography, ceramics, furniture and many other areas, house items spanning nearly 5,000 years of art. Displays are arranged by both geography and material. Individual galleries are devoted to the museum's outstanding collections of Japanese, Chinese and Korean artifacts, and also to such subjects across different periods. The museum's many highlights include the 17th-century Great Bed of Ware, the stunning Ardabil Carpet from Iran, the exquisite *Three Graces* sculpture by Antonio Canova, and the almost life-size *Tippoo's Tiger* (1790), which conceals a mechanical organ. The central courtyard features the tranquil John Madejski Garden, which is also used for commissioned installations. The museum's restaurant is made up of three ornately designed rooms dating from the Victorian period. A programme of exhibitions, some of them free, complements the permanent displays, and there are regular lectures, daily tours and special events.

Command module from the Apollo 10 space mission, Science Museum

㉖ Science Museum

Exhibition Rd, SW7. **Map** A4. **Tel** 0870 870 4868. 🚌 14, 74, 414, C1. ⊖ South Kensington. **Open** 10am–6pm daily. **Closed** 24–26 Dec. 📷 for IMAX, special exhibitions and simulators only. 🎫 ♿ 🖼 📷 🌐 **sciencemuseum.org.uk**

Centuries of scientific and technological development lie at the heart of the Science Museum's extensive collections. The exhibits are a tribute to mankind's inventiveness and curiosity, and include looms and steam engines, spacecraft, aero engines, and the very first mechanical computers.

The Energy Hall dominates the ground floor and contains the still-operational Harle Syke Mill Engine of 1903. The Exploring Space and Making the Modern World displays include the Apollo 10 spacecraft that carried three astronauts to the moon in May 1969. The Information Age, on the second floor, tracks the exciting developments in communication and information technologies over the last 200 years. The pioneering NeXT computer is featured in this gallery. The Flight gallery, on the third floor, is packed with an array of flying contraptions: biplanes, fighter planes, and part of a jumbo jet. The Wellcome Wing offers four floors of interactive technology, including "Who Am I?", an exhibition exploring the science of being human. The wing has an IMAX 3D cinema and a breathtaking simulator ride.

Many of the exhibits are aimed specifically at young people. In the basement, the Garden is an interactive space for 3–6 year olds, while the Wonderlab: The Statoil Gallery, on the third floor, offers an excellent hands-on experience for older children. Different days are for different age groups, so should be checked in advance, and there is a charge for entry, except for school visits during term time.

Elegant Italianate courtyard with an elliptical pool at the John Madejski Garden in the Victoria and Albert Museum

For hotels and restaurants in this region see p174 and pp184–5

The fascinating Mammals section in the Blue Zone at the Natural History Museum

❷ Natural History Museum

Cromwell Rd, SW7. **Map** A4.
Tel 020 7942 5000. 🚌 14, 74, 414, C1.
🚇 South Kensington. **Open** 10am–5:50pm daily (to 10:30pm last Fri of month). **Closed** 24–26 Dec. 🅿 ♿
♿ ⊘ ▯ 📷 🆆 nhm.ac.uk

This cathedral-like building's richly sculpted stonework conceals an iron and steel frame, a construction technique that was revolutionary when the museum opened in 1881. Inside, the imaginative displays tackle fundamental issues such as the ecology and evolution of the planet, the origin of species and the development of human beings – all explained through the latest technology and interactive techniques.

The museum is divided into four sections: the Blue, Green, Red and Orange Zones. The Blue Zone showcases mammals great and small (and a few that are extinct), fish, amphibians and reptiles, and takes a trip round the DNA and brain of humans. One of the most popular exhibits in this zone is the Dinosaur Gallery with lifelike animatronic models of dinosaurs. The Vault, in the Green Zone, contains a dazzling collection of the finest gems, crystals, metals and meteorites from around the world. Pride of place in the Red Zone's Earth Hall is the most complete Stegosaurus skeleton ever discovered. The Darwin Centre, in the Orange Zone, is a modern extension to the museum and the largest curved structure in Europe. The eight-storey-high cocoon houses the museum's vast collection of insects and plant specimens.

Portobello Road Market

Stretching for over 3 km (2 miles) through fashionable Notting Hill, Portobello Road is a characterful street of Victorian terraced shops and houses that is home to one of London's most vibrant and popular markets. It derives its name from the Porto Bello Farm, purchased by developers in the mid-19th century, which itself was named after a British naval victory of 1739. It was originally a general provisions market until the 1940s, when antique and bric-a-brac traders joined in. Today, it is probably the most famous antique market in the world, open on Saturdays (9am–7pm) with some dealers also operating on Fridays. There are also plenty of great fashion and fresh produce stalls here during the rest of the week (apart from Thursday afternoons). Halfway along the road, under the Westway flyover, is Portobello Green, a hub for clothing – both new and vintage – which is open Friday to Sunday. Further ahead, there's a rich array of food and drink on offer, from Caribbean street food to trendy cocktail bars and old-fashioned pubs. Notting Hill Gate and Ladbroke Grove are the nearest Underground stations.

Colourful antique shop selling a variety of collectables at the Portobello Road Market

❷ Royal Albert Hall

Kensington Gore, SW7. **Map** A4.
Tel 020 7589 8212 (box office).
🚇 South Kensington. **Open** varies according to event. Box office: 9am–9pm daily. **Closed** 24–26 Dec. 🅿 ♿
♿ ▯ 📷 🆆 royalalberthall.com

The network of Victorian cultural and educational institutions in South Kensington – popularly referred to as Albertopolis – was the brainchild of Queen Victoria's husband Prince Albert, who died before many of them were completed.

The vast oval hall named after him was opened in 1871, and has mainly functioned as a

Joseph Durham's statue of Prince Albert (1858) in front of the Royal Albert Hall

concert venue, although it has hosted a wide variety of other events over the years, including political rallies, stand-up comedy and sporting contests. Today, it is probably most famous for the popular annual summer season of classical music concerts that are known as the "Proms".

Environs
A short walk to the north of the Albert Hall, in Kensington Gardens, is the grandiose **Albert Memorial**. Designed by leading Victorian architect George Gilbert Scott and completed in 1875, it is made up of a vast decorative Gothic canopy within which sits a gilded statue of Prince Albert sculpted by John Foley.

A sculptural frieze at the base celebrates 169 great artistic figures. Eight large allegorical sculptures stand at the corner of the memorial and at the base of the steps leading up to it: four representing industry; the other four the Empire.

🏛 **Albert Memorial**
Kensington Gardens, W2. **Open** dawn–dusk. 📷 🆆 royalparks. org.uk

KENT AND SUSSEX

England's southeast corner has been a point of arrival for newcomers throughout history, including Iron Age Celts, Romans, Saxons, Christian missionaries and countless European visitors. Some landed on the region's long beaches while others arrived through its many fine harbours. A gentle climate, lush green countryside and close proximity to the capital city have made this region an ideal base for settlers and tourists alike.

The great white chalk cliffs of Dover and Beachy Head are the foremost symbols of the Kent and Sussex coast. Inland, green fields and woodlands are divided by three great chalk ridges running east to west, the North and South Downs and, between them, the slightly lower Weald. Iron Age people were the only settlers to prefer the tops of the Downs for the security given by their high altitude; later inhabitants all preferred the softer settings lower down.

The Romans arrived in Kent in the 1st century AD and built towns and villas between the coast and their new city of Londinium. A notable example of one of these villas is Fishbourne, near Chichester.

In the 6th century, St Augustine came to Kent to convert the Anglo-Saxons to Christianity, and he made Canterbury the centre of the English Church. Kent and Sussex have other fine churches, notably the cathedrals at Chichester and Rochester.

As London consolidated its status as a national hub, the counties between the city and the coast became favoured locations for monarchs and aristocrats to build their country homes, and so Kent and Sussex have an exceptional range of romantic castles and grand mansions, such as majestic Arundel Castle and Knole, with its 365 rooms and deer park. Kent is also known as the "Garden of England" due to the fertility of its fruit farms and the beauty of its spectacular gardens, from world-famous examples such as Sissinghurst to small gems like Ightham Mote.

Around the coast, ports such as Dover, Hastings and Rye – now far from the sea – grew rich in the Middle Ages on continental trade. More recently, this shoreline became one of the first centres of the seaside holiday, with long shingle beaches and a range of resorts from brash Margate to the jewel of the coast, bohemian Brighton.

Walkers following the South Downs Way at spectacular Beachy Head, near Eastbourne in East Sussex

◀ Brighton's majestic Royal Pavilion, transformed into a pleasure palace by King George IV

Exploring Kent and Sussex

The counties of Kent and Sussex are among the most densely populated parts of England, but around the countryside it is still easy to find peaceful corners, especially on the South Downs. Here and in many parts of Kent, such as Ashdown Forest, there are wonderful opportunities for walking. Historic towns, castles, stately mansions and gardens are spread all around the region, particularly from southeast London down to Rye. Outside London, Canterbury and Brighton are enticing urban centres, but smaller towns such as Chichester or Rye can also be enjoyable places to stay. The seaside resorts around the coast offer a choice of atmospheres, from sedate Bexhill to far more buzzing Brighton. You can also find wild places with spectacular landscapes, as on the cliffs near Eastbourne or on the marshes of Romney and Dungeness.

Sights at a Glance

1. Rochester
2. Chartwell
3. Knole
4. Hever Castle
5. Ightham Mote
6. Royal Tunbridge Wells
7. Leeds Castle
8. Sissinghurst
9. Wakehurst Place
10. *Ashdown Forest p71*
11. *Canterbury pp72–3*
12. Whitstable
13. Margate
14. Deal
15. Dover

16. Romney Marsh
17. *Rye pp78–9*
18. Winchelsea
19. Bodiam Castle
20. Hastings
21. Eastbourne
22. Charleston
23. Lewes
24. *Brighton pp82–3*
25. Steyning

26. Arundel Castle
27. Petworth House
28. Chichester
29. *South Downs and South Downs Way pp86–7*

St Malo, Santander, Bilbao, Caen, Cherbourg, Le Havre, Channel Islands

0 kilometres 10

0 miles 10

Colourful wooden beach huts on the seafront in Brighton, Sussex

For hotels and restaurants in this region see pp174–5 and pp185–6

Getting Around

The motorway network – the M25 around London, the M2 and M20 into Kent, and the M23 into Sussex – makes it easy to drive into this area from London. Along the Sussex coast, the A27 connects all the main towns. Note, though, that all these roads can get very congested in summer and at weekends, so plan accordingly. A comprehensive rail network serves all the main towns, especially from London, and there are excellent local bus services to smaller places, particularly around Brighton.

Boats docked at the Ramsgate marina in Kent

Key

▬ Motorway
▬ Dual carriageway
▬ Main road
╍╍╍ Other road
╍╍╍ Railway
▬ County border
△ Peak

Moated Bodiam Castle, built in the 14th century to defend Sussex against French invasion during the Hundred Years' War

For additional map symbols *see back flap*

View of Rochester Castle and Cathedral from across the River Medway

❶ Rochester

Kent. **Map** E1. 27,000
95 High St; 01634 338141.
3rd Sun. Dickens Festival: Jun; Dickens Christmas Festival: Dec.

Clustered at the mouth of the River Medway are Rochester, Chatham and Gillingham, all rich in naval history, but none more so than Rochester, which occupied a strategic position on the London to Dover road.

England's tallest Norman keep is at **Rochester Castle**, worth climbing for views over the Medway. The town's long history, from the Romans to Nelson's era, is visible in its historic streets. Rochester Cathedral, begun in 1080, has a fine Norman nave and crypt.

Rochester Castle
Castle Hill. **Tel** 01634 335882.
Open 10am–4pm daily (Apr–Sep: to 6pm). **Closed** 1 Jan & 24–26 Dec. grounds only.
EH W **english-heritage.org.uk**

Environs
The **Historic Dockyard**, located in Chatham, is now a naval museum and has a submarine and other historic warships. Nearby **Fort Amherst** was built in 1756 to protect the dockyard from attack, and has 1,800 m (5,906 ft) of tunnels that were hewn by Napoleonic prisoners of war.

Historic Dockyard
Main Gate Rd, Chatham. **Tel** 01634 823800. **Open** 10am–4pm daily (Apr–Sep: to 6pm). **Closed** Dec–mid-Feb.
except parts of ships.
W **thedockyard.co.uk**

Fort Amherst
Dock Rd, Chatham. **Tel** 01634 847747.
Open Grounds: dawn–dusk daily.
for tours only. Tunnels: 11am & 2pm daily (11am in winter).
W **fortamherst.com**

❷ Chartwell

Mapleton Rd, Westerham, Kent.
Map D1. **Tel** 01732 868381.
Sevenoaks or Oxted, then taxi.
Open House: Mar–Oct: 11:30am–5pm daily; Nov–Feb: 11am–3pm. Gardens & Studio: times vary, check website.
Closed 24 & 25 Dec. limited.
NT W **nationaltrust.org.uk**

This grand Victorian house was the home of Sir Winston Churchill from the 1920s until his death in 1965, and is full of reminders of the great man. Before he became prime minister in 1940, he expended a lot of his energy on improving Chartwell, and with Lady Churchill he created a magnificent garden, with lakes, a rose garden and gorgeous views over the Kent Weald. There is also the famous wall he built himself when he took up bricklaying as a hobby. His greatest hobby, though, was painting, and his specially built studio is lined with beautiful landscapes and portraits he painted at Chartwell and on his international travels.

After he died, Lady Churchill left the house almost immediately, and the main rooms are still preserved almost exactly as the couple left them. Enormously atmospheric, they are full of books, family photos, cigar stubs, letters, memorabilia and gifts from various world figures, giving a rich flavour of his life and personality.

❸ Knole

Sevenoaks, Kent. **Map** D1.
Tel 01732 462100. Sevenoaks, then taxi. **Open** Showrooms: Mar–Oct: noon–4pm Tue–Sun & public hols. Tower: 10am–5pm daily (to 4pm in winter). Park: dawn–dusk daily. limited to Great Hall and park. NT
W **nationaltrust.org.uk**

One of England's grandest private houses, this stunning Elizabethan mansion was built in the 15th century.

In 1566, Knole was acquired by Thomas Sackville, Earl of Dorset, a favourite of Elizabeth I,

Charles Dickens (1812–70)

Photo of Charles Dickens

Considered the greatest English novelist of the Victorian era, Charles Dickens was born in Portsmouth, but moved to Chatham aged 5. He set many of his stories – in particular *Great Expectations* – in the Rochester area. Although he later moved to London, Dickens kept up his Kent connections and spent his last years at his country home at Gad's Hill, near Rochester. The town celebrates the famous connection with an annual Dickens festival each June.

who extended the house. His descendants have lived here ever since, including the writer Vita Sackville-West (1892–1962).

The mansion's design echoes the calendar, with 365 rooms, 52 staircases, 12 entrances and seven courtyards. The house is full of treasures, including paintings by Anthony van Dyck, a magnificent 17th-century staircase and antique furniture. A lovely 405-ha (1,000-acre) medieval deer park, with a large herd of sika and fallow deer, encircles the house.

Knole is currently undergoing renovation and some show-rooms are closed to the public.

❹ Hever Castle

Edenbridge, Kent. **Map** D1. **Tel** 01732 865224. 🚆 Edenbridge, then taxi. **Open** Castle: Apr–Oct & Dec: noon–6pm daily; Nov–Mar: noon–4:30pm Wed–Sun. Gardens: Apr–Oct & Dec: 10:30am–6pm daily; Nov–Mar: 10:30am–4:30pm Wed–Sun. Last adm: 90 mins before closing. 🐾 📷 ♿ limited. 🖼 📷 📱 🌐 **hevercastle.co.uk**

This moated castle, the oldest parts of which date back to 1270, is famous as the child-hood home of Anne Boleyn, the doomed second wife of Henry VIII, who was executed for adultery. Hever was her family's castle, and the king often visited her here.

In 1903, Hever was bought by millionaire William Waldorf Astor, who restored it as a country mansion, building a

Neo-Tudor village alongside for guests and servants. Inside the house, visitors can see Anne Boleyn's bedroom and many other apartments, while the lovely gardens are filled with sculptures, grottoes and imaginative topiary. Hever also hosts jousting and other events.

One of the three outdoor mazes in the lush gardens of Hever Castle

❺ Ightham Mote

Ivy Hatch, near Sevenoaks, Kent. **Map** D1. **Tel** 01732 810378. 🚆 Sevenoaks, then taxi. **Open** House: Mar–Oct: 11am–5pm daily; Nov: 11am–3pm Sat & Sun; Dec: 11am–3pm daily. Gardens: Mar–Oct: 10am–5pm daily; Nov–Dec: 10am–3:30pm daily. Last adm: 30 mins before closing. **Closed** Jan, Feb, 24 & 25 Dec. 🐾 ♿ limited. 🖼 📷 NT 🌐 **nationaltrust.org.uk**

A little-known gem, nestled in a lush green valley, Ightham (pronounced "item") is the most complete medieval manor house in England,

with parts of it dating back to the 1320s. Its stone-and-timber building contains over 70 rooms and encloses a grand courtyard (complete with a Grade 1 listed 19th-century dog kennel). Rooms are decorated in a range of styles dating from across the centuries, including a 15th-century chapel with an ornate 16th-century painted oak ceiling, and a drawing room adorned with hand-painted 18th-century Chinese wallpaper. The house is surrounded by a placid moat, crossed by three bridges, and is set in beautifully manicured gardens.

For 300 years, the manor was home to the Selby family, who were involved in the Gunpowder Plot to blow up Parliament in 1605 (see p36). It is said that the ghost of Dorothy Selby, who accidentally gave away the plotters to the authorities, still lives in Ightham's tower.

Environs

Another extraordinary historic relic, in the countryside not far east of Ightham, is **Old Soar Manor**. It was once part of a larger estate, built around 1290, that was home to a medieval knight. Although parts of the stone manor have been lost over the centuries, Old Soar still retains several evocative rooms, a chapel and latrines.

🏠 Old Soar Manor

Plaxtol, Kent. **Tel** 01732 810378. **Open** Apr–Sep: 10am–6pm Sat–Thu. **Closed** Oct–Mar. NT 🌐 **nationaltrust.org.uk**

The west front of Ightham Mote, a moated medieval manor house

❻ Royal Tunbridge Wells

Kent. **Map** D2. 57,000.
The Corn Exchange, the Pantiles; 01892 515675. 2nd & 4th Sat.
visittunbridgewells.com

Mineral springs believed to have healing properties were discovered at Tunbridge in 1606, and the surrounding village developed to become one of England's first fashionable spa towns, aided by royal patronage that began with King Charles I and Queen Henrietta Maria in the 1630s. At the centre of old Tunbridge is the Pantiles *(see p193)*, a colonnaded promenade built between 1680 and 1697. It is now home to independent shops, restaurants and antique dealers.

Environs

Just 11 km (7 miles) to the north is the manor house of **Penshurst Place**, which features a magnificent Baron's Hall dating from 1341 and is set amid gorgeous gardens. It is a favourite location for historical films.

Penshurst Place
Penshurst. **Tel** 01892 870307.
Open House & Toy Museum: mid-Feb–Mar: noon–4pm Sat & Sun; Apr–Oct: noon–4pm daily. Gardens & Grounds: Apr–Oct: 10:30am–6pm daily. **Closed** Nov–mid-Feb (House & Gardens). limited for the house.
penshurstplace.com

The elegant Pantiles, 17th-century arcades in Royal Tunbridge Wells

Majestic Leeds Castle, seen from across its exceptionally broad moat

❼ Leeds Castle

Maidstone, Kent. **Map** E1. **Tel** 01622 765400. Bearsted then taxi or (Apr–Sep) shuttle bus. **Open** Apr–Sep: 10am–6pm daily; Oct–Mar: 10am–5pm daily. **Closed** 4 & 5 Nov, 25 Dec.
leeds-castle.com

Often considered to be the most beautiful castle in England, Leeds is surrounded by one of the country's largest moats, which reflects the warm stone colours of the castle's crenellated turrets. Begun in the 1120s, the castle was inhabited until 1974.

Leeds has royal connections going back to 1278, when it became a favourite residence of King Edward I. Henry VIII gave it to his first queen, Catherine of Aragon, although when staying here he often visited Anne Boleyn at nearby Hever *(see p69)*. Leeds passed out of royal ownership in 1552. Its last private owner, Lady Baillie, lavishly redecorated the interiors in the 1920s.

The estate's attractions include an exhibition of arms and armour, the historic Culpeper kitchen garden, playgrounds and a mini-train. Visitors can stay in rooms in a 16th-century tower or a "Knight's Glamping" campsite.

❽ Sissinghurst

Cranbrook, Kent. **Map** E2. **Tel** 01580 710700. Staplehurst then taxi.
Open Estate: dawn–dusk daily. Gardens: mid-Mar–Oct: 11am–5:30pm daily. **Closed** 24 & 25 Dec (Estate).
limited. NT
nationaltrust.org.uk

The most famous and influential of all the region's many gardens was begun by poet and writer Vita Sackville-West (1892–1962), who had grown up at Knole *(see pp68–9)*, and her husband, the diplomat and author Harold Nicholson (1886–1968). They acquired the 16th-century Sissinghurst Castle in the 1930s.

Working as an "artist-gardener", Sackville-West spurned traditional ideas of formal garden design and instead created different garden "rooms" around the old house, each with plants chosen by colour, texture and season to match a particular theme, most spectacularly in the celebrated White Garden. These gardens and the estate's meadows are interlinked so as to present a range of vistas. Inside the house, the library is full of items collected by Vita and Harold, and the Elizabethan Tower offers a lovely overview of the gardens.

❾ Wakehurst Place

Ardingly, West Sussex. **Map** D2.
Tel 01444 894066. Haywards Heath, then bus or taxi. **Open** Mar–Oct: 10am–6pm daily; Nov–Feb: 10am–4:30pm daily. **Closed** 24 & 25 Dec.
kew.org/visit-wakehurst

Spread across 188 ha (465 acres), this "country extension" of the Royal Botanical Gardens (Kew Gardens) in London is the largest and most varied of the many spectacular gardens in the Kent and Sussex Weald. Offering an array of vibrant colours at every time of year, the displays here are spread around an Elizabethan mansion that hosts related exhibitions. The fascinating range of natural environments includes woodlands, lakes, natural water gardens and rare Himalayan gardens. A special highlight is the Millennium Seed Bank, a comprehensive conservation scheme dedicated to preserving over 24,000 plant species.

Environs

Nearby are another two lovely gardens. **Sheffield Park** is considered one of the most celebrated works of "Capability" Brown *(see p25)*, with four inter-connected lakes arranged to present different vistas in each season. **Nymans** is a more intimate garden, created in the

1890s by the Messel family. It is set around a Neo-Gothic mansion, now partly in ruins.

🌿 Sheffield Park
Uckfield, East Sussex. **Tel** 01825 790231. **Open** 10am–5pm daily. **Closed** 24 & 25 Dec. 🅿️ ♿ 🛍️ 📷 **NT** **W** nationaltrust.org.uk

🌿 Nymans
Handcross, West Sussex. **Tel** 01444 405250. **Open** Gardens: Mar–Oct: 10am–5pm daily; Nov–Feb: 10am–4pm daily. House: Mar–Oct: 11am–4pm daily. **Closed** 24 & 25 Dec. 🅿️ 📷 ♿ 🛍️ 📷 **NT** **W** nationaltrust.org.uk

The ruins of a 19th-century mansion in the stunning gardens at Nymans

⑩ Ashdown Forest

Once a hunting reserve, Ashdown Forest is a broad expanse of wild, ancient heathland, intermixed with dense woods and hilltop clumps of tall pines. The forest is closely associated with A A Milne (1882–1956), who lived in Hartfield during the 1920s while he wrote his *Winnie the Pooh* stories. With his young son – the model for Christopher Robin – he explored the woods, and many of "the enchanted places" featured in the stories can be found here.

⑥ Ashdown Forest Centre
On one of the highest points in the forest, the centre provides information on walks, wildlife and other features of the area.

Key
▬▬ Tour route
═══ Other road

⑤ Wych Cross and Ashdown Forest Llama Park
The park offers llama rides. There are also cafés and a shop selling llama-wool products.

Tips for Drivers
Starting point: Hartfield.
Length: 20 km (12 miles).
Stopping-off points: Pubs serve food in each village. The Gallipot Inn in Upper Hartfield and the Hatch Inn in Coleman's Hatch are particularly recommended. Pooh Corner has a cozy tearoom.

① Hartfield
This little village is home to the Pooh Corner shop and tearoom, a must-visit for Winnie the Pooh fans.

② Poohsticks Bridge
This is where Milne invented the game of Poohsticks, which involves dropping twigs on one side of the bridge and seeing how fast they come out on the other.

③ Gill's Lap
The woods and heaths around Gill's Lap are at the heart of the Pooh stories, from the Enchanted Place Memorial, a plaque in honour of A A Milne and the illustrator E H Shepard, to the 100-Acre Wood.

④ Nutley Windmill
Over 300 years old, this wooden mill is one of only a handful still functioning in Britain.

A sculpture of Jesus at Christ Church Gate, Canterbury Cathedral

⓫ Canterbury

Kent. **Map** F1. 🚉 51,000. 🛳 🚌
ℹ The Beaney House of Knowledge, 18 High St; 01227 862162. 🚩 Wed & Fri. 🆆 canterbury.co.uk

Its location on the London to Dover route meant Canterbury was an important Roman town even before the arrival of St Augustine in 597, sent by the pope to convert the Anglo-Saxons to Christianity. The town soon became the centre of the Christian Church in England.

With the building of the cathedral and the martyrdom of Thomas Becket *(see p35)*, Canterbury became a religious centre. Today, the town is a UNESCO World Heritage Site.

Just east of St Augustine's Abbey is St Martin's Church, the oldest church in the English-speaking world. St Augustine first worshipped here, and the church is still used as a place of worship. It has impressive Norman and Saxon stonework.

A 10-minute walk west, the **Canterbury Roman Museum** offers a glimpse into the city's ancient past. Nearby, the Poor Priests' Hospital, founded in the 1100s, is now the **Canterbury Heritage Museum**. Five minutes away stands Westgate (1380), an imposing medieval gatehouse with two massive towers.

🏛 **Canterbury Roman Museum**
Longmarket, Butchery Lane. **Tel** 01227 785575. **Open** 10am–5pm daily. 🚫
♿ 🆆 canterburymuseums.co.uk

🏛 **Canterbury Heritage Museum**
Stour St. **Tel** 01227 475202. **Open** 11am–5pm Wed–Sun. **Closed** Jan. 🚫
📷 🆆 canterburymuseums.co.uk

Canterbury Cathedral

To match Canterbury's growing ecclesiastical rank as a major centre of Christianity, the first Norman archbishop, Lanfranc, ordered a new cathedral to be built on the ruins of the Anglo-Saxon cathedral in 1070. It was enlarged and rebuilt many times and as a result embraces examples of all styles of medieval architecture. The most poignant moment in its history came in 1170 when Thomas Becket was murdered here. Four years after his death a fire devastated the cathedral and the Trinity Chapel was built to house Becket's remains. The shrine quickly became an important religious site and until the Dissolution of the Monastaries the cathedral was one of Christendom's chief places of pilgrimage.

Nave
At 60 m (197 ft), this extended aisle makes Canterbury one of the longest medieval churches.

Main entrance

KEY

① **The southwest porch** (1426) may have been built to commemorate the victory at Agincourt.

② **Great Cloister**

③ **Chapter House**

④ **The circular Corona Chapel**

⑤ **Trinity Chapel**

⑥ **St Augustine's Chair**

⑦ **The quire** (choir), completed in 1184, is one of the longest in England.

⑧ **The Great South Window** has four stained-glass panels (1958) designed by Erwin Bossanyi.

★ **Medieval Stained Glass**
This depiction of the 1,000-year-old Methuselah is a detail from the south-west transept window.

Geoffrey Chaucer (c.1345–1400)

Considered the first great English poet, Geoffrey Chaucer was a courtier and civil servant. He wrote *The Canterbury Tales* (c.1387–1400), a witty and rumbustious account of a group of pilgrims travelling from London to Becket's shrine. The pilgrims represent a cross-section of 14th-century English society and the tales remain one of the greatest and most entertaining works of early English literature.

An illustration in *The Canterbury Tales*

VISITORS' CHECKLIST

Practical Information
11 The Precincts, Canterbury.
Map F1. **Tel** 01227 762862.
Open 9am–5pm Mon–Sat (to 5:30pm in summer), 12:30–2:30pm Sun; call ahead. **Closed** for services & concerts, Good Friday, 24 & 25 Dec. 🅿 🛍 🎧 ♿ 🚻 8am daily; 5:30pm Mon–Fri; 3:15pm Sat; 11am & 3:15pm Sun. 📷
W **canterbury-cathedral.org**

Bell Harry Tower
The central tower was built in 1498 to house a bell donated 100 years previously by Henry of Eastry. The fan vaulting is a superb example of the late Perpendicular style.

★ **Site of the Shrine of St Thomas Becket**
This Victorian illustration portrays Becket's canonization. The Trinity Chapel was built to house his tomb, which stood here until it was destroyed in 1538. The spot is now marked by a lighted candle.

★ **Black Prince's Tomb**
A bronze effigy marks the tomb of Edward III's son, who died in 1376.

The magnificent Trinity Chapel in Canterbury Cathedral ▶

Colourful shops on Harbour Street in Whitstable's town centre

⑫ Whitstable

Kent. **Map** F1. 🏠 30,000. 🚅 🚌
ℹ The Whitstable Shop, 34 Harbour
St; 01227 770060. 🛒 Thu, 2nd &
4th Sat. 🎣 Oyster Festival: late Jul.
W canterbury.co.uk/canterbury-
district/Whitstable.aspx

Celebrated for its oysters since
Roman times, Whitstable is
the prettiest of the old fishing
towns on the North Kent coast,
with brightly painted buildings,
atmospheric alleyways, a busy
little harbour and a long shingle
beach lined with colourful huts.

The town's relaxed charm
has made it a popular weekend
escape, with plenty of lively
restaurants specializing in local
fish and seafood, especially
during the bustling Oyster
Festival each July. There are also
many unusual shops where
artists and craftspeople sell their
creations. On the beach, the walk
westwards is especially lovely.

Environs
To the west, the characterful old
town of Faversham was also
once an important river port,
but its narrow creek is now
mainly used by yachts. From the
River Swale, medieval streets run
up to the lively Market Square
and the 16th-century Guildhall.

Modern Faversham is famous
for its beer, brewed from local
Kent hops. **Shepherd Neame**,
founded in the 16th century,
is the oldest continually
operating brewery in Britain.
It offers guided tours, including
tastings, which should be
booked in advance. Visitors
should note that children under
12 years are not admitted.

🍺 Shepherd Neame
17 Court St, Faversham. **Tel** 01795
542016. **Open** 10:30am–4:30pm
Mon–Sat. 🅿 🅲 times vary,
check website for details. 🅿
W shepherdneame.co.uk

⑬ Margate

Kent. **Map** F1. 🏠 55,000. 🚅 🚌
ℹ The Droit House, Stone Pier;
01843 577577. 🛒 last Sun of the
month. **W** visitthanet.co.uk

On the north side of the Isle
of Thanet, Margate is a classic
English seaside resort, with
a long sandy beach, big
boisterous amusement parks
and other attractions. Recently
the town has modernized
its image with **Turner
Contemporary**, an arts centre
that celebrates Margate's
connections with artist J M W
Turner. It is set in a spectacular
modern building that hosts
cutting-edge exhibitions.

Just west of the town is
Quex Park, an attractive park
set around an elegant 19th-
century mansion. It also houses
the engaging **Powell-Cotton
Museum**, which features
predominantly African art
and artifacts, as well as unique
wildlife dioramas.

🏛 Turner Contemporary
Rendezvous. **Tel** 01843 233000.
Open 10am–5pm Tue–Sun. 🅰 🅳
🅿 **W** turnercontemporary.org

🏛 Quex Park and
Powell-Cotton Museum
Birchington. **Tel** 01843 842168.
Open Museum & Gardens: 10am–
5pm Tue–Sun. House: Apr–Oct:
1–4pm Tue–Sun. 🅿 🅰 🅳 🅿
W quexpark.co.uk

Environs
On the east side of Thanet,
Broadstairs is a calmer alternative to Margate. Dickens
often came here to write – his
landlady was the inspiration
for Betsy Trotwood in *David
Copperfield*. Her house, where
he stayed, is now the **Dickens
House Museum**, with his writing
desk and other exhibits.

Just south of Thanet is
Richborough Roman Fort. Now
a large grassy site with several
ruined buildings 3 km (2 miles)
inland, this was where Claudius's
Roman invaders *(see p34)* first
landed in AD 43 before taking
control of Britain.

🏛 Dickens House Museum
2 Victoria Parade, Broadstairs.
Tel 01843 861232. **Open** Easter–mid-
Jun & mid-Sep–Oct: 1–4:30pm daily;
mid-Jun–mid-Sep: 10am–4:30pm
daily; Nov: 1–5pm Sat, 1–4:30pm Sun.
🅰 🅿 **W** dickensmuseum
broadstairs.co.uk

🏰 Richborough Roman Fort
Richborough Rd, near Sandwich.
Tel 01304 612013. **Open** Apr–Sep:
10am–6pm daily; Oct: 10am–5pm
daily; Nov–Mar: 10am–4pm Sat &
Sun. **Closed** 1 Jan & 24–26 Dec.
🅰 🅳 with assistance. 🅿 🄴🄷
W english-heritage.org.uk

Turner and Margate

Often considered the greatest
of all English painters, Joseph
Mallord William Turner (1775–
1851) was a Londoner, but
first visited Margate when
he was 11, attending school
there for a while. As an adult
he returned and painted the
town's harbour and seascapes
time and again. Obsessed
with the qualities of light, he
said that "the skies over Thanet
are the loveliest in Europe".
The site of the house where
he stayed is now fittingly
occupied by the Turner
Contemporary art centre.

Margate, painted by Turner in 1822

⓮ Deal

Kent. **Map** F1. 🏔 33,000. 🚢 🚌
🛈 Town Hall, High St; 01304 369576.
🛍 Wed, Fri & Sat. **W** deal.gov.uk

The town of Deal is full of historic maritime associations: it is thought this is where Julius Caesar made the first Roman landing in England in 55 BC, and it was a major naval base up to the time of Nelson. The hazardous Goodwin Sands sandbank offshore meant that Deal's sailors needed to be especially skilful, but they were also notorious smugglers.

Today, the 18th-century Old Town has plenty of charm, with enjoyable pubs and restaurants, and there's a huge shingle beach with a modern pier that is perfect for strolling and fishing. Two fortresses – massive Deal Castle in the middle of the beach and Walmer Castle further south – were built by Henry VIII in the 1540s to ward off invaders.

🏰 Deal Castle

Marine Rd. **Tel** 01304 372762.
Open Apr–Sep: 10am–6pm daily; Oct: 10am–5pm daily; Nov–Mar: 10am–4pm Sat & Sun. **Closed** 1 Jan & 24–26 Dec. 🚫 ♿ limited. 📷 EH
W english-heritage.org.uk

🏰 Walmer Castle

Kingsdown Rd. **Tel** 01304 364288.
Open mid-Feb–Mar: 10am–4pm Wed–Sun; Apr–Sep: 10am–6pm daily; Oct: 10am–5pm daily; Nov–mid-Feb: 10am–4pm Sat & Sun. **Closed** 1 Jan & 24–26 Dec 🚫 🖥 📷 EH
W english-heritage.org.uk

⓯ Dover

Kent. **Map** F2. 🏔 32,000. 🚢 🚌 🚌
🛈 Dover Museum, Market Sq; 01304 201066. 🛍 Tue. **W** whitecliffs country.org.uk

Its proximity to France makes Dover the leading port for cross-Channel travel, whether by ferry or the nearby Channel Tunnel at Folkestone. Its famous white cliffs are an iconic British landmark. Dover's strategic position and harbour has meant it has had an important military role. Built on the site of an earlier Saxon fort, **Dover Castle** helped defend the English coast from the 1180s, when Henry II first built the keep, right up to World War II, when it served as the command post for the Dunkirk evacuation. Exhibits in the castle and the labyrinth of tunnels dug during the Napoleonic Wars *(see p37)* cover all these periods.

🏰 Dover Castle

Castle Hill. **Tel** 01304 211067.
Open mid-Feb–Mar: 10am–4pm Wed–Sun; Apr–Sep: 10am–6pm daily; Oct: 10am–5pm daily; Nov–mid-Feb: 10am–4pm Sat & Sun. **Closed** 1 Jan & 24–26 Dec. 🚫 📷 of tunnels. ♿ limited. 🖥 📷 EH **W** english-heritage.org.uk

The stunning white cliffs of Dover towering over the English Channel

⓰ Romney Marsh

Kent. **Map** E2. 🚢 Ashford, Folkestone. 🚌 Hythe. 🛈 Dymchurch Rd, New Romney; 01797 369487.
Open Apr–Oct: 10am–5pm daily; Nov–Mar: 10am–4pm Wed–Sun.
W theromneymarsh.net

Vast flat horizons and the constant presence of wind and water make the 260 sq km (100 sq miles) of Romney Marsh a pleasant retreat in densely populated southern England. Until Roman times the area was entirely covered by sea at high tide. Over time, the marshes were gradually reclaimed from the sea, forming an expanse of wetlands and boggy, fertile fields particularly suitable for the Romney Marsh sheep, bred for the quality of their wool.

Ideal for easy walking and cycling, the flat marshes are also full of birdlife, and the Visitor Centre has detailed information on bird-watching routes. The tiny marsh villages have unusual medieval churches, some built with separate towers to prevent the buildings from sinking into the soft soil. One of the best ways to see the area is by steam train. **Romney, Hythe & Dymchurch Light Railway**, opened in 1927, runs down the east side of the marsh from Hythe.

🚂 Romney, Hythe & Dymchurch Light Railway

Hythe Station. **Tel** 01797 362353.
♿ 🖥 📷 **W** rhdr.org.uk

Environs

At the end of the steam railway line, but standing apart from Romney Marsh, is the lonely Dungeness headland. An almost desert-like spit of shingle, which formed an island before the draining of the marshes, it has a nuclear power station and a lighthouse. Dungeness is also a nature conservation area, with a unique range of plants, insects and birds. The village here is one of the most eccentric in the area, with some houses made from driftwood and old railway coaches.

A Romney, Hythe & Dymchurch Light Railway steam train stopping in Dungeness

⑰ Street-by-Street: Rye

This charming fortified town was added to the original Cinque Ports in the 12th–13th centuries. A storm in 1287 diverted the River Rother so that it met the sea at Rye, and for more than 300 years the town was one of the most important Channel ports. However, in the 16th century the harbour began to silt up and the town is now 3 km (2 miles) inland. Rye's fortifications were built following frequent attacks by the French in the 14th century – on one occasion the city was almost completely burned to the ground.

★ Mermaid Street
This delightful cobbled street, with its huddled houses jutting out at unlikely angles, has hardly altered since it was rebuilt in the 15th century.

The Mint
was where coins were produced during the reign of King Stephen.

The Mermaid Inn is Rye's largest medieval building. In the 1750s it was the headquarters of a notorious group of smugglers called the Hawkhurst gang.

Strand Quay
The brick-and-timber warehouses here survive from the prosperous days when Rye was a thriving port.

Lamb House
This fine Georgian house was built in 1722. George I stayed here when he was stranded in a storm, and author Henry James (1843–1916) lived here.

St Mary's Church
The church's turret clock (1561)
is believed to be the oldest
working clock in the country.

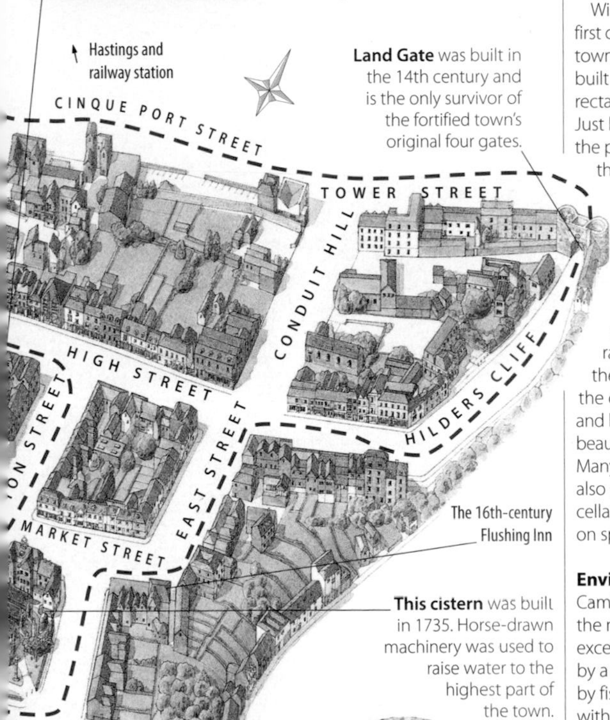

**Hastings and
railway station**

Land Gate was built in
the 14th century and
is the only survivor of
the fortified town's
original four gates.

CINQUE PORT STREET

TOWER STREET

CONDUIT HILL

HIGH STREET

HILDERS CLIFF

EAST STREET

MARKET STREET

The 16th-century
Flushing Inn

This cistern was built
in 1735. Horse-drawn
machinery was used to
raise water to the
highest part of
the town.

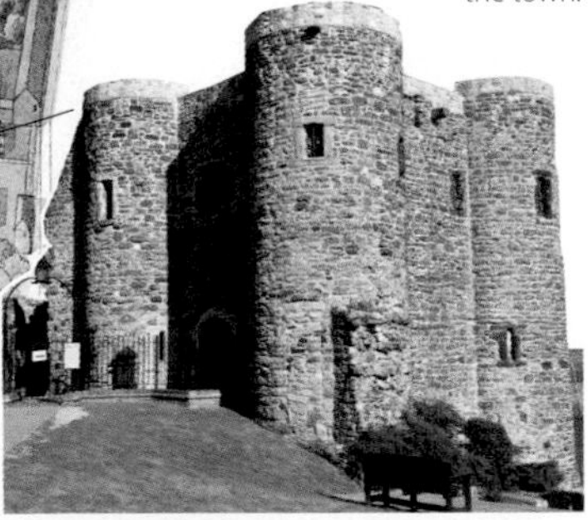

SQUARE

Key

— Suggested route

0 metres   50
0 yards   50

★ **Ypres Tower**
Built as a castle around 1250, and later used as
a private house and a prison, this is now Rye's
museum. It offers fine views of the town.

🔟 Winchelsea

East Sussex. **Map** E2. 🚏 2,200 🚉 🚌
🔲 winchelsea.net

Just 3 km (2 miles) to the
south of Rye is the small town
of Winchelsea, which is set above
one of the finest beaches on the
southeast coast. At the behest
of Edward I, the town was moved
to its present position in 1288,
after most of the Old Town on
lower land to the southeast was
drowned by the same storm that
diverted the River Rother in 1287.

Winchelsea is probably Britain's
first coherently planned medieval
town. Although not all of it was
built as originally planned, its
rectangular grid survives today.
Just beyond the edges of
the present-day town are
the remains of three of the
original gates – showing
just how big Winchelsea
was when first envisaged.
The Church of St Thomas
Becket dates back to the
same period as the town's
medieval gates. Several
raids by the French during
the 14th century damaged
the church, but it was rebuilt
and has well-preserved,
beautifully carved tombs.
Many of Winchelsea's houses
also still have their medieval
cellars, which can be visited
on special guided tours.

Environs

Camber Sands, to the east of
the mouth of the Rother, is an
excellent beach and is backed
by a row of dunes. Once used
by fishermen, it is now popular
with swimmers and windsurfers.

The ruins of **Camber Castle**
are west of the beach, near Brede
Lock. It was one of the forts built
by Henry VIII when he feared an
attack by the French. The castle
was built on the edge of the sea,
but it became stranded inland
as the river silted up. During the
Civil War, in 1642, Parliament
supporters dismantled the
castle to prevent it from being
used by the Royalists.

🏛️ **Camber Castle**
Camber. **Tel** 01797 227784. **Open** Jul–
Sep: 2pm first Sat of the month for 🅿️
only. EH 🔲 english-heritage.org.uk

Bridge leading to the main entrance of the imposing 14th-century Bodiam Castle

⑲ Bodiam Castle

Near Robertsbridge, East Sussex.
Map E2. **Tel** 01580 830196. 🚃 Battle then taxi. **Open** 10:30am–5pm daily.
Closed 24 & 25 Dec. 🅿️ ♿ limited.
📷 📸 **NT** **W** nationaltrust.org.uk

Surrounded by its wide moat, this castle, with its portcullis, spiral staircases and battlements, is one of the most romantic in England. It was begun in 1385 for knight Sir Edward Dalyngrigge, who was given permission to build it by King Richard II because it was thought it would help defend Sussex against French invasions. The castle saw action during the Wars of the Roses in 1483 and again during the Civil War in 1643–4, after which Parliamentary soldiers removed its roof to prevent it from being used by Royalist troops. Since the 19th century it has been preserved and restored as a ruin.

Environs

To the east is **Great Dixter**, a 15th-century manor restored in 1910. The late Christopher Lloyd created a lovely garden here.

🏠 Great Dixter

Northiam, near Rye. **Tel** 01797 252878.
Open House: late Mar–Oct: 2–5pm Tue–Sun. Garden: 11am–5pm Tue–Sun. Nursery Garden: open all year. 🅿️ ♿ limited. 📷 📸 **W** greatdixter.co.uk

⑳ Hastings

East Sussex. **Map** E2. 🚶 90,000. 🚃 🚌 🏨 Aquila House; 01424 451111. 🌙 Fri. **W** visit1066country.com

This fascinating seaside town was one of the first Cinque Ports *(see p36)* and is still a thriving fishing port, as illustrated by

the unique tall wooden "net shops" on the beach, where for hundreds of years fishermen have stored their nets.

In the 19th century, the area west of the Old Town was built as a seaside resort. Further east, the characterful streets of the old fishermen's quarter have remained intact. On either side of the Old Town there are "cliff railways", or funiculars, to the tops of West Hill and East Hill, which offer superb views. At the top of West Hill are the ruins of **Hastings Castle**, built by William the Conqueror soon after his victory at Battle. As well as the ruins, visitors can see an audiovisual display, "The 1066 Story". Further down the hill, the **Smugglers Adventure** exhibit evokes the world of 18th-century smugglers.

🏰 Hastings Castle

West Hill. **Tel** 01424 422964. **Open** Apr–Oct: 10am–5pm daily. 🅿️ 📸 **W** smugglersadventure.co.uk

🏛 Smugglers Adventure

St Clement's Caves, West Hill. **Tel** 01424 422964. **Open** mid-Feb–Easter: 10am–4pm daily; Easter–Oct: 10am–5pm daily. 🅿️ 📸 **W** smugglersadventure.co.uk

Environs

Just 11 km (7 miles) from the town of Hastings is Battle, built as its name suggests on the site of

the clash that transformed English history in 1066. The square is dominated by the gatehouse of **Battle Abbey**, founded by William the Conqueror to give thanks for his victory and to supposedly atone for the blood that had been spilled. The abbey was closed in the Dissolution *(see p36)*, and is mostly a ruin. From the gatehouse visitor centre, a well-marked walk takes visitors around the ruins and the battlefield.

🏰 Battle Abbey

High St, Battle. **Tel** 01424 775705.
Open Easter–Sep: 10am–6pm daily; Oct: 10am–5pm daily; Nov–Mar: 10am–4pm Sat & Sun; mid-Feb: 10am–4pm daily; late Feb–Easter: 10am–4pm Wed–Sun. **Closed** 1 Jan & 24–26 Dec. 🅿️ 🍽 ♿ 📷 📸 **EH** **W** english-heritage.org.uk

Steep West Hill cliff railway heading up to Hastings Castle at the top

㉑ Eastbourne

East Sussex. **Map** D2. 🚶 105,000. 🚃 🚌 **i** Cornfield Rd; 01323 415415. **W** visiteastbourne.com.

With its pier and beachside promenade, Eastbourne is a classic Victorian seaside resort. It is also the starting point of the South Downs Way *(see pp86–7)*,

Battle of Hastings, *Bayeux Tapestry*

Battle of Hastings

In 1066, William the Conqueror and his invading army from Normandy landed at Pevensey near Eastbourne, aiming to take Winchester and London. Hearing that the Saxon King Harold and his army were camped near Hastings, William confronted them there on 14 October. He won the battle after Harold was mortally wounded. This last successful invasion of England is depicted on the *Bayeux Tapestry*, which is kept in France.

and an excellent base for touring the South Downs. The path begins at Beachy Head, the 163-m (536-ft) chalk cliff just west of the town. From here there is a bracing clifftop walk to Birling Gap, with views to the Seven Sisters, another row of massive cliffs that end abruptly when they meet the River Cuckmere. The cliffs are part of the **Seven Sisters Country Park**, a 280-ha (690-acre) area of chalk cliffs and downland marsh.

Seven Sisters Country Park
Exceat, near Seaford. **Tel** 0345 608 0193. **Open** Visitor Centre: Mar & Nov: 11am–4pm Sat & Sun; Apr–Sep: 10:30am–4:30pm daily; Oct: 11am–4pm daily. limited. **sevensisters.org.uk**

Environs
Bexhill-on-Sea, 19 km (12 miles) east of Eastbourne, features the Art Deco **De La Warr Pavilion**, commissioned by a town mayor in 1935. Recently restored, it hosts art exhibitions, and the café is popular for its fabulous views. To the west, north of Seven Sisters, is the village of Alfriston, with an ancient market cross and a 15th-century inn, the Star. Nearby is the 14th-century **Clergy House**, which became the first National Trust property in 1896.

De La Warr Pavilion
Marina, Bexhill-on-Sea. **Tel** 01424 229111. **Open** 10am–5pm daily. to concerts. **dlwp.com**

Clergy House
The Tye, Alfriston. **Tel** 01323 871961. **Open** mid-Mar–Oct: 10:30am–5pm Sat–Wed; Nov–mid-Dec: 11am–4pm Sat & Sun. NT **national trust.org.uk**

⑫ Charleston
Firle, near Lewes. **Map** D2. **Tel** 01323 811626. Lewes then taxi. **Open** Mar–Jun & Oct: 1–6pm Wed–Sat, 1–5:30pm Sun; Jul–Sep: noon–6pm Wed–Sat, noon–5:30pm Sun. **Closed** Nov–Feb. obligatory in house, booking advisable. except upper floor of house. Charleston Festival: May. **charleston.org.uk**

An artistic time capsule, this pretty, secluded farmhouse is inseparable from the circle of avant-garde artists, designers and writers known as the Bloomsbury Group – after the area of London in which they first met in the early 1900s (see p57). Members included novelist Virginia Woolf, her husband Leonard, writers Lytton Strachey and E M Forster, and economist J M Keynes. In 1916, Virginia Woolf's sister Vanessa Bell and her lover Duncan Grant, both artists, moved to this Sussex farmhouse, and in the following years it became the group's favourite country retreat.

Over the years, Bell and Grant, with help from their family and friends, decorated the house with post-Impressionist-style paintings, textiles and ceramics. The house soon amassed an art collection that includes works by Picasso, Derain and Renoir among others. The grounds also feature a distinctive walled garden created by Bell and Grant.

The house and garden have been carefully preserved and restored as they were when the Bells left, and host varied artistic events, including an arts festival every year in May.

The imposing Lewes War Memorial, located at the top of School Hill

⑬ Lewes
East Sussex. **Map** D2. 17,000. 187 High St; 01273 483448. Fri. **staylewes.info**

The ancient town of Lewes was a vital strategic site for the Saxons. William the Conqueror built a wooden castle here in 1067, but this was soon replaced by the stone **Lewes Castle**, the ruins of which can be visited today. In 1264 Lewes was the site of a major battle in which Simon de Montfort defeated Henry III.

The impressive Tudor **Anne of Cleves House** is a museum of local history, although Anne of Cleves, Henry VIII's fourth wife, never actually lived here.

The town is famed for its celebrations of Guy Fawkes Night on 5 November (see p30).

Lewes Castle
High St, Lewes **Tel** 01273 486290. **Open** daily; times vary, check website. **sussexpast.co.uk**

Anne of Cleves House
52 Southover High St. **Tel** 01273 474610. **Open** late Feb–Dec: 10am–5pm daily. limited. **sussexpast.co.uk**

Environs
East of Lewes is Glyndebourne, the site of a private opera house which hosts the famous annual opera festival (see p28). Further south, in Rodmell, is **Monk's House**, another Bloomsbury Group residence. In 1919 Woolf and her husband bought this house as a country retreat.

Monk's House
Rodmell. **Tel** 01273 474760. **Open** House: Apr–Oct: 1–5pm daily. Garden: Apr–Oct: noon–5:30pm Wed–Sun. NT **nationaltrust.org.uk**

Spectacular view of the Seven Sisters, a series of dramatic chalk cliffs near Birling Gap

㉔ Street-by-Street: Brighton

As the nearest South Coast resort to London, Brighton is perennially popular, but has always been more sophisticated than brash neighbours such as Margate. Brighton has famously attracted actors and artists, and the spirit of the Prince Regent lives on, not only in the magnificence of his Royal Pavilion, but in the city's buzzing nightlife, unusual shops, thriving gay community and progressive politics – Brighton has Britain's only Green Member of Parliament.

The Old Ship Hotel, built in 1559, was later bought by Nicholas Tettersells with the money given to him by Charles II as a reward for helping him escape to the safety of France during the Civil War *(see p36).*

i360

Inaugurated in 2016, this breathtaking "vertical cable car" is a sleek glass pod that rises 137 m (450 ft) up a giant silver needle to provide superb 360° vistas. At the foot of the needle is a fine beachside restaurant, and inside the pod is the "Skybar", where visitors can enjoy an array of locally sourced drinks. The Skybar is also open at night for a unique view of the stars over the sea.

Brighton's i360 observation tower

Brighton Museum and Art Gallery
This lovely museum and art gallery has wonderfully varied exhibits ranging from seaside souvenirs to refined modern art.

★ **Brighton Pier**
Opened in 1899, this typical Victorian seaside pier now caters for modern visitors with arcade games, restaurants and great funfair rides.

| 0 metres | 100 |
| 0 yards | 100 |

Key
— Suggested route

The Theatre Royal, one of England's most historic theatres, opened in 1807. It often presents first performances of new plays before they move to the West End in London.

Brighton Museum and Art Gallery

CHURCH STREET

NORTH STREET

GRAND PARADE

OLD STEINE

OLD STEINE

MARINE PARADE

MADEIRA DRIVE

The Sea Life Centre is the oldest continually operating aquarium in the world. It first opened in 1872, and now hosts modern exhibits on marine life, including a shark pool.

VISITORS' CHECKLIST

Practical Information
Brighton, East Sussex. **Map** D2.
🚉 280,000. 🅻 Brighton Centre,
King's Rd; 01273 290337. 🅰
🅲 International Arts Festival: May.
🅦 visitbrighton.com

Transport
🚆 Brighton. 🚌 Pool Valley.

Brighton Dome
Built as the stables of the Royal Pavilion, this Indian-style domed building is now a concert hall and arts venue.

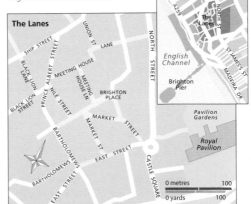

★ **Royal Pavilion**
A lavish mix of Indian, Islamic and Chinese styles, constructed with British materials, the Prince Regent's fantastic Oriental pleasure palace helped make Brighton a fashionable resort.

The Lanes

SHIP STREET
UNION ST
LANE
BLACK LION LANE
PRINCE ALBERT STREET
MEETING HOUSE LANE
MEETING HOUSE LN
NORTH STREET
BLACK LION STREET
NILE STREET
BRIGHTON PLACE
MARKET STREET
MARKET ST
EAST STREET
BARTHOLOMEWS
EAST STREET
CASTLE SQUARE

A259
The Lanes
NORTH ST
ST JAMES'S ST
MADEIRA DR
English Channel
Brighton Pier
Pavilion Gardens
Royal Pavilion

0 metres   100
0 yards   100

The Lanes
A maze of independent shops today, the Lanes were the original streets of the fishing village of Brighthelmstone *(see p37)*.

Brighton: Royal Pavilion

As sea bathing became fashionable at the end of the 18th century, Brighton was transformed into England's most fashionable seaside resort. Its gaiety soon appealed to the rakish Prince of Wales, who became George IV in 1820. After he secretly married Mrs Fitzherbert in 1785, it was here that they conducted their liaison. He rented a former farmhouse near the shore and had it enlarged by Henry Holland. In 1815, George employed John Nash to transform the house into a lavish Oriental palace, the expansion reflecting the change in his status from Prince of Wales to Regent and then King. Completed in 1823, the exterior has remained largely unaltered. Queen Victoria sold the Pavilion to the town of Brighton in 1850.

★ Banqueting Room
Fiery dragons feature in many of the interior schemes. A particularly colourful one dominates the centre of the Banqueting Room's extraordinary ceiling, which has a huge crystal chandelier suspended from it.

★ Great Kitchen
The Prince's epic banquets required a kitchen of huge proportions. The vast ranges and long shelves of gleaming copper pans were used by famous chefs of the day.

KEY

① **The exterior**, partly built in Bath stone, is a mix of Indian, Islamic and European styles.

② **Eight original torchères**, oil lamps supported by a vertical base, decorate the Banqueting Room. Made of Spode china stoneware, they are adorned with dragons, dolphins and lotus flowers.

③ **The banqueting table**, which seats 24 people, is laid for a splendid feast.

④ **Banqueting Room Gallery**

⑤ **South Gallery**

⑥ **The eastern façade**

⑦ **Queen Victoria's bedroom** is decorated with an exquisite hand-painted chinoiserie wallpaper.

⑧ **The central dome** is an imposing onion dome decorated with delicate tracery. Nash drew heavily from Islamic buildings such as the Taj Mahal, but called this design his "Hindu style".

⑨ **Music Room Gallery**

⑩ **Yellow Bow Rooms**

⑪ **Cast iron domes**

Saloon
The original farmhouse that stood on the site was transformed into a villa by architect Henry Holland. The saloon, decorated with Chinese wallpaper, was the central room of the villa.

The Prince of Wales and Mrs Fitzherbert

The Prince of Wales was only 23 years old when he fell in love with Maria Fitzherbert, a 29-year-old Catholic widow, and secretly married her. They lived in the farmhouse that later became the Pavilion, and were the toast of Brighton society until George's official marriage to Caroline of Brunswick in 1795. Mrs Fitzherbert moved into a small house nearby, and stayed in Brighton for another 40 years.

Portrait of
Mrs Fitzherbert

VISITORS' CHECKLIST

Practical Information
Old Steine, Brighton. **Map** D2.
Tel 03000 290900. **Open** Apr–
Sep: 9:30am–5:45pm daily;
Oct–Mar: 10am–5:15pm daily
(last adm: 45 mins before closing).
Closed 25 & 26 Dec. 🅿 📷
🔊 ♿ limited. 🖥 📸
🌐 **brightonmuseums.org.uk**

Long Gallery
Mandarin figures which can nod their heads line the pink-and-blue walls of this 49-m (161-ft) gallery.

The Music Room
A 70-piece orchestra played for the Prince's guests in this exquisitely decorated room with crimson and gold murals.

Plan of the Royal Pavilion

Both Holland and Nash made additions and changes to the original farmhouse. The upper floor contains bedrooms, such as the Yellow Bow Rooms, which George's brothers used.

Key to Floorplan
- ▢ Ground floor
- ▢ First floor

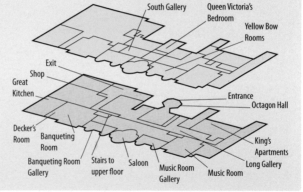

South Gallery
Queen Victoria's Bedroom
Yellow Bow Rooms
Exit
Shop
Great Kitchen
Entrance
Octagon Hall
Decker's Room
Banqueting Room
Banqueting Room Gallery
Stairs to upper floor
Saloon
Music Room Gallery
Music Room
King's Apartments
Long Gallery

㉕ Steyning

West Sussex. **Map** D2. 6,000 ⌂
9 Causeway, Horsham; 01403 211661.
W steyningsouthdowns.co.uk/visit

This lovely little town below the downs is full of timber-framed houses from the Tudor era and earlier. In Saxon times, Steyning was an important port on the River Adur, and a splendid 12th-century church is evidence of its medieval prosperity. In the 14th century the river silted up, but the town later became an important coaching stop. Standing out on the side of Steyning are the gaunt ruins of a Norman motte-and-bailey defensive fort, Bramber Castle. Also in Bramber, once a separate village, is **St Mary's House**, a timber-framed manor built around 1470, with fine panelled rooms and a garden.

St Mary's House
Bramber. **Tel** 01903 816205.
Open May–Sep: 2–6pm Thu, Sun &
public hols (also Wed in Aug).
W stmarysbramber.co.uk

㉖ Arundel Castle

Arundel, West Sussex. **Map** C2.
Tel 01903 882173. **Open** Apr–Oct:
10am–5pm Tue–Sun (also Mon in Aug).
W arundelcastle.org

Dominating the riverside town below, the vast hilltop Arundel Castle was initially built for a Norman earl in 1067. In the 16th century its owners, the Fitzalans, merged by marriage with the family of the Dukes of Norfolk, who after the Protestant

The medieval Arundel Castle, home of the
Dukes of Norfolk, dominating the skyline

Reformation (see p36) remained Roman Catholic. The castle was damaged in the Civil War (see p36), but was later restored and a Victorian mansion added.

㉗ Petworth House

Petworth, West Sussex. **Map** C2.
Pulborough then taxi. **Tel** 01798
342207. **Open** House: Apr–early Nov:
11am–5pm daily; mid-Nov–Mar:
10am–3pm daily. Park: Mar–early Nov:
10am–5pm, Nov–Feb: 10am–3:30pm
daily. **NT**
W nationaltrust.org.uk

The 17th-century Petworth House was immortalized in a series of paintings by Turner (see p76), who was often welcomed as a guest by his friend and patron, the third Earl of Egremont (1751–1837). Many of Turner's works form part of Petworth's art collection, which also includes works by Titian. The deer park around the house was landscaped by "Capability" Brown (see p25).

㉙ South Downs and South Downs Way

The South Downs are a range of steep chalk ridges extending across Sussex into Hampshire. The South Downs Way trail runs along the tops of the downs for 160 km (100 miles) from Eastbourne to Winchester, providing views over the Weald countryside to the north, and southwards down to the sea. There are lovely walks around beauty spots along the path. Iron Age hillforts are also dotted across the downs, built to take advantage of the high ground.

0 kilometres 10

0 miles 10

Old Winchester Hill
At the summit of this hill there is an Iron Age fort, and within it there are barrows – earth mounds with tombs – dating back to 4000 BC.

Weald and Downland Open Air Museum
The museum is home to a fascinating collection of historic rural buildings from across Kent and Sussex.

㉘ Chichester

West Sussex. **Map** C2. 🚉 27,000.
🚤 🚌 *i* The Novium, Tower St;
01243 775888. 🗓 1st & 3rd Fri of
month. 🎭 Arts Festival: Jun–Jul.
w visitchichester.org

This well-preserved market town,
with a 16th-century market cross
at its centre, is dominated by its
Cathedral, consecrated in 1108.
Inside, there are carved stone
panels from the 1120s and a
stained-glass window by Marc
Chagall (1887–1985). Nearby
is the cathedral's unusual 15th-
century detached bell tower.
Chichester was an important
Roman town, and sections of
its 3rd-century Roman city walls
can still be seen. In the town
centre is the **Pallant House
Gallery**, which has a collection
of modern British art.

🏰 **Chichester Cathedral**
West St. **Tel** 01243 782595. **Open** 7am–
6pm Mon–Sat, 7:15am–5pm Sun.
🎫 ⚖ ⛪ 🖥 �️ **w** chichester
cathedral.org.uk

Interior of Chichester Cathedral, with the
1966 altar tapestry designed by John Piper

🏛 **Pallant House Gallery**
9 North Pallant. **Tel** 01243 774557.
Open 10am–5pm Tue–Sat (to 8pm
Thu), 11am–5pm Sun & public hols.
🖼 ⚖ ⚖ 🖥 🛍 **w** pallant.org.uk

Environs

Bosham is a charming village
set on Chichester Harbour. Its
Saxon Holy Trinity Church is
thought to have been used by
King Cnut *(see p119)*. The church
appears in the famous Bayeux
Tapestry *(see p80)*, as King
Harold heard Mass here
before sailing to Normandy.
  Closer to Chichester is
Fishbourne Roman Palace,
the largest Roman villa in Britain.
Discovered in the 1960s, it was
built around AD 75 and had
over 100 rooms. To the north is
Goodwood House, built in the
18th-century and home to the
Duke of Richmond. Goodwood
is also well known for its sporting
events, with a motor-racing
circuit that hosts the Festival
of Speed in June and July, and
a horse-racing track that is the
venue for the annual Glorious
Goodwood festival in late July.

🏰 **Fishbourne Roman Palace**
Roman Way. **Tel** 01243 785859.
Open Mar–Oct: 10am–5pm daily;
Feb & Nov–Dec: 10am–4pm daily. 🖼
⚖ 🖥 🛍 **w** sussexpast.co.uk

🏛 **Goodwood House**
Goodwood. **Tel** 01243 755000. **Open**
late Mar–Jul & Sep–Oct: 1–5pm Sun &
Mon; Aug: 1–5pm Sun–Thu. 🖼 🎫 ⚖
⚖ 🖥 🛍 🖼 **w** goodwood.com

Key

▬▬ Motorway
▬▬ Main road
- - - South Downs Way
△ Peak

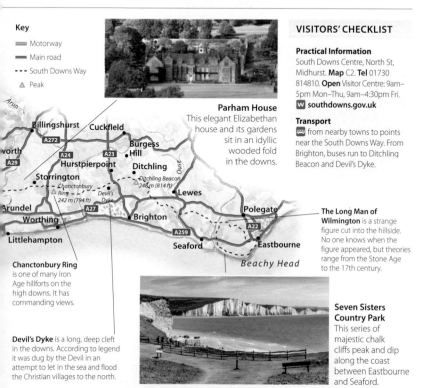

Parham House
This elegant Elizabethan
house and its gardens
sit in an idyllic
wooded fold
in the downs.

Billingshurst Cuckfield
  A272
  Burgess
worth Hill
  A24 A23
  A29 Hurstpierpoint Ditchling
  Storrington Ditchling Beacon
  Chanctonbury 248 m (814 ft)
  Ring Devil's
  242 m (794 ft) Dyke Lewes
Arundel
  Worthing A27 Brighton Polegate
Littlehampton Seaford A22
  A259 Eastbourne
  Beachy Head

Arun
Ouse

Chanctonbury Ring
is one of many Iron
Age hillforts on the
high downs. It has
commanding views.

Devil's Dyke is a long, deep cleft
in the downs. According to legend
it was dug by the Devil in an
attempt to let in the sea and flood
the Christian villages to the north.

VISITORS' CHECKLIST

Practical Information
South Downs Centre, North St,
Midhurst. **Map** C2. **Tel** 01730
814810. **Open** Visitor Centre: 9am–
5pm Mon–Thu, 9am–4:30pm Fri.
w southdowns.gov.uk

Transport
🚌 from nearby towns to points
near the South Downs Way. From
Brighton, buses run to Ditchling
Beacon and Devil's Dyke.

**The Long Man of
Wilmington** is a strange
figure cut into the hillside.
No one knows when the
figure appeared, but theories
range from the Stone Age
to the 17th century.

**Seven Sisters
Country Park**
This series of
majestic chalk
cliffs peak and dip
along the coast
between Eastbourne
and Seaford.

HAMPSHIRE AND SALISBURY PLAIN

A unique mix of natural features gives this region its distinctive landscapes, from the great rolling chalk plateau of Salisbury Plain to green river valleys and the huge natural harbours facing the Isle of Wight. They have formed the backdrop to a fascinating mix of people throughout history, from the builders of prehistoric Stonehenge and medieval cathedrals to 18th-century mariners and famous novelists.

Although often empty-looking to modern eyes, around 5,000 years ago the downs of Salisbury Plain were home to early settlers who created the mysterious stone circles of Stonehenge and Avebury and other prehistoric sites, from West Kennet Long Barrow to Silbury Hill. From Roman times onwards the grasslands of the plain provided pasture for sheep, whose wool was exported across Europe, making towns such as Bradford-on-Avon and Devizes wealthy.

Saxon settlers arrived in the 4th century, and occupied the valleys around the plain. Winchester, on the River Itchen, was the capital of Saxon Wessex and the first capital of England. In 1079, William the Conqueror made a corner of Hampshire a royal hunting reserve known as the New Forest; it has preserved its woods and heathlands ever since.

Later aristocrats built magnificent country mansions set in glorious parks and gardens, such as Beaulieu, Stourhead, Bowood and Longleat, which is now best known for its wild animal park. Hampshire's quiet, leafy villages have a special charm, and several provided the setting for the stories of one of the county's most famous residents, Jane Austen. Winchester and Salisbury have two of England's finest medieval cathedrals, and there are beautiful lesser-known churches nearby such as Romsey Abbey.

Many of the region's rivers run south into natural harbours. Thanks to these, cities such as Southampton and Portsmouth have played a central role in Britain's maritime history, from the earliest days of sailing ships to the era of transatlantic liners. The Solent, between the coast and the Isle of Wight, is also the historic home of competitive yachting, and its many harbours are a paradise for sailing fans.

The stunning 14th- and 15th-century Perpendicular Gothic nave of Winchester Cathedral, the longest cathedral in England

◀ A bird's-eye view of yachts racing in Cowes Week, one of the longest-running international regattas, which takes place on the Solent

Exploring Hampshire and Salisbury Plain

The counties of Hampshire and Wiltshire offer a great range of scenery. In eastern Hampshire, country lanes wind along wooded valleys, such as those of the Test and the Itchen, and weave between villages and unusual features such as the sudden ravines of the "Hangers". Southampton, Portsmouth and their neighbouring coastal towns make up the region's most populated area, from where ferries run to the Isle of Wight. The nearby New Forest is much loved by walkers and pony riders. Further north, the majestic spire of Salisbury Cathedral can be seen from the rolling grasslands of Salisbury Plain, on which stand the prehistoric sites of Stonehenge and Avebury. In the northwest, the downs give way to honey-stoned towns such as Corsham and Bradford-on-Avon.

Sights at a Glance

1. Chawton
2. Selborne and the Hangers
3. *Winchester pp92–3*
4. Portsmouth
5. Southampton
6. *Isle of Wight p95*
7. Romsey
8. Beaulieu
9. Lymington
10. *New Forest p97*
11. *Salisbury pp100–101*
12. *Stonehenge pp102–3*
13. Old Sarum
14. Avebury
15. Bowood House
16. Devizes
17. Lacock
18. Corsham
19. Bradford-on-Avon
20. Longleat
21. *Stourhead pp106–7*

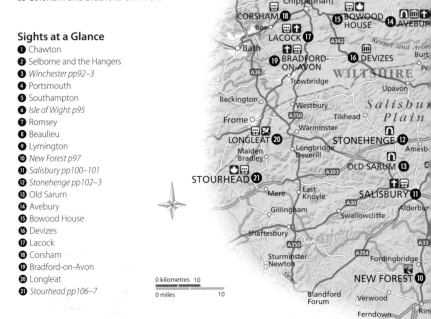

The chalk Needles and Trinity Lighthouse, the Isle of Wight's most famous landmarks

For hotels and restaurants in this region see pp176–7 and pp186–8

Purple heather in bloom in the New Forest National Park

Getting Around

Rail services run through major towns and some smaller destinations, including towns in the New Forest. Regional buses run mainly from Winchester, Salisbury and Southampton. Local buses are infrequent elsewhere, so you will need a car to explore rural areas. Two major motorways run into this region from London – the M4, running west across the top of Salisbury Plain, and the M3, which runs south to Winchester and Southampton. The often-congested M27 connects Portsmouth, Southampton and the New Forest.

Key

━━━ Motorway
━━━ Dual carriageway
━━━ Main road
∷∷∷∷ Other road
∼∼∼∼ Railway
━━━ County border

The majestic 13th-century Salisbury Cathedral

For additional map symbols *see back flap*

❶ Chawton

Hampshire. **Map** B2. 🏛 380. 🚋 Alton, then bus or taxi. 🚌 **ℹ** The Library, The Square, Petersfield; 01730 268829. **w** visit-hampshire.co.uk

This pretty, tranquil village, with its woods, ponds and old cottages, is famed as the site of **Jane Austen's House**, where the author lived with her mother and sister for the last eight years of her life. Before she came here she was unknown. At Chawton she completed novels such as *Sense and Sensibility* and *Pride and Prejudice*, and wrote all her other major novels. The house has a lovely garden and features items such as the Austens' dinner service and Jane's writing table.

Just outside the village is **Chawton House**, a magnificent 1580s manor house that once belonged to Austen's brother Edward, who added a pretty walled rose garden. The house is now a centre for the study of women's writing between 1600 and 1830, with a unique library of related works.

🏛 **Jane Austen's House**
Chawton Village Green. **Tel** 01420 83262. **Open** Jan–mid-Feb: 10:30am–4:30pm Sat & Sun; mid-Feb–May & Sep–Dec: 10:30am–4:30pm daily; Jun–Aug: 10am–5pm daily. **Closed** 24–26 Dec. 🅿 🚻 ground floor only. 📷 **w** jane-austens-house-museum.org.uk

🚻 **Chawton House**
Chawton. **Tel** 01420 541010. **Open** House: late Mar–Oct: noon–4:30pm Mon–Fri, 11am–5pm Sun & public hols. Library: by appt all year. **Closed** Nov–late Mar. 🅿 🚻 ground floor only. 📷 **w** chawtonhouse.org

The idyllic village of Selborne, seen from the woodlands on the nearby Hangers

❷ Selborne and the Hangers

Hampshire. **Map** B2. 🏛 650. 🚋 Alton, then bus or taxi. 🚌 **ℹ** The Library, The Square, Petersfield; 01730 268829. **w** visit-hampshire.co.uk

Eastern Hampshire has a unique landscape made up of a series of precipitous, cliff-like tall ridges called Hangers because they are so steep that trees and bushes seem to hang from them rather than stand on top. On one of the highest Hangers is the village of Selborne, where naturalist Gilbert White was parish priest for over 40 years, chronicling flora and fauna and every aspect of local life in his 1789 *Natural History of Selborne*. An idyllic Georgian rectory, **Gilbert White's House** is now an inspirational museum. The house was later owned by the family of Captain Lawrence Oates, who died on the 1912 Scott Expedition to Antarctica, and there are also exhibits on Oates's polar exploration and family. Away from the museum, Selborne has a zigzag path, laid out by Gilbert White, which descends the Hanger.

The Hangers are great for walking, with superb views. A circular path snakes around Hawkley, one of the prettiest villages, and the 33-km (21-mile) Hangers Way runs all the way from Alton to Petersfield.

🏛 **Gilbert White's House**
The Wakes. **Tel** 01420 511275. **Open** Jan–mid-Feb: 10:30am–4:30pm Fri–Sun; mid-Feb–late Mar, Nov & Dec: 10:30am–4:30pm Tue–Sun; late Mar–Jun, Sep & Oct: 10:30am–5pm Tue–Sun; Jul–Aug: 10:30am–5pm daily. **Closed** 25–31 Dec. 🅿 🚻 ground floor & gardens only. 📷 📷 **w** gilbertwhiteshouse.org.uk

❸ Winchester

Hampshire. **Map** B2. 🏛 45,000. 🚋 🚌 **ℹ** Guildhall, High St; 01962 840500. 🗓 Wed–Sat. 🎷 Jazz Festival: Sep; Wine Festival: Nov. **w** visitwinchester.co.uk

Capital of the early Saxon kingdom of Wessex, Winchester was also the chief city of the Anglo-Saxon kings of England until the Norman Conquest. William the Conqueror built one of his first English castles here. The only surviving part of the medieval castle is the **Great Hall**, from the 1230s, with its famous Round Table. According to legend, the wizard Merlin made the table for King Arthur

Jane Austen (1775–1817)

One of England's most popular writers, Jane Austen was happiest when she was living in Hampshire. She was born at Steventon near Basingstoke, where her father was a parish priest, and began writing very young. In 1801 the Austens moved to fashionable Bath. Reverend Austen died in 1805, and in 1809 Jane relocated with her mother and sister to her brother's estate at Chawton. In 1817 she moved to Winchester, but died soon after. Her gravestone in Winchester Cathedral famously does not mention her writing.

English novelist Jane Austen

(see p156), with a shape that was meant to ensure that no knight could claim precedence. The Winchester Table actually dates from the 13th century, and was painted in the 1520s for Henry VIII.

Old Winchester is charming. **Westgate Museum** is one of two surviving 12th-century gatehouses in the city wall, and features a painted ceiling made to celebrate the marriage of Queen Mary I and Philip of Spain in 1554. The room above the gate was a prison, and still has some of the prisoners' graffiti.

The town is an ecclesiastical centre. Wolvesey Castle, now a ruin, was once the palace of the

Part of the ruins of Wolvesey Castle, the medieval Bishop's Palace, Winchester

cathedral's bishops. South of the city, the **Hospital of St Cross** is an almshouse, dating from the 1130s. Visitors still claim the "Wayfarer's Dole", a cup of ale and bread given out since medieval times.

Great Hall
Castle Ave. **Tel** 01962 846476.
Open 10am–5pm daily. **Closed** 25 & 26 Dec & for public events.
w hants.gov.uk

Westgate Museum
High St. **Tel** 01962 869864.
Open mid-Feb–Mar: 10am–4pm Sat, noon–4pm Sun; Apr–Oct: 10am–5pm Sat, noon–5pm Sun. **Closed** Nov–mid-Feb.
w hampshireculturaltrust.org.uk

Hospital of St Cross
St Cross Rd. **Tel** 01962 878218.
Open Apr–Oct: 9:30am–5pm Mon–Sat, 1–5pm Sun; Nov–Mar: 10:30am–3:30pm Mon–Sat. **Closed** 25 Dec. by appt. limited.
w hospitalofstcross.co.uk

Winchester Cathedral

A church was built on the site of Winchester Cathedral in 648, but the present building was begun in 1079. It was a Benedictine monastery, and much of the Norman architecture remains despite modifications that went on until the early 16th century.

VISITORS' CHECKLIST

Practical Information
The Close. **Tel** 01962 857200.
Open 9:30am–5pm Mon–Sat, 12:30–3pm Sun.
w winchester-cathedral.org.uk

Choirstalls (c.1308)
These magnificent oak benches are England's oldest choirstalls.

The Lady Chapel (c.1500) was rebuilt by Elizabeth of York (1486–1503) after her son was baptized in the cathedral.

Anglers' Window
Author Izaac Walton (c.1594–1683) is depicted in this pretty 1914 stained-glass window.

The Perpendicular nave Is the highlight of the building.

Jane Austen's grave

Norman chapterhouse

Visitors' centre

Main entrance

The 12th-century black Tournai marble font

Prior's Hall

The Close originally housed domestic buildings for the Priory of St Swithun – the name of the site before it became Winchester Cathedral. Most of the buildings were destroyed during the Dissolution *(see p36)*.

View of Portsmouth's Old Town with the spectacular Spinnaker Tower in the background

❹ Portsmouth

Hampshire. **Map** B2. 🗺 210,000. 🚆 🚌 🛳 *i* D-Day Museum, Clarence Esplanade; 023 9282 6722. 🛍 Thu, Fri & Sat. **w** visitportsmouth.co.uk

A vital naval port for centuries, Portsmouth is a bustling, vibrant waterfront city with a fascinating history. **Portsmouth Historic Dockyard** contains the city's most important sights, with a range of maritime attractions. One is the hull of the *Mary Rose*, the greatest of Henry VIII's warships, which capsized on its maiden voyage as it left to fight the French in 1545. Recovered from the seabed in 1982, it is exhibited along with many of the 19,000 16th-century objects that have been raised from the wreck in a museum which opened in 2013.

The Dockyard's most famous exhibit is HMS *Victory*, the flagship on which Admiral Nelson was killed at Trafalgar in 1805 *(see p37)*. Here, visitors get a vivid idea of life at sea in the age of sail. The 19th-century HMS *Warrior* and World War I gunboat the *M.33* are nearby, along with a special exhibit on the 1916 Battle of Jutland, the National Museum of the Royal Navy and a series of other interactive attractions. Portsmouth's other major military memorial is the **D-Day Museum**, which contains the *Overlord Embroidery*, depicting the World War II Allied landings in Normandy in 1944.

Among the city's less-warlike attractions are the **Charles Dickens Birthplace Museum**,

the modest house where the famous Victorian novelist was born in 1812, and the striking **Spinnaker Tower**, which rises 170 m (558 ft) above Portsmouth, with magnificent views over the harbour and beyond.

Portchester Castle, on the north edge of the harbour, was fortified in the 3rd century and is the best example of Roman sea defences in northern Europe. Around 1100, the Normans used the Roman walls in a new castle, which Henry V used as a base before the Battle of Agincourt.

🏛 **Portsmouth Historic Dockyard**
Victory Gate, HM Naval Base. **Tel** 023 9283 9766. **Open** Apr–Oct: 10am–5:30pm daily; Nov–Mar: 10am–5pm daily. **Closed** 24–26 Dec. 🚫 🚭 limited. 🖊 🖥 📷 **w** historic dockyard.co.uk

Memorial to the Pilgrim Fathers, Southampton

🏛 **D-Day Museum**
Clarence Esplanade. **Tel** 023 9282 6722. **Open** Apr–Sep: 10am–5:30pm daily; Oct–Mar: 10am–5pm daily. NB: closed for refurbishment until spring 2018. 🚫 🚭 🖥 📷 **w** dday museum.co.uk

🏛 **Charles Dickens Birthplace Museum**
393 Old Commercial Rd. **Tel** 023 9282 1879. **Open** late Mar–Sep: 10am–5:30pm Fri–Sun; also 7 Feb (Dickens's birthday). Last adm: 30 mins before closing. 🚫 📷 **w** charles dickensbirthplace.co.uk

❄ **Spinnaker Tower**
Gunwharf Quays. **Tel** 023 9285 7520. **Open** Jul–Aug: 9:30am–6pm daily; Sep–late Jul: 10am–5:30pm daily. 🚫 🚭 🖥 📷 **w** spinnakertower.co.uk

🏰 **Portchester Castle**
Church Rd. **Tel** 02392 378291. **Open** late Mar–Sep: 10am–6pm daily; Oct: 10am–5pm daily; Nov–late Mar: 10am–4pm Sat & Sun. **Closed** 1 Jan & 24–26 Dec. 🚫 🚭 limited. 📷 **EH** **w** english-heritage.org.uk

❺ Southampton

Hampshire. **Map** B2. 🗺 255,000. ✈ 🚆 🛳 🚌 🛳 🚢 Fri & Sat.

This city has been a flourishing port since the early Middle Ages. Its city walls, extended by King Edward III in the 14th century, show its importance as a medieval royal harbour. Southampton – like Portsmouth – was one of the ports where the *Mayflower* called before it sailed to America with the Pilgrim Fathers in 1620. In the 19th century, it became Britain's foremost departure point for transatlantic liners sailing to America – the *Titanic* left from here on its maiden and ultimately tragic voyage in 1912.

A well-marked walk runs around the remains of the city walls, which include the Bargate, the most elaborate surviving medieval gatehouse in England. It still has its 13th-century drum towers and is decorated with beautifully intricate 17th-century armorial carvings.

Southampton's maritime past is showcased in the **SeaCity Museum**, with absorbing interactive displays on the city's role as "gateway to the world", including special exhibits on ocean liners and the *Titanic*, with a large-scale model of the ship.

🏛 **SeaCity Museum**
Havelock Rd. **Tel** 023 8083 3007. **Open** 10am–5pm daily (last adm: 1 hr before closing). **Closed** 1 Jan & 24–26 Dec. 🚫 🚭 🖥 📷 **w** seacitymuseum.co.uk

❻ Isle of Wight

A little England in miniature, the diamond-shaped Isle of Wight prides itself on its tranquillity and a sense of being slightly apart from the bustle of the mainland. For a small island, it has remarkably varied scenery and plenty of historical associations, from prehistoric settlers to King Charles I and Queen Victoria. The north coast is a paradise for sailing enthusiasts, particularly around Cowes, the birthplace of modern regattas.

VISITORS' CHECKLIST

Practical Information
Hampshire. **Map** B3. 🛈 The Guildhall, High St, Newport; 01983 521555; 🅦 visitisleofwight.co.uk

Transport
🚢 from Southampton to East Cowes, Portsmouth to Fishbourne and Lymington to Yarmouth (passenger-only ferries from Southampton and Portsmouth to Cowes and Ryde).

Cowes has been the home of yacht racing since the 19th century. In August, the Cowes Week races feature boats from all over the world.

Osborne House was the favourite home of Queen Victoria and her husband Prince Albert. It is still furnished largely as they left it.

Ryde is the island's largest town. It has long sandy beaches beside Britain's oldest traditional seaside pier, begun in 1813.

Yarmouth
With a castle built by Henry VIII, Yarmouth is one of the most picturesque of the island's small harbours.

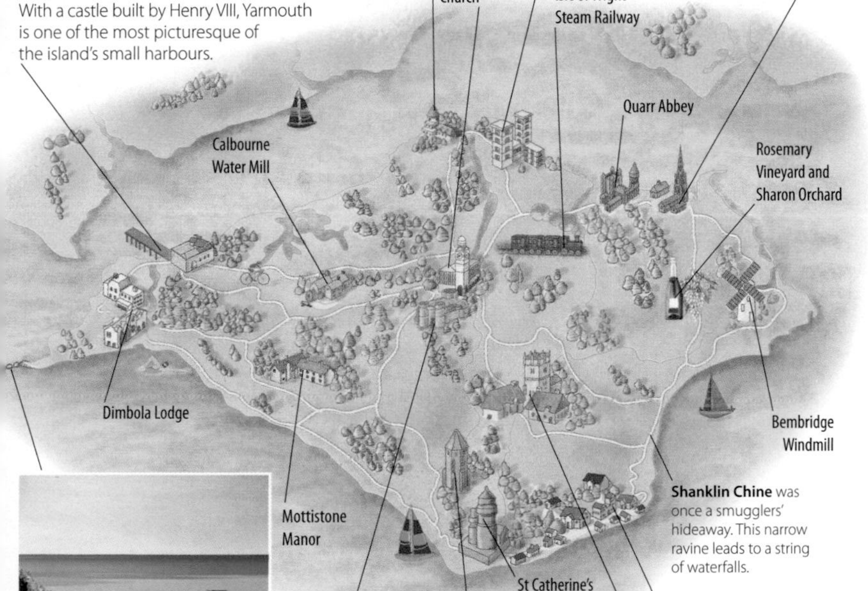

Whippingham Church

Isle of Wight Steam Railway

Quarr Abbey

Calbourne Water Mill

Rosemary Vineyard and Sharon Orchard

Dimbola Lodge

Bembridge Windmill

Mottistone Manor

Shanklin Chine was once a smugglers' hideaway. This narrow ravine leads to a string of waterfalls.

The Pepper Pot

St Catherine's Lighthouse

Godshill's church was reportedly built on a hill after, according to legend, the stones used to build it were moved here by God from their original position at the bottom of the hill.

Ventnor is a tranquil town on a steep bay with an unusually sunny microclimate.

Carisbrooke Castle
Set on a hill above Newport, this castle is famous as the place where King Charles I was imprisoned by Parliament before his execution in 1649.

The Needles
These jagged rock pinnacles are a symbol of the island, and there are superb views of them from the cliffs and beaches at nearby Alum Bay.

The interior of Romsey Abbey, a fine example of British Norman architecture

❼ Romsey

Hampshire. **Map** B2. 🚂 18,000. 🚊 🚌 𝒊 Church St; 01794 512987. 🛒 Tue, Fri & Sat. **W** visitromsey.co.uk

This charming market town grew up around **Romsey Abbey**, built around 1130 on the remains of an older Saxon church. The Norman church has a nave of simple columns and rounded arches.

Nearby, the heritage centre at **King John's House** combines a 19th-century gun shop with a Tudor-era extension built onto one of the oldest surviving houses in England, with graffiti left by medieval knights in 1306.

On the edge of Romsey is **Broadlands**, an elegant 1730s Palladian mansion set in a park landscaped by "Capability" Brown (*see p25*). It was the home of the Victorian prime minister Lord Palmerston and later of Earl Mountbatten.

🏠 Romsey Abbey
Church Lane. **Tel** 01794 513125. **Open** 7:30am–6pm Mon–Sat, 9am–6pm Sun. 🎴 🚻 🚹 📷 **W** romseyabbey.org.uk

🏛 King John's House
Church St. **Tel** 01794 512200. **Open** 10am–4pm Mon–Sat. 🚫 🚻 limited. 🖥 📷 **W** kingjohnshouse.org.uk

🏰 Broadlands
Broadlands Park. **Tel** 01794 505080. **Open** Jul & Aug: 1–4pm Mon–Fri. 🚫 🎴 🚫 🖥 📷 **W** broadlands estates.co.uk

Environs
North of Romsey runs the River Test, renowned for fly-fishing and flanked by the Test Way footpath.

About 8 km (5 miles) north of Romsey, **Mottisfont Abbey** is a historic house with sections that date from the 13th to the 18th century. Inside is a permanent art collection with works by Degas, as well as a room decorated in the 1930s by artist Rex Whistler. The house has gorgeous gardens.

🏛 Mottisfont Abbey
Near Romsey. **Tel** 01794 340757. **Open** House & Gallery: Mar–Oct: 11am–5pm daily; Nov–Feb: 10am–4pm daily. Gardens: Mar–Oct: 10am–5pm daily; Nov–Feb: 10am–dusk daily. **Closed** 24 & 25 Dec. 🚫 🚻 **NT** **W** nationaltrust.org.uk

❽ Beaulieu

Hampshire. **Map** B2. 🚂 850. 🚊 Beaulieu Rd. 🚌 **W** thenewforest. co.uk

The Beaulieu estate is one of Britain's most popular aristocratic homes. **Palace House**, once the gatehouse of Beaulieu Abbey, has been home to the Montagu family since 1538. Parts of the house were built in the 13th century, but it was renovated in the Victorian era in Neo-Gothic style. The vast estate can be toured by monorail and sights include an *Alice in Wonderland*-themed topiary garden and an exhibit on monastic life in the ruins of the original abbey (founded in 1204 by King John for Cistercian monks).

The most famous attraction of Beaulieu is the **National Motor Museum**. Established by the current Lord Montagu's father in 1952, it is home to one of the world's finest collections of vintage vehicles. A single ticket is valid for all the attractions.

🏛 Palace House and National Motor Museum
Beaulieu. **Tel** 01590 612345. **Open** late May–Sep: 10am–6pm daily; Oct–late May: 10am–5pm daily. **Closed** 25 Dec. 🚫 🚻 🖥 📷 **W** beaulieu.co.uk

Environs
South of Beaulieu, **Buckler's Hard** is a well-preserved village built by Lord Montagu in the 18th century. It was once a centre for shipbuilding, using timber from the New Forest to construct hulls for Royal Navy vessels, but fell into decline when sailing ships gave way to steam. Today, a maritime museum hosts exhibitions on shipwright skills. Boat cruises are also available.

🏛 Buckler's Hard
Beaulieu. **Tel** 01590 616203. **Open** late Mar–Sep: 10am–5pm daily; Oct–late Mar: 10am–4:30pm daily. **Closed** 25 Dec. 🚫 🚻 limited. 🚫 🖥 📷 **W** bucklershard.co.uk

❾ Lymington

Hampshire. **Map** B2. 🚂 6,000. 🚊 Mill Lane. 🚌 🛒 Sat. **W** thenewforest.co.uk

With a Georgian high street, cobbled lanes, restaurants and a busy Saturday market, Lymington has plenty of charm. Its location on the Solent facing the Isle of Wight, with ferries across, makes it a popular sailing harbour, and there are three marinas. Near the harbour is the **Sea Water Baths**, an open-air seawater swimming pool built in 1833.

Sea Water Baths
Bath Rd. **Tel** 01590 678882. **Open** Apr–Jul: 2:30–6pm Mon–Fri, 10am–6pm Sat & Sun; Jul–Sep: 10am–6pm daily. 🚫 🚻 🖥 **W** lymington seawaterbaths.org.uk

The Neo-Gothic towers and gables of Palace House, Beaulieu

⑩ New Forest

The New Forest got its name when it was made a new royal hunting preserve by William the Conqueror shortly after he seized England in 1066. Now a national park, it retains some ancient laws – especially the right for local inhabitants to graze animals across the entire forest. These include the famous New Forest ponies, which roam freely through the villages. The gorgeous mix of heath and woodland scenery is home to a range of birds and England's largest deer herds.

⑦ Fordingbridge
A bridge was first built over the River Avon here in the early 13th century.

⑧ Rufus Stone
This iron-clad stone marks the spot where cruel King William II – known as Rufus because of his red face – is said to have been killed.

⑨ Minstead
This little village of old thatched cottages was a favourite of Sir Arthur Conan Doyle, creator of Sherlock Holmes, who is buried in the churchyard.

Key

━━ Tour route

┅┅ Other road

0 km 2
0 miles 2

① Lyndhurst
The "Capital of the New Forest" contains the Queen's House, site of the Verderer's Court, which administers the traditional Forest laws.

Cadnam · Fritham · Frogham · A338 · Rockford · A31 · New Forest National Park

② Bolderwood
A narrow lane leads to the Bolderwood Deer Sanctuary, the best place to see deer in the forest.

⑥ Ringwood
A market has been held here every Wednesday since 1226. The town has a long tradition of beer-making, now kept up by the Ringwood Brewery.

⑤ Burley
This village's main street has a timeless feel, with its low-roofed cottages and freely roaming ponies.

③ Rhinefield Ornamental Drive
A road lined with rhododendrons, azaleas and some of the only American sequoias and redwoods to be found in England.

Tips for Drivers

Starting point: Lyndhurst.
Length: 77 km (48 miles).
Stopping-off points: Each town and village has cafés and pubs serving food. In Fordingbridge, the George is located beside the River Avon and the historic bridge. **Information:** New Forest Centre, Lyndhurst; 023 8028 3444; www.newforestcentre.org.uk **Transport:** New Forest Tour offers bus tours on three routes (www.thenewforesttour.info).

④ Brockenhurst
Ponies, cattle and donkeys are often seen drinking peacefully at the river ford in the centre of one of the prettiest New Forest villages. It is a popular base for pony treks into the countryside.

⓫ Salisbury

The "new" city of Salisbury was founded in 1220, when the hilltop settlement of Old Sarum was abandoned – being too arid and windswept – in favour of a new site among the lush water meadows where the rivers Avon, Nadder and Bourne meet. Locally sourced Purbeck marble and Chilmark stone were used for the construction of a new cathedral, which was built mostly in the early 13th century, over the remarkably short space of 38 years. Its magnificent landmark spire – the tallest surviving in England – was an inspired afterthought added in 1280–1310.

🏠 The Close

Mompesson House: **Tel** 01722 335659. **Open** mid-Mar–Oct: 11am–5pm daily. 🅿 🚫 limited. 💻 **NT** **W** **nationaltrust.org.uk**
Salisbury and South Wiltshire Museum: **Tel** 01722 332151. **Open** Apr–Oct: 10am–5pm Mon–Sat, noon–5pm Sun; Nov–Mar: 10am–5pm Mon–Sat. 🅿 🚫 limited. 💻 📷 **W** **salisbury museum.org.uk**

The spacious close, with its schools, almshouses and clergy housing, makes a fine setting for Salisbury Cathedral. Among the elegant buildings here are the Matrons' College, built in 1682 as a home for widows and unmarried daughters of the clergy, and the 13th-century Malmesbury House, with its early Georgian façade, fronted by wrought-iron gates. There is also the famous Mompesson House, built by a wealthy family in 1701. The handsomely furnished rooms of this house give an indication of life for the close's inhabitants in the 18th century. Other buildings of interest in the area include the Medieval Hall, the Wardrobe (now a military museum) and the Cathedral School, housed in the 13th-century Bishop's Palace and famous for the choristers who sing there.

The medieval King's House is now the Salisbury and South Wiltshire Museum. It displays archaeological finds from Old Sarum, Stonehenge and other prehistoric sights (*see p102*).

City Centre

Church of St Thomas: St Thomas's Sq. **Tel** 01722 322537. **Open** 8am–5pm daily (to 4pm in winter). 🚫 🕿 📷 **W** **stthomassalisbury.co.uk**
Salisbury Guildhall: Market Pl. **Tel** 01722 342860. **Open** 9am–5pm Mon–Fri. **Closed** public hols. 🅿 for special exhibitions. 🚫 limited. **W** **salisburyguildhall.co.uk**

Salisbury's medieval centre developed with areas devoted to different trades, perpetuated in street names such as Fish Row and Butcher Row. The busy High Street is home to

Salisbury Cathedral

The cathedral was mainly built between 1220 and 1258. It is a fine example of Early English Gothic architecture, typified by tall, sharply pointed lancet windows. The extraordinary spire, 123-m- (404-ft-) tall, still contains some of the original timber and scaffolding used to build it.

The Cloisters
The cathedral has the largest cloisters in England. They were added between 1263 and 1284 in the Decorated style.

The Chapter House
Notable for its octagonal shape, the chapter house has stone friezes showing scenes from the Old Testament. It also displays an original copy of Magna Carta.

Choirstalls

Bishop Audley's Chantry was built to honour a former bishop and is one of several chapels around the altar.

The Trinity Chapel contains the tomb of St Osmund, who was the bishop of Old Sarum from 1078 to 1099.

The Poultry Cross market, at the junction of Silver Street and Minster Street

the 13th-century Church of St Thomas, which has a lovely carved timber roof (1450), and a late 15th-century Doom painting, showing Christ seated in judgment and demons seizing the damned. In nearby Silver Street, Poultry Cross was built in the 14th century as a covered poultry market. An intricate network of alleys lined with fine timber-framed houses fans out from this

point. In the Market Place the Guildhall is an unusual cream stone building built in 1787–95 and now used for civic functions.

Environs

The nearby town of Wilton is renowned for its carpet industry, founded by the 8th Earl of Pembroke using French Huguenot refugee weavers. The town's church (1844) is an excellent example of Neo-Romanesque architecture, incorporating marble columns from a 13th-century shrine that once stood in Santa Maria Maggiore church in Rome. It also features Flemish Renaissance woodwork, German and Dutch stained glass, and Italian mosaics.

Wilton House has been home to the Earls of Pembroke since it was converted from a nunnery after the Dissolution *(see p36)*. The house, largely rebuilt by Inigo Jones in the 17th century, includes one of the original Tudor towers, a fine collection

of art and a landscaped park with a Palladian bridge (1737). The Single and Double Cube Rooms, so-called because of their perfect proportions, have magnificent frescoed ceilings and gilded stucco work, and were designed to hold a series of family portraits by the Flemish artist Anthony van Dyck.

🏛 Wilton House
Wilton. **Tel** 01722 746700. **Open** Easter weekend, May–Aug: 11:30am–5pm Sun–Thu & public hol Sat. 🎫 ♿ ✏
📷 🅦 **wiltonhouse.co.uk**

The West Front
The stunning façade is decorated by rows of symbolic figures and saints in niches.

The graceful spire soars to a height of 123 m (404 ft).

A roof tour takes visitors up to an external gallery at the base of the spire, with views of the town and Old Sarum.

The clock, dating from 1386, is the oldest working clock in Europe.

North transept

The Nave
Divided into ten bays by columns of Purbeck marble, the nave has three levels – a tall pointed arcade, an open gallery and a clerestory.

Stained-Glass Windows
Numerous decorated windows depict stories from the Bible.

⑫ Stonehenge

Built in several stages from about 3000 BC, Stonehenge is Europe's most famous prehistoric monument. We can only guess at the rituals that took place here, but the alignment of the stones leaves little doubt that the circle is connected with the sun and the passing of the seasons, and that its builders possessed an understanding of both arithmetic and astronomy. Despite popular belief, the circle was not built by the Druids, an Iron Age priestly cult in Britain from around 250 BC – Stonehenge was abandoned more than 1,000 years before this time.

The Heel Stone casts a long shadow straight to the heart of the circle on Midsummer's Day.

The Avenue forms a ceremonial approach to the site.

The Slaughter Stone, named by 17th-century antiquarians who believed Stonehenge to be a place of human sacrifice, is one of a pair marking the entrance to the interior.

The Outer Bank, dug around 3000 BC, is the oldest known phase of Stonehenge.

The remains of Stonehenge's Horseshoe of Sarsen Trilothons

Building of Stonehenge

Stonehenge's builders must have been able to command immense resources and vast numbers of people to transport and erect the stones. One method is explained here.

A sarsen stone was moved on rollers and levered into a pit.

With levers supported by timber packing, it was gradually raised.

The stone was pulled upright by about 200 men hauling on ropes.

Wiltshire's Other Prehistoric Sites

The open countryside of Salisbury Plain is extraordinarily rich in prehistoric sites. North of Stonehenge, Silbury Hill is Europe's largest prehistoric earthwork, but despite extensive excavations its purpose remains a mystery. Built out of chalk blocks around 2400 BC, the hill covers 2 ha (5 acres) and rises to a height of 40 m (131 ft). Nearby, West Kennet Long Barrow was built around 3600 BC. It is the biggest chambered tomb in England, with numerous stone-lined "rooms". Other prehistoric sites in Wiltshire include Cley Hill, an Iron Age hillfort, and the Membury Hillfort, one of the largest hillforts in the country. Visitors can see ceremonial bronze weapons and other finds excavated around Stonehenge and the other local prehistoric sites in the museum in Salisbury *(see p100)* and the main museum in Devizes *(see p104)*.

Silbury Hill, a prehistoric chalk mound

⑬ Old Sarum

Castle Rd. **Map** A2. **Tel** 01722 335398. **Open** Apr–Sep: 10am–6pm daily; Oct–Mar: 10am–4pm daily. **Closed** 1 Jan & 24–26 Dec. 🅿 ♿ limited. 📷 EH
W **english-heritage.org.uk**

The remains of this prehistoric settlement lie within the massive ramparts of a 1st-century Romano-British hillfort. The Norman founders of Old Sarum built their own motte-and-bailey castle inside this ready-made fortification. Above ground, nothing remains of the town that once sat within the ramparts. The town's occupants moved to the fertile river valley site that became Salisbury during the early 12th century.

The Sarsen Circle was erected around 2500 BC and is capped by lintel stones held in place by mortise and tenon joints.

The Bluestone Circle was built around 2500 BC out of some 80 slabs quarried in the Preseli Hills in south Wales.

Horseshoe of Sarsen Trilothons

Horseshoe of Bluestones

Reconstruction of Stonehenge

This illustration shows what Stonehenge probably looked like about 4,000 years ago, when the last phase of construction was completed.

The pit around the base was packed tightly with stones and chalk.

Alternate ends of the lintel were levered up.

The weight of the lintel was supported by a timber platform.

The lintel was then levered sideways on to the upright stones.

---

⑭ Avebury

Wiltshire. **Map** A1. 🚂 500. 🚌 Swindon, then bus. ℹ️ Green St; 01672 539250. **Open** dawn–dusk daily. 🅴🅷 🅽🆃 🆆 **english-heritage.org.uk** 🆆 **nationaltrust.org.uk**

Built in 2800–2200 BC, the Avebury Stone Circles surround the village of Avebury and were probably once some form of religious monument. Although the stones used are smaller than those at Stonehenge, the circles are larger. Villagers smashed many of the stones in the 18th century, believing the site to be a place for pagan sacrifice.

The original form of the circles is best appreciated by a visit to the **Alexander Keiller Museum**, named after the archaeologist who excavated Avebury. Situated to the west of the site, the museum illustrates the construction of the circles. There is also an exhibition explaining Avebury's changing landscape and a special children's area.

Just off Avebury High Street is St James's Church. Dating from around 1000, the building still has its tall, narrow Saxon nave. It also contains a Norman font carved with sea monsters, and a rare 15th-century choir screen.

🏛 Alexander Keiller Museum
Off High St. **Tel** 01672 538016.
Open Apr–Oct: 10am–6pm daily; Oct–Mar: 10am–4pm daily. **Closed** 1 Jan, 24 & 25 Dec. 🆋🅴🅷🅽🆃

Neolithic stones forming part of the Avebury Stone Circles

⑮ Bowood House

Calne, Wiltshire. **Map** A1. **Tel** 01249 812102. 🚂 Chippenham, then taxi. 🚌 **Open** Apr–Oct: 11am–6pm daily (last adm: 1 hr before closing). **Closed** Oct–late Mar. 🚫 🎫 by appt. ♿ limited. 🅿 🛒 📷 🌐 **bowood.org**

This grand mansion was built for the Shelburne-Lansdowne family in the mid-18th century, with magnificent interiors by Robert Adam. Some sections were demolished in the 1950s, but the remaining house is still impressive. In addition to the rich collection of paintings, sculpture and jewellery, visitors can see the laboratory where Joseph Priestley (invited to Bowood by his patron Lord Shelburne) discovered oxygen in 1774. Gorgeous formal and walled gardens surround the house, while the lake-filled grounds – landscaped by "Capability" Brown (see p25) – include a Doric temple, cascades and playgrounds. The estate also has a golf course, a luxurious hotel and a spa.

⑯ Devizes

Wiltshire. **Map** A1. 🔲 12,000. 🚌 ℹ️ Wiltshire Museum; 41 Long St; 01380 800400. 🛒 Thu. 🌐 **devizes.org.uk**

This historic town once held markets almost every day in its broad Market Place. The regular market is now only held on

Historic buildings lining Market Place in the town of Devizes

Thursdays, but there are many special markets at other times. The Market Cross has a plaque with the cautionary tale of Ruth Pierce, who in 1753 said that God should strike her down if she cheated her neighbours on the price of wheat, and almost immediately dropped dead. Georgian houses, some of the town's 500-plus listed historic buildings, surround the Market Place.

On Long Street, the **Wiltshire Museum** contains an array of archaeological finds from Avebury (see p103), Stonehenge (see pp102–3) and other prehistoric sites on Salisbury Plain.

🏛 Wiltshire Museum

41 Long St. **Tel** 01380 727369. **Open** Mar–Oct: 10am–5pm Mon–Sat, noon–4pm Sun; Nov–Feb: 10am–5pm Tue–Sat. 🚫 ♿ 📷 🌐 **wiltshiremuseum.org.uk**

⑰ Lacock

Wiltshire. **Map** F3. 🔲 1,200. 🚂 Chippenham, then taxi. 🎭 Scarecrow Festival: late Mar.

Maintained in its pristine state by the National Trust, the charming village of Lacock has provided the backdrop to many films and TV series, including the Harry Potter films and historic drama Downton Abbey.

The River Avon forms the boundary to the churchyard, where stone figures look down from the 14th-century Church of St Cyriac. Inside the church is the Renaissance-style tomb of Sir William Sharington (1495–1553), who acquired **Lacock Abbey** after the Dissolution (see p36) and made it his residence.

The abbey later passed to the Talbot family, and in the late 18th century John Ivory Talbot had it remodelled in the then-fashionable Gothic Revival style. William Henry Fox Talbot, one of the pioneers of photography, took one of the world's first photographic images from the South Gallery window in 1835, creating the first-ever negative. Part of the abbey is occupied by the Fox Talbot Museum, which explores Fox Talbot's role in the history of photography.

🏛 Lacock Abbey

Lacock. **Tel** 01249 730459. **Open** Abbey: Mar–Oct: 11am–5pm daily; Nov–Feb: 11:30am–3:30pm Sat & Sun (also Thu & Fri in Dec). Museum & Grounds: Mar–Oct: 10:30am–5:30pm daily; Nov–Feb: 11am–4pm daily. **Closed** 1 Jan, 25 & 26 Dec. 🚫 ♿ limited. 🛒 📷 NT 🌐 **national trust.org.uk**

Salisbury Plain

Extending over 780 sq km (300 sq miles), Salisbury Plain is a huge chalk plateau of rolling hills or downlands, filling most of Wiltshire and part of Hampshire. From the early Middle Ages, its broad grasslands were largely used as sheep pasture, but in prehistoric times this was one of the first extensively inhabited parts of Britain, as is reflected in its wealth of world-famous archaeological sites, such as Stonehenge and Avebury. Since World War II, around half the plain has been a military training area closed to the public, which curiously has preserved much of its wild vegetation and fauna.

Panoramic view of the rolling hills and grasslands of Salisbury Plain

⑱ Corsham

Wiltshire. **Map** F3. 🚶 13,000.
🚆 Chippenham, then taxi. 🚌
ℹ️ 31 High St; 01249 714660. 🏛️ Tue.
🌐 **corshamheritage.org.uk**

Corsham's streets are lined with stately Georgian houses in Cotswold stone, reflecting its historic wealth as a wool-weaving centre.

Near the town centre is the entrance to **Corsham Court**, a gracious Elizabethan mansion that like Lacock has often been used as a film location. Built in the 1580s, it has been the home of the Methuen family since 1745. The superb picture gallery contains a remarkable collection of mostly Italian, Flemish and English paintings, including works by famous artists such as Van Dyck, Salvator Rosa and Joshua Reynolds.

The extensive grounds, designed by "Capability" Brown *(see p25)*, are home to a muster of peacocks, which roam freely and add colour to the mansion's impressive stone façade.

🏛️ **Corsham Court**
Corsham. **Tel** 01249 712214. **Open**
Apr–Sep: 2–5:30pm Tue–Thu, Sat & Sun; Oct–Nov & Jan–Mar: 2–4:30pm Sat & Sun (last adm: 30 mins before closing). **Closed** Dec. 🔲🔲🔲🔲
🌐 **corsham-court.co.uk**

A colourful peacock strutting past Corsham Court's elegant main façade

⑲ Bradford-on-Avon

Wiltshire. **Map** F3. 🚶 9,500. 🚆 🚌
ℹ️ Westbury Gardens; St Margaret St; 01225 865797. 🏛️ 3rd Thu & last Sun of month. 🌐 **bradfordonavon.co.uk**

Bradford's quiet, narrow lanes make it an ideal place for a leisurely stroll. This lovely town is full of beautiful honey-coloured Cotswold-stone houses, which were built by wealthy wool and cloth merchants in the 17th and 18th centuries. One particularly fine Georgian example is the 1770s Abbey House, located on Church Street.

St Laurence Church is a remarkably complete Saxon church, which was probably built around the year 1000.

It was first converted into a school. Later it was used as a workshop and then a cottage after larger medieval churches were built nearby. It was only rediscovered as a church in the 1850s, when a vicar recognized its characteristic carvings and roof.

The Town Bridge was first built in the Middle Ages but widened in the 17th century. At one end is a curious dome-shaped stone cell. Originally a chapel, it was used as a lockup for vagrants and troublemakers in the 18th century.

A short walk away is the 14th-century **Tithe Barn**. This was once used for collecting church taxes ("tithes") – in the form of crops or livestock – from local peasants.

Nearby, running alongside a series of converted mills, is the Kennet and Avon Canal, which was once used for transporting cloth and textile materials to and from the town. Today, companies offer popular boat excursions along the waterways.

🏛️ **St Laurence Church**
10 Church St. **Open** Apr–Sep: 10am–6pm daily; Oct–Mar: 10am–4pm daily.

🏛️ **Tithe Barn**
Pound Lane. **Open** 10:30am–4pm daily. **Closed** 1 Jan & 24–26 Dec.
♿ EH 🌐 **english-heritage.org.uk**

Bradford-on-Avon's iconic medieval Town Bridge and lockup, set over the River Avon

Visitors feeding giraffes at the famous safari park at Longleat

⑳ Longleat

Warminster, Wiltshire. **Map** A2.
Tel 01985 844400. 🚂 Frome, then taxi. **Open** House & Safari Park: mid-Feb–Mar & Nov–Dec: Fri–Mon; Apr–Oct: daily; times vary, check website for details. 🅿 📷 ♿ 🚻 🖥 📷
ⓦ longleat.co.uk

The architectural historian John Summerson coined the term "prodigy house" to describe the exuberance and grandeur of Elizabethan architecture that is so well represented at Longleat. The house was started in 1540, when John Thynne bought the ruins of a priory on the site for £53. Over the centuries, subsequent owners have added their own touches. These include the Breakfast Room and Lower Dining Room (dating from the 1870s and modelled on the Venetian Doge's Palace) and erotic murals painted by the present owner, the 7th Marquess of Bath. Today, the Great Hall is the only remaining room from Thynne's time.

In 1949, the 6th Marquess was the first landowner in Britain to open his stately home to the public. In 1966, a large part of the estate, landscaped by "Capability" Brown (see p25), was turned into the world's first safari park outside Africa, where lions, tigers, baboons, giraffes and many other wild animals roam freely. This, along with further additions such as enclosures for smaller animals, a large hedge maze, a "Jungle Express" mini-train and an Adventure Castle, have made Longleat one of England's most popular estates.

㉑ Stourhead

Stourhead is among the finest examples of 18th-century landscape gardening in Britain. The garden was begun in the 1740s by Henry Hoare (1705–85), who inherited the estate and transformed it into a breathtaking work of art. He created the lake, surrounding it with rare trees and plants, and Neo-Classical Italianate temples, grottoes and bridges. The Palladian-style house, built by Colen Campbell, dates from 1721–5.

Pantheon
Modelled on the Pantheon in Rome, this elegant temple was designed by architect Henry Flitcroft (1679–1769) in 1753. It was intended as a visual centrepoint for the garden and a place for the Hoare family to entertain their guests.

KEY

① **The reception** has a helpful visitor information centre.

② **Pelargonium House** contains a collection of over 100 species of the pelargonium plant and its cultivars.

③ **Stourton village** was incorporated into Hoare's overall design.

④ **The Temple of Flora** (1744) is dedicated to the Roman goddess of flowers.

⑤ **The Grotto** is an artificial cave with a pool and a life-size statue of the guardian of the River Stour, sculpted by John Cheere in 1748.

⑥ **Gothic Cottage** (1806)

⑦ **Iron Bridge**

⑧ **A walk** of 3 km (2 miles) around the lake provides artistically contrived vistas.

⑨ **Turf Bridge**

★ **Temple of Apollo**
Inspired by Italian originals and dedicated to the sun god Apollo, this circular temple was designed by Henry Flitcroft.

The Lake
Stourhead's famous lake was created by damming the River Stour in the 1750s. The path around it evokes the journeys of Aeneas in Virgil's *Aeneid*.

VISITORS' CHECKLIST

Practical Information
Stourton, Wiltshire.
Map A2. **Tel** 01747 841152.
Open Gardens: Apr–Oct: 9am–6pm daily; Nov–Mar: 9am–5pm daily. House: Mar–early Nov: 11am–4:30pm daily. 🖼 🅿
🚻 limited. 🚫 🖥 🏠 NT
W **nationaltrust.org.uk/stourhead**

Transport
🚆 Gillingham (Dorset), then taxi.

Colourful Shrubs
Fragrant rhododendrons bloom in the spring, and azaleas explode into colour later in the summer. There are also many fine cypresses, Japanese pines and other exotic trees.

★ **Stourhead House**
Restored after a fire in 1902, the house contains fine Chippendale furniture. The art collection reflects Henry Hoare's Classical tastes and includes *The Choice of Hercules* (1637) by Nicolas Poussin.

Entrance and car park

St Peter's Church
The parish church contains monuments to the Hoare family. The medieval Bristol Cross, nearby, was brought from Bristol in 1765.

DORSET AND SOMERSET

With the long, sandy beaches of Bournemouth, the rural cottages of the Isle of Purbeck and the wild scenery of Exmoor, Dorset and Somerset are home to some of the country's most beautiful landscapes, lively coastal resorts and historic cities. The region's natural highlights, including the ancient fossil-rich Jurassic Coast, Cheddar Gorge and the Durdle Door rock arch, are among England's most iconic sights, while the cities of Bristol, Bath and Dorchester have histories as ancient and fascinating as any in the country.

This sleepy, rural region has a surprisingly rich history. First inhabited in Neolithic times, it was later settled by the Celts, who founded strongholds such as Dorchester's vast Maiden Castle. However, it was the Romans who really put the area on the map when they built England's first spa resort at Bath in the 1st century AD – an amazing feat of construction that is remarkably intact today. Once the Romans left, the southwest of England became a stronghold of Celtic resistance, with the mythical King Arthur leading the fight against the Saxons in the early 6th century – legend suggests that he and his queen Guinevere were buried at Glastonbury Abbey.

The region's biggest city, Bristol became Britain's main transatlantic port after John Cabot, a Genoese navigator and explorer, set off from there to explore America in 1497 – the city's grand buildings are a testament to the wealth acquired from the subsequent slave, tobacco and wine trades. In the 18th century, the spa waters of Bath came back into fashion with the Georgians, who built the stunning Palladian-style town that we see today, while George III's regular visits to Weymouth kick-started its 200-plus years as a popular seaside resort. With the arrival of the railway line in the 19th century, Bournemouth became one of the country's most fashionable places to bathe.

Equally impressive is the region's geology. The UNESCO World Heritage Jurassic Coast encompasses most of Dorset's shoreline, a rugged series of coves and cliffs whose rock falls reveal ancient fossils. Neighbouring Somerset's mild climate produces Cheddar cheese and cider apples for which the region is famous. It boasts dramatic features, too, from the deep Cheddar Gorge to the plunging cliffs and valleys of Exmoor.

Grand sweep of the Royal Crescent, with a row of terraced houses once owned by the city's wealthy elite, in historic Bath

◀ A section of the stunning 153-km (95-mile) fossil-rich coastline of the Jurassic Coast, a World Heritage Site

Exploring Dorset and Somerset

The south of the region is home to the fine seaside resorts of Bournemouth, Swanage and Weymouth, as well as the picture-postcard town of Lyme Regis in the heart of the Jurassic Coast. Head inland to find pretty villages nestling in a rural landscape that inspired literary figures such as Samuel Taylor Coleridge and Thomas Hardy. The north coastline backs onto the wild scenery of Exmoor National Park, where ponies roam free. Wildlife can also be found in the wetlands of the Somerset Levels. The revitalized port of Bristol is famed as the home of graffiti artist, Banksy. Nearby is the Georgian town of Bath, while to the south lie the cathedral city of Wells and mystical Glastonbury, famous for its music festival.

Sights at a Glance

1. Bournemouth
2. Poole Harbour
3. Wimborne Minster
4. Isle of Purbeck
5. Corfe Castle
6. Lulworth
7. Weymouth
8. Isle of Portland
9. Abbotsbury
10. Bridport
11. Charmouth
12. Lyme Regis
13. *Jurassic Coast Tour pp116–17*
14. Dorchester
15. Maiden Castle
16. Cerne Abbas
17. Shaftesbury
18. Sherborne
19. Montacute House
20. Taunton
21. Bridgwater and the Quantocks
22. *Cheddar Gorge p121*
23. *Exmoor National Park pp122–3*
24. Somerset Levels
25. Glastonbury
26. *Wells Cathedral pp124–5*
27. *Bristol pp126–7*
28. *Bath pp128–31*

Key

— Motorway
— Dual carriageway
— Main road
⋯ Other road
⋯ Railway
— County border

Boats docked at the harbour in front of Weymouth's atmospheric Old Town

For hotels and restaurants in this region see p177 and pp188–9

Getting Around

Bath, Bristol, Bournemouth, Poole, Dorchester and Weymouth are all served by fast mainline trains from London, with other major towns linked by regional rail routes, long-distance coach services and local buses. However, once visitors leave the main towns and head into the countryside, a car is the best way to get around. Dorset is one of the few counties in England without a single motorway. It is possible to explore it on foot or by bike along the network of long-distance cycle routes and footpaths that crisscross the region.

Holidaymakers enjoying views of the coastline from the famous Cobb, the harbour wall at Lyme Regis

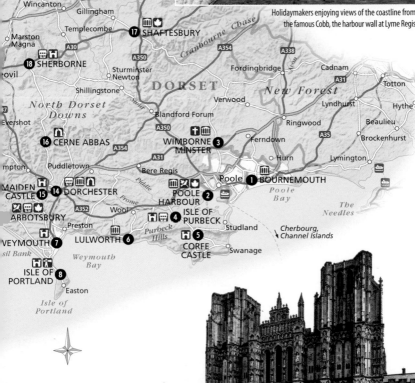

West façade of the magnificent Wells Cathedral, built between 1175 and 1490

For additional map symbols *see back flap*

Bournemouth's 300-m- (984-ft-) long pier, one of the town's most iconic landmarks

❶ Bournemouth

Dorset. **Map** A3. 🄰 195,000. ✈ 🚢
🚇 **i** Pier Approach; 01202 451 734.
w bournemouth.co.uk

The popularity of Bournemouth as a seaside resort is due to an almost unbroken sweep of sandy beach, extending from the mouth of Poole Harbour to Hengistbury Head. Most of the seafront is built up with seaside villas and hotels. To the west there are clifftop parks and gardens, with beautiful wooded river ravines known as chines.

In central Bournemouth the amusement arcades, casinos, nightclubs and shops cater to the city's many visitors. There's also **PierZip**, the world's only pier-to-land zip wire.

Nearby, the **Russell-Cotes Art Gallery and Museum**, housed in a late Victorian villa, has an extensive collection, with fine Oriental and Victorian artifacts.

PierZip
Bournemouth Pier, Pier Approach.
Tel 01202 983983. **Open** Jul–Sep: 10am–9pm daily; times vary, check website. 🈲 **w** rockreef.co.uk

🏛 Russell-Cotes Art Gallery and Museum
Russell-Cotes Rd. **Tel** 01202 451800.
Open 10am–5pm Tue–Sun. 🈲 ♿
w russellcotes.com

Environs
The magnificent **Christchurch Priory**, east of Bournemouth, is 95 m (310 ft) in length – one of the longest churches in England. It was rebuilt between the 13th and 16th century. The original

nave, from around 1093, is an impressive example of Norman architecture, but the highlight is the intricate stone reredos, which features a Tree of Jesse, tracing the lineage of Christ. Next to the Priory are the ruins of a Norman castle.

Between Bournemouth and Christchurch, Hengistbury Head is well worth climbing for grassland flowers and sea views.

⛪ Christchurch Priory
Quay Rd, Christchurch. **Tel** 01202 485804. **Open** 9:30am–5pm Mon–Sat, 2:15–5:30pm Sun. 🈲 ⛪
w christchurchpriory.org

❷ Poole Harbour

Dorset. **Map** A3. 🄰 150,000.
🚢 🚌 🚲 🚲 **i** 4 High St; 01202 262600. 🚢 Thu & Sat.
w pooletourism.com

One of the largest natural harbours in the world, Poole Harbour covers an area of 36 sq km (14 sq miles). It is

very shallow, averaging just half a metre (2 ft) in depth, making it ideal for kite- and wind-surfing. Giant cross-Channel ferries glide through specially dredged channels to its principal settlement, Poole, which developed from the 13th century, and was initially a sheltered haven for fishermen, timber traders and the odd pirate.

Although most of today's skyline was built in the late 20th century, the attractive Old Town around Poole Quay gives a sense of the town's history. Its medieval buildings have now been converted into restaurants, bars and hotels.

Visitors can learn more about the town's history at the **Poole Museum**, set in a converted 18th-century warehouse, which includes a 10-m (30-ft) log boat dating back to 295 BC. Boat trips depart from the quay to destinations around the harbour, the most popular being **Brownsea Island**, a verdant, wooded islet, where the only residents are

Luxury houses stretching along the Sandbanks peninsula in Poole

For hotels and restaurants in this region see p177 and pp188–9

red squirrels and a rich array of birdlife. Clearly marked trails spread out across the island, with some passing the site of the world's first ever Scout camp, set up by Robert Baden Powell in 1907.

Virtually enclosed, Poole Harbour joins the sea next to Poole's premier address, Sandbanks, a sand spit boasting some of the most expensive real estate in the country. Its appeal is easy to understand, with harbour views on one side and a stretch of golden sands on the other. A chain ferry at the end of the spit takes cars and passengers across the harbour mouth to the Isle of Purbeck.

Near Sandbanks is **Compton Acres**. This varied and colourful ornamental garden, conceived as a museum of different garden styles, is regarded as one of the finest privately owned gardens in southern England.

🏛 **Poole Museum**
4 High St. **Tel** 01202 262600.
Open Apr–Oct: 10am–5pm daily; Nov–Mar: 10am–4pm Tue–Sat, noon–4pm Sun. **Closed** 1 Jan, 25 & 26 Dec.
♿ 🚻 📷 **w** poolemuseum.co.uk

🏞 **Brownsea Island**
Poole. **Tel** 01202 707744. 🚢 from Poole Quay (every 30 min). **Open** Feb–mid-Mar: 10am–4pm Sat & Sun; mid-Mar–Oct: 10am–5pm daily. 🚶 🚍 walking tours. ♿ limited. 🚻 📷 **NT**
w nationaltrust.org.uk

🌿 **Compton Acres**
164 Canford Cliffs Rd. **Tel** 01202 700778.
Open Easter–Oct: 10am–6pm daily; Nov–Easter: 10am–4pm daily. **Closed** 1 Jan, 25 & 26 Dec. 🚻 ♿ limited. 🚍 📷 **w** comptonacres.co.uk

❸ Wimborne Minster

High St, Wimborne, Dorset. **Map** A2.
Tel 01202 884753. 🚍 **Open** Mar–24 Dec: 9:30am–5:30pm Mon–Sat, 2:30–5:30pm Sun; 25 Dec–Feb: 9:30am–4pm Mon–Sat, 2:30–5:30pm Sun. ♿ 🏥 Sun am & 6:30pm. 📷 🚍 Fri–Sat. **w** wimborneminster.net

The fine church of Wimborne Minster was founded in 705 by Cuthburga, sister of King Ina of Wessex. It fell prey to marauding Danish raiders in the 10th

Library at Kingston Lacy, a country house near Wimborne Minster

century, and the imposing grey edifice that can be seen today dates from after 1043, when the church was refounded by Edward the Confessor *(see p43)*. Stonemasons made use of the local Purbeck marble, carving beasts, biblical scenes and distinctive zigzag patterns.

Set in the 16th-century house opposite the Minster, the **Priest's House Museum** explores the rich history of rural East Dorset through different period rooms, including a 17th-century hall and a working Victorian kitchen.

🏛 **Priest's House Museum**
High St. **Tel** 01202 882533. **Open** Jan–Mar, Nov & Dec: 10am–4pm Mon–Sat; Apr–Oct: 10am–4:30pm Mon–Sat. **Closed** 24 Dec–5 Jan. 🚍 ♿ limited.
🚍 📷 **w** priest-house.co.uk

Environs
Designed for the Bankes family after the destruction of Corfe Castle *(see p114)*, **Kingston Lacy** was acquired by the National Trust in 1981. This quiet, forgotten corner of Dorset can be explored using paths and "green lanes" that date back to Roman and Saxon times. The fine 17th-century house on the estate has an excellent collection of paintings, including works by Velázquez, Rubens, and Titian.

🏡 **Kingston Lacy**
On B3082. **Tel** 01202 883402.
Open House: from 11am daily (closing times vary). Gardens: 10am–6pm daily.
🚍 ♿ limited. 🚻 📷 **NT**
w nationaltrust.org.uk

❹ Isle of Purbeck

Dorset. **Map** A3. 🚉 Wareham. 🚢 Shell Bay, Studland. 🛈 Swanage; 01929 422885. **w** swanage.gov.uk

The so-called Isle of Purbeck is in fact a peninsula, and is the source of the famous crystalline grey limestone, known as Purbeck marble, from which Corfe Castle and surrounding houses were built.

The island is also fringed with unspoiled beaches, part of the World Heritage Jurassic Coast *(see pp116–17)*. Studland Bay, with its white sand and its sand-dune nature reserve, rich in birdlife, has been rated one of Britain's best. The geology of the peninsula changes to the southwest at Kimmeridge, where the muddy shale contains fossils and oil.

The main resort in the area is Swanage, the port from where Purbeck stone was transported by ship to London, to be used for everything from street paving to church building. Unwanted masonry from demolished buildings was shipped back and used in the town – this is how Swanage got its wonderfully ornate Town Hall façade, which was originally designed in 1670 by Edward Jerman, a pupil of Christopher Wren, for the Mercers' Hall in London. The repurposed façade features cherubs holding cloths for the Virgin Mary, the emblem of the Mercer's Company.

Striking stone façade of the Town Hall in Swanage, on the Isle of Purbeck

Dramatic Durdle Door, a natural limestone arch near Lulworth Cove

🏛 Lulworth Heritage Centre

Main Rd. **Tel** 01929 400587.
Open Mar–Oct: 10am–6pm daily;
Nov–Feb: 10am–4pm daily. ♿ 📷
W lulworth.com

❼ Weymouth

Dorset. **Map** F5. 🚇 55,000 🚊
🚌 🚏 🚋 🅿 Apr–Oct: Thu.
W visit-dorset.com

Weymouth's popularity as a seaside resort began in 1789, when King George III (1738–1820) paid the first of many summer visits to its glorious sandy beach. His statue is a prominent feature on the seafront. Here, gracious Georgian terraces look across to the beautiful expanse of Weymouth Bay, which hosted the sailing events in the 2012 Olympic Games.

To the south of the beach lies the distinctive **Jurassic Skyline**, a tower with a rotating glass pod that rises to a height of 53 m (174 ft), giving superb views of the town and coast. On the other side of the lifting Town Bridge, the Old Town has an earthier, more traditional character, with its fishing boats, old seamen's inns and boat trips.

A short walk from the Old Town leads to the Victorian **Nothe Fort**, where displays of World War II memorabilia recall the time when the town played

❺ Corfe Castle

Dorset. **Map** A3. **Tel** 01929 481294.
Open Apr–early Oct: 10am–6pm daily;
Mar & late Oct: 10am–5pm daily; Nov–Feb: 10am–4pm daily. 🖥 📷 NT W nationaltrust.org.uk

The spectacular ruins of Corfe Castle romantically crown a jagged pinnacle of rock above the picturesque village that shares its name. The castle has dominated the landscape since the 11th century, first as a royal fortification, then as the picturesque ruins seen today.

In 1635 the castle was bought by Sir John Bankes, whose wife and her retainers – mostly women – courageously held out here against 600 Parliamentary troops in a six-week siege during the Civil War (see p36). The castle was eventually taken through treachery and in 1646 Parliament voted to have it "slighted" – deliberately blown up to prevent it being used again. From the ruins there are stunning views over the Isle of Purbeck.

The ruins of Corfe Castle, which dates from Norman times

❻ Lulworth

Dorset. **Map** F5. 🚌

Sheltered Lulworth Cove is one of the prettiest and most popular coastal spots in Dorset, an almost circular shingle bay fringed by tall cliffs. A collection of former fishermen's houses nestle at the top of the bay, now occupied by bustling restaurants and cafés.

The **Lulworth Heritage Centre**, near the main car park, explains the unusual coastal geology of the area, including Durdle Door, Dorset's iconic rock arch. The arch can be reached by road or via a 30-minute walk along the coast path. The steps down to the shingle beach are very steep, but the views are well worth the effort.

King George III and Weymouth

Visible on the road from Weymouth to Osmington is a dramatic image of a mounted George III, carved into the chalk of the rolling downs. The monarch is commemorated in the resort he first visited in 1789 to recover from

A band performing for George III at Weymouth

illness – possibly porphyria, a hereditary illness that causes mental problems. His doctors recommended a salt-water cure, and he enjoyed his swims from a bathing machine on Weymouth beach so much that he decided to buy Gloucester Lodge (now private apartments) on the Esplanade for his visits to the town. A band would play "God Save the King" as he emerged from the water. Now he is best remembered as the mentally unstable king in Alan Bennett's *The Madness of King George*, though many historians claim that he suffered from bipolar disorder, and argue that he should be best remembered as a popular king, known for his love of rural life.

host to over 500,000 troops in advance of the 1944 D-Day Landings. The fort also provides fine views from its ramparts and the adjacent Nothe Gardens.

❄ Jurassic Skyline
The Quay. **Tel** 0871 282 9242. **Open** from 11am daily (closing times vary). 🎫 ⑂ 🅦 jurassicskyline.com

🏰 Nothe Fort
Barack Rd. **Tel** 01305 766626. **Open** Feb & Oct school hols: 11am–4:30pm daily; Apr–Sep: 10:30am–5:30pm daily. 🎫 ⑂ 🖥 🎬 🅦 nothefort.org.uk

❽ Isle of Portland
Dorset. **Map** F5. 🚠 12,000. 🚌

A rocky lump rising dramatically above the coast, the Isle of Portland has been described as the Gibraltar of England. Many of the world's finest buildings, including St Paul's Cathedral *(see pp58–9)*, have been constructed using the Portland stone that has been quarried here for centuries. There are spectacular views from the top of the island, which is home to two forts. The brooding Verne Citadel still serves as a prison, but it is possible to visit the other, **Portland Castle**, built under Henry VIII to protect the harbour. At the southern tip of the island is Portland Bill, an attractive headland capped by the **Portland Bill Lighthouse**, built in 1906. Visitors can climb to the top for spectacular views.

🏰 Portland Castle
Liberty Rd. **Tel** 01305 820539. **Open** Apr–Jun: 10am–5pm daily; Jul–Aug: 10am–6pm daily. 🎫 ⑂ 🖥 🎬 🇪🇭 🅦 english-heritage.org.uk

🗼 Portland Bill Lighthouse
Portland Bill. **Tel** 01305 821050. **Open** May–Sep: 10am–5pm daily; Oct, Mar–Apr: 10am–5pm Tue–Sun; Nov–Feb: 10am–3pm Sat & Sun. **Closed** 24 & 25 Dec. 🎫 🎬 🅦 trinityhouse.co.uk

Portland Bill Lighthouse, which commands stunning views from the Isle of Portland

❾ Abbotsbury
Dorset. **Map** F5. 🚠 500. 🛈 West Yard Barn, West St; 01305 871130. 🅦 abbotsbury-tourism.co.uk

The name Abbotsbury recalls the town's 11th-century Benedictine abbey, of which little but the huge tithe barn, built around 1400, remains. Nobody knows when the **Swannery** here was

founded, but the earliest records date to 1393. Mute swans come to nest here in June, attracted by the reed beds along the Fleet, a brackish lagoon protected from the sea by a high ridge of pebbles called Chesil Beach. Its wild atmosphere is appealing, although strong currents make swimming too dangerous.

The tithe barn now forms part of a **Children's Farm** where kids can get close to a range of animals, including ponies.

The **Abbotsbury Subtropical Gardens** are home to a large number of exotic plants, many of which had been newly discovered by botanists in South America and Asia when they were first introduced.

On a hilltop above the village is St Catherine's Chapel. Visitors can enjoy stupendous views of the abbey ruins from here.

🦢 Swannery
New Barn Rd. **Tel** 01305 871858. **Open** mid-Mar–Oct: 10am–5pm daily. 🎫 ⑂ 🎬

🐄 Children's Farm
Church St. **Tel** 01305 871817. **Open** mid-Mar–mid-Sep: 10am–5pm daily; mid-Sep–mid-Oct: 10am–5pm Sat & Sun. 🎫 ⑂ limited.

🌿 Abbotsbury Subtropical Gardens
Off B3157. **Tel** 01305 871387. **Open** Apr–Oct: 10am–5pm daily; Nov–Mar: 10am–4pm daily. **Closed** 19 Dec–1 Jan. 🎫 ⑂ limited. 🖥 🎬

The peaceful village of Abbotsbury, seen from St Catherine's Chapel on a hilltop above the village

Sheer cliffs along the rugged Jurassic Coast in West Bay

⑩ Bridport

Dorset. **Map** E5. 🚇 14,600. 🚌
ℹ️ Town Hall, Bucky Doo Sq, South St;
01308 424901. 🗓️ Wed & Sat.

The market town of Bridport was famed for its rope-making until the late 1700s, and its unusually wide streets date from the time when rope was hung between houses to be twisted. Today it has something of a foodie reputation thanks to a plethora of fine restaurants and a twice-weekly market. The town was a major port until the river silted up, but visitors can still walk alongside the River Brit to the nearest coast, West Bay, a fishing village with a broad shingle

beach and towering sandstone cliffs, which formed the iconic backdrop to the popular British TV series *Broadchurch*.

⑪ Charmouth

Dorset. **Map** E5. 🚇 1,300.
🗓️ Jun–Sep: Mon.

A handsome village set on a pretty hillside next to the coast, Charmouth is famed for its landslips: its dramatic coastal cliffs frequently fall into the sea, revealing fossils by the bucket-load. In 2000, a fossilized scelidosaurus was found here, the only known example of this herbivorous dinosaur, while tiny fossils of belomnites (an extinct, squid-like creature) lie loose on Charmouth's attractive beach. Organized fossil tours take place from the **Heritage Coast Centre** next to the main car park. Visitors can also walk along

⑫ Jurassic Coast Tour

The 153-km- (95-mile-) long Jurassic Coast is the only natural site in England with UNESCO World Heritage status. The area was given this accolade because of its extraordinary geology; incredibly rich in fossils, it reveals to scientists a landscape that has varied from swamp to arid desert over a period of 185 million years.

③ **Charmouth**
A favoured haunt of Austen, this town is great for fossil hunting, with new specimens exposed beneath one of Europe's largest coastal landslip areas.

Key

━━ Tour route
═══ Other road

① **Orcombe Point**
The reddish sandstone at Orcombe Point dates back 250 million years. The Geoneedle is an impressive landmark here.

Tips for Drivers

Tour length: 146 km (91 miles).
Stopping-off points: Lulworth Cove Visitor Centre (call 01929 400352) details the geology and history of the coastline. Sample the seafood at The Hive Beach Café in Burton Bradstock.

② **Lyme Regis**
Dorset's prettiest coastal harbour town is known for its fossils, coastal walks and the 13th-century Cobb.

the coastal path to the top of the Golden Cap, the highest cliff on the South Coast at 191 m (627 ft).

🏛 Heritage Coast Centre
Lower Sea Lane. **Tel** 01297 560772. **Open** Easter–Oct: 10:30am–4:30pm daily; Nov–Easter: 10:30am–4:30pm Fri–Mon. 🚗 ♿ 🅿 🆆 **charmouth. org/chcc**

Groups hunting for fossils on the beach below the crumbling cliffs, Charmouth

⓬ Lyme Regis
Dorset. **Map** E5. 🚉 3,600. 🛈 Church St; 01297 442138. 🆆 **lymeregis.org**

This is the most picturesque resort along the Jurassic Coast. It takes its name (Regis) from the Royal Charter given by Edward I in 1284, and was a fashionable sea-bathing spot for the gentry in the late 18th and early 19th centuries. Jane Austen set parts of her novel *Persuasion* here. Today it is a mix of fishermen's cottages and Victorian and Georgian townhouses, though its most famous structure is the Cobb, a 13th-century breakwater curling round the harbour. Visitors can walk out along its massive walls, dodging waves that often crash over when the seas are high. Lyme Regis is also known for its fossils – it was

Mary Anning plaque, Lyme Regis Museum

here that pioneer fossil collector Mary Anning and her brother Joseph unearthed a 9-m- (20-ft-) long fossilized ichthyosaur in 1811. Her home is now the **Lyme Regis Museum**, which traces the history of the town, including its role in the Monmouth Rebellion in 1685, when the Duke of Monmouth James Scott landed here in an unsuccessful attempt to overthrow King James II.

Southwest of Lyme Regis, the South West Coast Path runs through the Undercliff, a wooded nature reserve that has grown up on former landslips.

🏛 Lyme Regis Museum
Bridge St. **Tel** 01297 443370. **Open** Easter–Oct: 10am–5pm Mon–Sat, 11am–5pm Sun; Nov–Easter: 11am–4pm Wed–Sun & school hols. **Closed** 25 & 26 Dec 🖉 limited. 🆆 **lymeregismuseum.co.uk**

---

④ West Bay
There are terrific walks above and below the distinctive golden cliffs of West Bay.

⑤ Wears Hill
The former Iron Age hillfort here provides superb views across the Fleet Lagoon.

⑥ Chesil Beach and the Fleet Lagoon
With some 29 km (18 miles) of pebbles, Chesil Beach provides a natural barrier between the sea and the Fleet Lagoon.

⑧ Durdle Door and Lulworth Cove
The coastline's geology can be best viewed at Durdle Door and Lulworth Cove's crescent bay.

⑨ Swanage
Visitors can enjoy fish and chips on the beach at this typical English seaside resort.

⑩ Old Harry Rocks
A short walk from the pretty village of Studland are the dramatic chalk stacks of Old Harry Rocks.

Askerswell
A35
Littlebredy
Burton Bradstock ⑤
A354   A352
Broadway
B3157
A353
⑥
Weymouth
A354
⑦
Southwell

Frome
A352
Wool
Owermoigne
⑧
Lulworth Cove

Wareham   Poole Harbour
⑪
Corfe Castle   B3351
⑩
A351
Worth ·   ⑨
Matravers

⑦ Isle of Portland
Connected to the mainland by a causeway, this peninsula is known for its sailing and diving.

⑪ Shell Bay
The sandy beach of Shell Bay marks the start of the 1,014-km (630-mile) South West Coast Path.

0 km   6
0 miles   6

Max Gate, home to Dorset's most famous author and poet, Thomas Hardy

⓮ Dorchester

Dorset. **Map** F5. 🚇 20,000 🚻
🚌 🛈 The Library, Charles St; 01305 267992. 🛍 Wed.

Many parts of Dorchester, the county town of Dorset, are still recognizable as the place Thomas Hardy described in his novel *The Mayor of Casterbridge* (1886). Hardy lived at **Max Gate**, where rooms are open to visitors, but the original manuscript of his famous novel and a re-creation of his study can be seen in the **Dorset County Museum** on the High Street. This impressive galleried Victorian building also houses fossils and exhibits on the nearby Jurassic Coast *(see p117)*, along with archaeological finds.

Nearby is the **Old Crown Court**, where the famous Tolpuddle Martyrs were sentenced to transportation for demanding a wage increase; later pardoned, they are credited with founding the Trade Union movement.

Dorchester is home to Britain's only example of a **Roman Town House**. The remains of this wealthy family villa include a fine mosaic and a Roman heating system. There are also finds from Iron Age and Roman sites on the outskirts of the town.

Just off Weymouth Avenue is Maumbury Rings, a Neolithic henge that was adapted for use as a Roman amphitheatre. It was later used for bear-baiting and executions, but it now hosts firework displays and other events.

A more recent Dorcester attraction is Brewery Square, a former brewery that has now been redeveloped into a

fashionable cultural quarter, comprising a cinema, theatre, arts centre and several shops and restaurants clustered around a central square.

🎬 Max Gate
Arlington Ave. **Tel** 01305 262538.
Open Mar–Oct: 11am–5pm daily; Nov–Mar: 10am–4pm Thu–Sun. 🚫 ♿ limited. **NT** **W** **nationaltrust.org.uk**

🏛 Dorset County Museum
High West St. **Tel** 01305 262735.
Open 10am–5pm daily (to 4pm in winter). 🚫 📷 for groups. ♿ 🍴 📷 **W** **dorsetcountymuseum.org**

🏛 Old Crown Court
58–60 High West St. **Tel** 01305 267992.
NB: closed for refurbishment until 2018. 🚫 📷

🏛 Roman Town House
Colliton Park. **Open** 24 hrs. ♿

Environs
Just to the west of Dorchester, Poundbury is an ambitious eco-friendly town built from scratch on part of the Duchy of Cornwall's estate. Prince Charles has played an active role in the development of the town, which boasts handsome sign-free squares and mock-Georgian townhouses.

To the east of the city is **Hardy's Cottage**, where the writer was born. His heart is buried with his family at Stinsford church – his body was given a public funeral

in Westminster Abbey *(see pp50–51)*. Further east, at the 15th-century **Athelhampton House**, there is a magnificent medieval hall and beautiful gardens with fountains, statues, pavilions and columnar yews.

🏛 Hardy's Cottage
Higher Bockhampton. **Open** mid-Mar–Oct: 11am–5pm daily; Nov–Mar: 10am–4pm Thu–Sun. 🚫 ♿ limited. 📱 📷 **NT** **W** **nationaltrust.org.uk**

🏛 Athelhampton House
Athelhampton. **Open** Mar–Oct: 10:30am–5pm Sun–Thu; Nov–Feb: 10:30am–dusk Sun. 🚫 ♿ limited. 🚫 **W** **athelhampton.co.uk**

⓯ Maiden Castle

Dorset. **Map** F5. **EH**
W **english-heritage.org.uk**

Just southwest of Dorchester, barely out of the town suburbs, is the massive Maiden Castle, parts of which date back to around 3000 BC.

It is one of Europe's largest Iron Age hillforts and from around 450 BC several hundred members of the Durotriges tribe resided in the safety of the fort, in a town situated on a flat plateau at the top of the hill. You can still see where the fort's concentric lines of earthen ramparts and ditches follow the contours of the hill. These were once fortified by a

Thomas Hardy (1840–1928)

The lyrical novels and poems of Thomas Hardy, one of England's best-loved writers, are set against the background of his native Dorset, which formed part of the area he called Wessex in his novels. The son of a stonemason, Hardy grew up in the village of Higher Bockhampton, near Dorchester. He started work as an architect in London before returning to Dorset to be a writer. The success of *Far from the Madding Crowd* (1874) allowed him to move to Max Gate in Dorchester, which he helped design. Vivid accounts of rural life in his novels record a key moment in history, when mechanization was about to destroy ancient farming methods, just as the Industrial Revolution had transformed towns a century before. Hardy's visual style has made novels such as *Tess of the D'Urbervilles* (1891) and *Jude the Obscure* (1895) popular with film-makers, and literary pilgrims are drawn to the villages and landscapes that inspired his fiction.

English poet and novelist Thomas Hardy

Aerial view of the impressive prehistoric Maiden Castle

series of wooden fences and staggered gates that would have made the hilltop nigh-on impregnable to invading forces – at least until AD 43, when the Romans defeated the tribe in a bloody battle. Despite their victory the Romans decided to settle in nearby Dorchester, building a temple on the hilltop in the 4th century that was later abandoned; the foundations survive today on a grassy hillock. Visitors can walk up the slopes to the top of Maiden Castle, now grazed by placid sheep that have little idea of the history that lies beneath their feet.

⑯ Cerne Abbas

Dorset. **Map** F5. 🚹 800. 🚌

Charming Cerne Abbas grew up around a Benedictine abbey, which was built in 987 and visited by kings John and Henry III. Though little of the abbey can still be seen, the village exudes history, with a magnificent medieval tithe barn and ancient cottages. Visitors can also see St Augustine's Well, the spring where St Augustine allegedly offered local shepherds a choice of water or beer. When they chose water, the saint struck the ground with his staff, making a spring gush from the ground. Ironically, the fresh water that bubbles up here subsequently supported a brewing trade that was so successful that the village once had 15 pubs.

Today, however, the village's most famous attraction is the Cerne Abbas Giant, a huge chalk figure carved into the hillside nearby. Many believe this 55-m-(180-ft-) high carving to be a fertility figure representing either the Roman god Hercules or an Iron Age warrior, though others argue he may be a much later caricature of Oliver Cromwell. The figure has now been fenced off to avoid erosion and is best seen from the well-signed viewpoint on the hillside opposite, or via the Giant's Walk, a marked 90-minute trail from the village.

⑰ Shaftesbury

Dorset. **Map** F4. 🚹 7,500. 🚌
ℹ️ 8 Bell St; 01747 853514. 🚌 Thu.
🌐 **shaftesburytourism.co.uk**

Set on a hilltop commanding far-reaching rural views, the attractive town of Shaftesbury dates from Anglo-Saxon times. King Alfred the Great founded Shaftesbury Abbey here in 880 as a Benedictine nunnery – the first religious centre to be built for women. It quickly became one of the wealthiest and most powerful abbeys in the south, but was dissolved under Henry VIII in 1539. Much of the surrounding town fell into disrepair during the years that followed. Little remains of the fortifications, 12 churches and four market crosses that once made this a town of some importance, although the 14th-century St Peter's Church is one survivor.

The foundations of the abbey now form part of the **Abbey Museum and Garden**, which explores the abbey's fascinating history, including details of King Cnut's death here in 1035. The king was believed to have been visiting the tomb of the Saxon king Edward the Martyr, who was buried in the abbey after his murder at Corfe Castle (*see p114*) in 978.

Today, Shaftesbury's cobbled streets and pretty 18th-century cottages are often used as a setting in films to give a flavour of English rural history. Its most famous sight is the picturesque Gold Hill, an extremely steep cobbled lane, which is lined on one side by quaint thatched cottages and, on the other, by a wall of the demolished abbey.

🏛️ **Abbey Museum and Garden**
Park Walk. **Tel** 01747 852910.
Open Easter–Oct: 10am–5pm daily.
♿ 📷 🌐 **shaftesburyabbey. org.uk**

Quaint cottages lining Gold Hill in the picture-postcard village of Shaftesbury

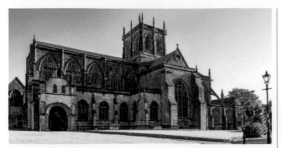

Sherborne Abbey Church features examples of various architectural styles

⑱ Sherborne

Dorset. **Map** F4. 🔁 10,000 🚆 🚌
ℹ️ 3 Tilton Court, Digby Rd; 01935
815341. 🚢 Thu. **W** visit-dorset.com

Few towns in England can rival Sherborne for its wealth of unspoiled medieval buildings. In 1550, Edward VI founded the Sherborne School, thereby saving the **Abbey Church** that might otherwise have been demolished in the Dissolution (see p36). Its most striking feature is the 15th-century fan-vaulted ceiling.

  Sherborne Castle, built by Sir Walter Raleigh (1552–1618) in 1594, anticipates Jacobean architecture with its flamboyant style. Raleigh also lived in the 12th-century **Old Castle**, which now stands in ruins, demolished during the Civil War (see p36).

🏛 Abbey Church
Abbey Close. **Tel** 01935 812452.
Open Apr–Oct: 8am–6pm daily;
Nov–Mar: 8am–4pm daily. 🅿 🎁 ♿
🚻 📷 **W** sherborneabbey.com

🏰 Sherborne Castle
New Rd. **Open** Easter–Oct: 11am–5pm
Tue, Thu, Sat & Sun. 🅿 ♿ limited. 📷
📷 **W** sherbornecastle.com

🏰 Old Castle
Off A30. **Tel** 01935 812730. **Open**
Easter–Oct: daily. 🅿 ♿ 📷 EH

⑲ Montacute House

Montacute. **Map** E4. **Tel** 01935
823289. **Open** House: mid-Mar–Oct:
11am–4:30pm daily. Gardens: Apr–
Oct: 11am–4:30pm daily; Nov–Feb:
11am–4pm Wed–Sun. 🅿 ♿ 📷 NT
W nationaltrust.org.uk

West of Sherborne stands the magnificent Elizabethan Montacute House, set in the picturesque village of the same name. The house was built in the late 16th century for the wealthy politician Sir Edward Phelips, and stayed in the same family until the early 20th century. It is noted for its Long Gallery, tapestries, and Tudor and Elizabethan portraits, which are loaned from the National Portrait Gallery. The house is set in 120 ha (300 acres) of grounds with formal gardens.

⑳ Taunton

Somerset. **Map** E4. 🔁 66,000. 🚆 🚌
ℹ️ Fore St; 01823 340470. 🚢 Thu, Fri
& Sat. **W** visitsomerset.co.uk

Pretty Taunton lies at the heart of a fertile region famous for its apples and cider, but it was the prosperous wool industry that financed the massive church of **St Mary Magdalene** (1488–1514), with its glorious tower.

  Taunton's castle was the setting for the notorious Bloody Assizes of 1685, when "Hanging" Judge Jeffreys dispensed harsh retribution on the Duke of Monmouth and his followers for an uprising against King James II. The charming 12th-century building houses the **Museum of Somerset**. A star exhibit is the Roman mosaic from a villa at Low Ham, depicting the story of Dido and Aeneas.

⛪ St Mary Magdalene
Church Sq. **Tel** 01823 272441.
Open 9:30am–3pm Mon–Fri,
9:30am–2pm Sat. 🚻 **W** stmary
magdalenetaunton.org.uk

🏛 Museum of Somerset
Taunton Castle. **Tel** 01823 255088.
Open 10am–5pm Tue–Sat.
W museumofsomerset.org.uk

㉑ Bridgwater and the Quantocks

Somerset. **Map** E4. 🔁 40,000. 🚆 🚌
🚢 Fri. 🎪 St Matthew's Fair: end of
Sep; Guy Fawkes Carnival: 1st Sun in
Nov. **W** bridgwatertown.com

Sedate Bridgwater grew as a bustling port and market town on the River Parrett. Its 16th-century **Blake Museum** details the town's history and its role in the Monmouth Rebellion.

  Bridgwater is also a useful base from which to explore the nearby Quantock hills. An Area of Outstanding Natural Beauty, the hills and surrounding countryside inspired the poet Samuel Taylor Coleridge (1772–1834). The pretty cottage where he wrote some of his best-known works lies in the village of Nether Stowey, 13 km (8 miles) west of Bridgwater.

  From here, a footpath known as the Coleridge Way runs west for 82 km (51 miles) through stunning Exmoor (see pp122–3) to the coastal town of Lynmouth.

🏛 Blake Museum
5 Blake St. **Tel** 01278 456127.
 Open Easter–Oct: 10am–4pm
Tue–Sat. 🅿 donation.
W bridgwatermuseum.org.uk

Somerset Cider

Somerset is one of the few English counties where farmhouse cider, or "scrumpy" (see p183), is still made using the traditional methods. Cider once formed part of the farm labourer's wages, and local folklore has it that unsavoury additives, such as iron nails, were added to give strength. Today, cider apple orchards flourish in the mild climate of the West Country. Scrumpy, made from fermented apples, can be extremely potent. Distilled cider brandy, matured for 20 years, is even stronger. Cider-making can be seen at Sheppy's farm, near Taunton.

Sheppy's Cider

㉒ Cheddar Gorge

Described as a "deep frightful chasm" by novelist Daniel Defoe in 1724, Cheddar Gorge is a spectacular ravine cut through the Mendip plateau by fast-flowing streams during the interglacial phases of the last Ice Age. Cheddar has given its name to a rich cheese that originates from here and is now produced worldwide. The caves in the gorge provide the perfect environment of constant temperature and high humidity for storing and maturing the cheese.

VISITORS' CHECKLIST

Practical Information
On B3135, Somerset. **Map** E4.
Caves & Gorge: **Tel** 01934 742343.
Open 10am–5pm daily. **Closed** 24
& 25 Dec. 🅿 entry with a Gorge
& Caves day ticket only. 🛈 🖼
🅰 only for museum. 🚻 📷
🎦 🆆 **cheddargorge.co.uk**
Cheddar Gorge Cheese Company:
The Cliffs. **Tel** 01934 742810.
Open 10am–3:15pm daily. 🅿
🅰 📷 🎦 🆆 **cheddargorge
cheeseco.co.uk**

Transport
🚌 from Weston-super-Mare
and Wells.

The B3135 road winds round the base of the 5-km (3-mile) gorge.

Cheddar Pink
This rare plant is among the astonishing range of plant and animal life that flourishes in the rocks.

A footpath follows the top of the gorge on its southern edge.

"Cheddar Man"
This famous 9,000-year-old skeleton is on display at the Museum of Prehistory, which looks at the prehistoric world of our ancestors.

The Gorge
This narrow, winding ravine with limestone rocks rises almost vertically on either side to a height of 140 m (460 ft).

Gough's Cave is noted for its cathedral-like proportions.

Cox's Cave contains unusually shaped stalactites and stalagmites.

A flight of 274 steps leads to the top of the gorge.

Cheddar Gorge Cheese Company
This is the only working Cheddar dairy in Cheddar. Visitors can see Cheddar being made, and taste and buy cheese in the store.

The Lookout Tower has far-reaching views over the area to the south and west.

㉓ Exmoor National Park

The 692 sq km (267 sq miles) of this national park offer a dramatically diverse landscape. Majestic cliffs plunge into the Bristol Channel along Exmoor's northern coast. Inland, rolling hills are grazed by hardy Exmoor ponies and England's only wild population of red deer. For walkers, the park offers 1,000 km (621 miles) of wonderful public paths, including the South West Coast Path. The moorland also offers less energetic attractions, including picturesque villages, seaside resorts, ancient castles and churches.

The Valley of the Rocks
A short walk west of Lynton, the Valley of Rocks is a dry gorge some 152 m (500 ft) above the sea. It is home to a series of sandstone outcrops eroded into fantastical shapes.

Heddon's Mouth
A 3-km (2-mile) walk through woodland along the Heddon Valley leads to the point where the River Heddon meets the sea. Set between some of England's highest cliffs, it is an attractive spot.

KEY

① **The village of Simonsbath** is a good starting point for walkers.

② **Combe Martin** is home to the Pack O'Cards Inn *(see p148)*.

③ **Parracombe's church** has a Georgian interior with boxed pews, a wooden pulpit and a carved screen.

④ **Watersmeet**, set in a beautifully wooded valley, is the spot where the River East Lyn and Hoar Oak Water join together in a tumbling cascade. There is also a tearoom with a pretty garden.

⑤ **Oare Church** commemorates the writer R D Blackmore, whose novel *Lorna Doone* (1869) is set in the area.

⑥ **Culbone Church**, a mere 10.6 m (35 ft) in length, claims to be Britain's smallest parish church.

⑦ **Selworthy** is a picturesque village of thatched cottages.

⑧ **Minehead** is a resort built around a quay. The West Somerset Railway runs from here to Bishop's Lydeard.

⑨ **Dunster** is a medieval village with an ancient castle and an unusual octagonal Yarn Market (c.1609), where local cloth was once sold.

⑩ **Tarr Steps** is an ancient "clapper" bridge built of stone slabs.

Martinho

Ilfracombe • Watermouth ②

Heddon Valley

③

A3123

A399

Patchole • Blackmoor Gat

B3220

A39

Arlington

A399

Brayford

Great Hangman
At 433 m (1,421 ft), the Great Hangman, England's highest sea cliff, lies on the South West Coast Path near the village of Combe Martin.

Exmoor Ponies
A native breed, the sturdy brown Exmoor ponies can be seen roaming freely around the spectacular moors. In spring and early summer, visitors should look out for the new-born foals.

Cliff Railway
Since the early 19th century, a water-powered funicular railway *(see p148)* has shuttled 263 m (862 ft) up a steep track between the picturesque coastal village of Lynmouth and Lynton, perched on the clifftop above. The short ride offers fabulous views of the spectacular Jurassic Coast.

VISITORS' CHECKLIST

Practical Information
Somerset/Devon. **Map** D4.
i Dulverton National Park Centre; 01398 323841.
w **exmoor-nationalpark.gov.uk**
Dunster Castle: **Tel** 01643 821314.
Open Mar–Oct: 11am–5pm daily.
🚫 ♿ 11:30am (Nov–Feb). ♿
🏠 NT w **nationaltrust.org.uk**
West Somerset Railway: **w** **west-somerset-railway.co.uk**

Transport
🚆 🚌 Tiverton Parkway then bus.

Porlock
This flower-filled village has a historic charm, with winding streets, thatched houses and a lovely old church.

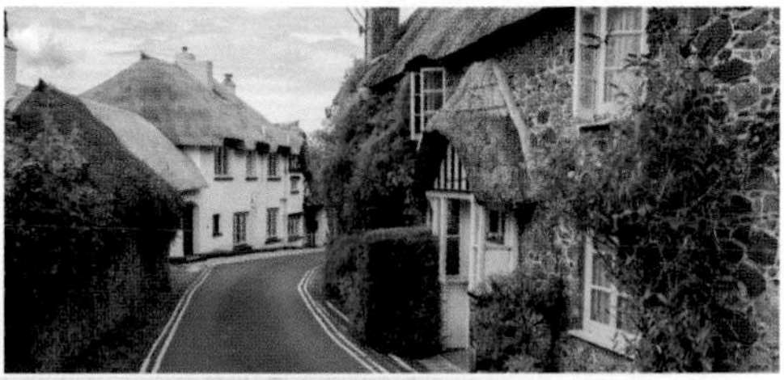

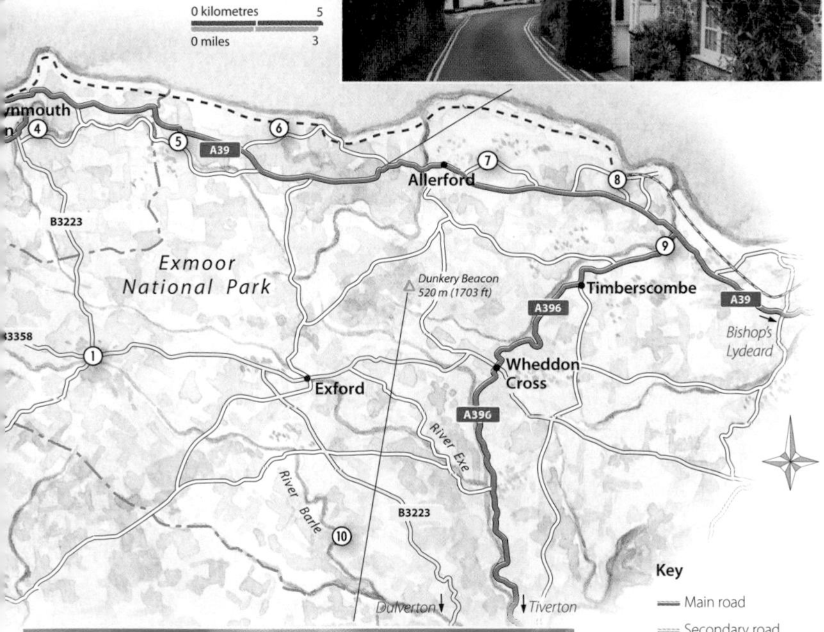

| 0 kilometres | 5 |
| 0 miles | 3 |

Exmoor National Park

Dunkery Beacon 520 m (1703 ft)

Allerford

Timberscombe

Bishop's Lydeard

Wheddon Cross

Exford

River Exe

River Barle

Dulverton↓   ↓Tiverton

Key
═══ Main road
═══ Secondary road
═══ Minor road
- - - South West Coast Path
△ Peak

Dunkery Beacon
Rising to a height of 519 m (1,703 ft), the summit of Dunkery Beacon is Exmoor's highest point. On a clear day, the views stretch as far as Wales to the north and Dartmoor to the south.

Path leading to the ruins of St Michael's Tower at the top of Glastonbury Tor

㉔ Somerset Levels

Somerset. **Map** E4. 🚆 Glastonbury. 🚌 Glastonbury.

The extensive Somerset Levels consist of ancient peat moors and grassland interspersed with dramatic hillocks such as the Glastonbury Tor, which some say was the mythical Isle of Avalon in Arthurian legend. Visible for miles around, the Tor is a hill crowned by St Micheal's Tower, which is all that remains of a 14th-century monastic church. The building was largely destoyed during the Dissolution of the Monasteries (see p36).

Though split by the Polden Hills, the Levels are prone to flooding and have been drained since the Middle Ages. Today, the wetlands – many formed from abandoned peat workings – are a magnet for wildlife. The various nature reserves at the beautiful Avalon Marshes are home to kingfishers, bitterns and great white egrets, and in the winter massive murmurations of starlings blacken the sky in wonderfully dramatic patterns.

There are excellent walks and cycle rides from the central **Avalon Marshes Centre**.

🏛 **Avalon Marshes Centre**
Shapwick Rd, Westhay. **Tel** 01458 860556. **Open** 10am–5pm daily.
📧 📷 🇼 avalonmarshes.org

㉕ Glastonbury

Somerset. **Map** E4. 🚶 9,000 🚌 ℹ️
The Tribunal, High St; 01458 832954.
🏠 Tue. 🇼 **glastonburytic.co.uk**

Shrouded in Arthurian myth and rich in mystical association, the town of Glastonbury was once one of the most important destinations for pilgrims in England. Today, thousands flock here for the annual music festival and for the summer solstice on Midsummer's Day (21 June).

Over the years, history and legend have become intertwined. In around 700, the monks who set up Glastonbury Abbey found it profitable to encourage the association between Glastonbury and the mythical "Blessed Isle" known as Avalon – alleged to be the last resting place of King Arthur (see p156) and the Holy Grail. The great abbey was left in ruins after the Dissolution. Despite this, some magnificent remains survive, including parts

㉖ Wells Cathedral

The charming town of Wells is named after St Andrew's Well, the clear sacred spring that bubbles up from the ground near the 13th-century Bishop's Palace, the residence of the Bishop of Bath and Wells. The cathedral was begun in the late 1100s, and is famous for its elaborate West Front and the "scissor arches" installed in 1338 to support the tower.

The Vicars' Close was built in the 14th-century for the Vicars' Choir. It is one of the oldest complete streets in Europe.

The spectacular West Front features 300 fine medieval statues of kings, knights and saints, many of them life-size.

Chapter House
From the north transept a doorway leads to a graceful flight of steps, which curves up to the octagonal Chapter House. The interior features delicate vaulting dating from 1306. The 32 ribs fanning from the central column create a beautiful palm-tree effect.

Chain Gate (1460)

Cloisters

Victorian laundry items at the Somerset Rural Life Museum in Glastonbury

of the Norman abbey church, the unusual Abbot's Kitchen (with its octagonal roof) and a Victorian farmhouse, now the **Somerset Rural Life Museum**. Growing in the grounds is a cutting from the Glastonbury thorn, which is believed to have miraculously grown from the staff of St Joseph of Arimathea.

According to myth, he was sent around AD 60 to convert England to Christianity. The thorn flowers at Christmas as well as in May.

The **Lake Village Museum**, on the High Street, has finds from the Iron Age settlements that once fringed the marshlands around Glastonbury Tor.

Somerset Rural Life Museum
Chilkwell St. **Tel** 01458 831197. **Open** Abbey Farm: 1–5pm Mon, 9am–5pm Tue–Fri. **Closed** 1 Jan, Good Fri, Easter, 25 Dec & public hols. limited.

Lake Village Museum
The Tribunal, High St. **Tel** 01458 832954. **Open** 10am–4pm Mon–Sat (to 3:15pm in winter). **Closed** 23 Dec–1 Jan.

Glastonbury Festival

Camping area at the Glastonbury Festival

In 1970, farmer Michael Eavis decided to host a music festival at Worthy Farm in Pilton, near Glastonbury. Little did he know that the event, which attracted 1,500 people, would grow into one of the world's largest contemporary music festivals. Today, the festival is held in late June and pulls in over 130,000 attendees. The extensive farmland location means that the site has become renowned for its mud, and Wellington boots are as ubiquitous here as the hundreds of tents across the site. The festival features theatre, comedy and performance artists, but the main draw is the quality of its music: top acts have ranged from David Bowie and Bob Dylan to Oasis, the Rolling Stones and Adele.

Bishops' Tombs
The tombs of past bishops circle the chancel. This marble tomb in the south aisle is that of Bishop Lord Arthur Hervey, who was Bishop of Bath and Wells from 1869 to 1894.

Bishop's Palace (1230–40)

13th-century ruins of the Great Hall

Moat
Swans on the moat are trained to ring a bell by the gatehouse when they want to be fed.

Path leading around the moat

㉗ Bristol

In 1497, John Cabot sailed from Bristol on his historic voyage to North America. The city, at the mouth of the Avon, became the main British port for transatlantic trade, pioneering the era of the ocean-going steam liner with the construction of Isambard Kingdom Brunel's SS *Great Britain*. Bristol flourished as a major trading centre, growing rich on the distribution of wine, tobacco and, from the 17th to the 19th century, slaves. Because of its docks and aero engine factories, Bristol was heavily bombed during World War II. In 2008, a multimillion-pound redevelopment programme was completed with the opening of Cabot Circus, a vast shopping centre. The old dock area has been brought back to life with bars, cafés, restaurants and art galleries lining the waterside.

Energy Tree, erected as part of Bristol's year as European Green Capital, in At-Bristol

The vaulted nave of St Mary Redcliffe, one of the largest parish churches in England

🏠 St Mary Redcliffe

Redcliffe Way. **Tel** 0117 231 0060.
Open 9am–5pm daily. 🚻 ♿ ▣
W stmaryredcliffe.co.uk

This magnificent 14th-century church was claimed by Queen Elizabeth I to be "the fairest in England". The church owes much to the generosity of William Canynges the Elder and Younger, both famous mayors of Bristol. Inscriptions on the tombs of merchants and sailors tell of lives devoted to trade. Look out for the Bristol maze roof boss in the north aisle.

🎭 King Street

Theatre Royal: **Tel** 0117 987 7877.
Open Box office: 10am–4pm Mon–Fri.
W bristololdvic.org.uk

The group of buildings on cobbled King Street include the 17th-century timber-framed Llandoger Trow inn. It is here that Daniel Defoe is said to have met Alexander Selkirk, whose true-life island exile served as the inspiration for Defoe's novel *Robinson Crusoe* (1719). Just up from here is the Theatre Royal, built in 1766 and home to the famous Bristol Old Vic.

🏛 Old Quarter

The oldest part of the city lies around Broad, King and Corn streets, known as the Old Quarter. The lively St Nicholas covered market, part of which occupies the Corn Exchange, was built by John Wood the Elder (*see p128*) in 1743. Outside are the Bristol Nails, four bronze 16th- to 17th-century pedestals which Bristol merchants used as tables when paying for goods – giving rise to the expression "to pay on the nail". St John's Gate, at the head of Broad Street, has medieval statues of Bristol's two mythical founders, King Brennus and King Benilus. Between Lewins Mead and Colston Street, Christmas Steps is a steep lane lined with specialist shops and cafés. The Chapel of the Three Kings at the top was founded in 1504.

Harbourside

Arnolfini: 16 Narrow Quay. **Tel** 0117 917 2300. **Open** 11am–6pm Tue–Sun. **W** arnolfini.org.uk
At-Bristol: Anchor Rd. **Tel** 0117 915 1000. **Open** 10am–5pm Mon–Fri, 10am–6pm Sat, Sun, public hols & Bristol school hols. 🅿
♿ ▣ 🍴 **W** at-bristol.org.uk

The renowned Arnolfini arts centre, on Narrow Quay, showcases contemporary art, drama, dance and cinema. On the Harbourside, At-Bristol combines an interactive science centre with a planetarium.

🏛 M-Shed

Princes Wharf, Harbourside. **Tel** 0117 352 6600. **Open** 10am–5pm Tue–Fri; 10am–6pm Sat, Sun & public hols. 🅿 for temporary exhibitions only. ♿
▣ 🍴 **W** bristolmuseums.org.uk

Housed in a 1950s harbourside transit shed, this museum focuses on the city's history. The story is told through film, photographs, objects and personal accounts. Temporary exhibitions take place regularly.

St Nicholas Market, home to the largest collection of independent retailers in Bristol

🏛 Brunel's SS Great Britain

Gas Ferry Rd. **Tel** 0117 926 0680.
Open 10am–4pm daily (Mar–Oct: to
5:30pm). **Closed** 24 & 25 Dec. 🅿
ticket valid for one year. 🎫 by appt.
♿ 🖥 📷 🌐 **ssgreatbritain.org**

Designed by Brunel, this was the
world's first large iron passenger
ship. Launched in 1843, she
travelled 32 times around the
world before being abandoned
in the Falkland Islands in 1886.
The ship has been fully restored
and now houses one of the most
important maritime museums.

🏛 Bristol Cathedral

College Green. **Tel** 0117 926 4879.
Open 8am–5pm Mon–Fri, 8am–
3:15pm Sat & Sun. 🔔 donation.
🎫 ♿ limited. 🏛 🖥 📷
🌐 **bristol-cathedral.co.uk**

Bristol's cathedral, begun in
1140, took an unusually long
time to build. Rapid progress
was made between 1298 and
1330, when the inventive choir
was rebuilt; the transepts and
tower were finished in 1515;
and another 350 years passed
before the Victorian architect G E
Street built the nave. Humorous
medieval carvings abound,
including a snail crawling across
the stone foliage in the Berkeley
Chapel and musical monkeys
in the Elder Lady Chapel. There
is also a fine set of wooden
misericords in the choir.

🏛 Georgian House

7 Great George St. **Tel** 0117 921 1362.
Open late Mar–Dec: 11am–4pm
Mon, Tue, Sat & Sun. 🌐 **bristol
museums.org.uk**

Daily life in a wealthy Bristol
merchant's house during the
1790s is reimagined in rooms
that include an elegant drawing
room and the servants' area.

🏛 Bristol Museum and Art Gallery

Queen's Rd. **Tel** 0117 922 3571.
Open 10am–5pm Tue–Sun.
Closed 1 Jan, 25 & 26 Dec. ♿ 🖥
📷 🌐 **bristolmuseums.org.uk**

Varied collections include ancient
Egyptian artifacts, dinosaur fossils,
Chinese glass and fine European
paintings, with works by Renoir
and Bellini. There are also works
by Bristol artists Francis Danby,
Sir Thomas Lawrence and the
celebrated graffiti artist Banksy.

Clifton

Bristol Zoo Gardens: College Rd.
Tel 0117 428 5300. **Open** 9am–5pm
daily. 🅿 ♿ 🖥 🌐 **bristolzoo.org.uk**

The hilltop suburb of Clifton
is home to ornate Regency
crescents. The Clifton Suspension
Bridge by Brunel, completed in
1864, perfectly complements the
steep Avon Gorge. Bristol Zoo
Gardens house over 400 exotic
and endangered species.

The Clifton Suspension Bridge across the Avon, linking Bristol and North Somerset

Bristol City Centre

① St Mary Redcliffe
② King Street
③ Old Quarter
④ Harbourside
⑤ M-Shed
⑥ Brunel's SS
   Great Britain
⑦ Bristol Cathedral
⑧ Georgian House
⑨ Bristol Museum
   and Art Gallery
⑩ Clifton

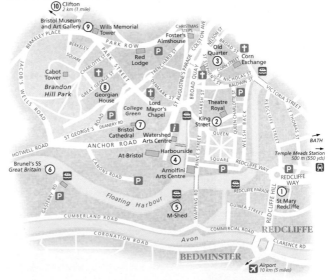

0 metres   250
0 yards   250

For keys to symbols see back flap

❷ Street-by-Street: Bath

Bath owes its magnificent Georgian townscape to the bubbling pool of water at the heart of the Roman Baths. The Romans transformed Bath into England's first spa resort and it regained fame as a spa town in the 18th century. At this time, two architects, John Wood the Elder and his son John Wood the Younger, designed many of the city's Palladian-style buildings. Many houses bear plaques recording the numerous famous people who have resided here.

Assembly Rooms and Museum of Costume

The Circus, designed by John Wood the Elder (1705–54), is a daring departure from the typical Georgian square.

← Royal Victoria Park

No. 1 Royal Crescent

No. 17 was home to famous English painter Thomas Gainsborough (1727–88).

The Jane Austen Centre *(see p130)* tells the story of the author's time in Bath through a permanent exhibition of film, costumes and books.

★ Royal Crescent
Hailed the most majestic street in Britain, this graceful arc of 30 houses (1767–74) is the masterpiece of John Wood the Younger. West of the Royal Crescent, the Royal Victoria Park (1830) is the city's largest open space.

Theatre Royal (1805)

Milsom Street
Milsom and New Bond streets feature some of Bath's most elegant shops. The striking buildings on Milson Street were once townhouses, and have now been converted into shops and offices.

Key
— Suggested route

| 0 metres | 100 |
| 0 yards | 100 |

For hotels and restaurants in this region see p177 and pp188–9

BENNETT ST

BROCK STREET

ROYAL CRESCENT

THE CIRCUS

GAY STREET

GEORGE

QUEEN

SQUARE

BARTON ST

BEAUFORD SQUARE

Pulteney Bridge

This charming bridge (1769–74), designed by Robert Adam, is lined with shops and links the city centre with the magnificent Great Pulteney Street. Look out for a rare Victorian pillar box on the east bank.

VISITORS' CHECKLIST

Practical Information
Bath. **Map** F3. 🚶 94,000.
ℹ️ Abbey Chambers,
Abbey Church Yard; 0844
847 5256. 🏪 Mon–Sat.
🎵 International Music
Festival: May–Jun.
🇼 visitbath.co.uk

Transport
✈️ Bristol, 32 km (20 miles) W
of Bath. 🚆 🚌 Dorchester St.

Museum of Bath
Architecture

★ **Roman Baths**
Built in the 1st century, this bathing complex is one of Britain's greatest surviving Roman structures.

★ **Bath Abbey**
This splendid abbey stands at the heart of the old city in the Abbey Church Yard, a paved courtyard enlivened by buskers. Its unique façade features stone angels climbing Jacob's Ladder to heaven.

Pulteney Bridge

Holburne
Museum

Parade Gardens
These gardens have a lovely view of Pulteney Bridge. Summer concerts are held in the bandstand.

The Pump Rooms were tearooms that once formed the social hub of the 18th-century spa community.

Sally Lunn's House (1482) is one of Bath's oldest houses.

Rail and
coach stations ↙

Exploring Bath

Set among the rolling green hills of the Avon Valley, the beautiful and compact city of Bath has a long history of tourism. For centuries, visitors have been drawn to the city's natural hot springs and thriving leisure industry. Today, the traffic-free heart of this lively city is full of museums, cafés and shops, while the elegant honey-coloured Georgian houses, so characteristic of Bath, form an elegant backdrop to city life.

Front entrance of the Holburne Museum of Art, the first public art gallery in Bath

⬆ Bath Abbey

Abbey Churchyard. **Tel** 01225 422462. **Open** 9:30am–5:30pm Mon–Fri, 9:30am–6pm Sat, 1–1:30pm & 4:30–5:30pm Sun. **Closed** during services, except Good Fri service. 🔊 donation. ♿ ⬆ 🏠 **W bathabbey.org**

The abbey was supposedly designed by divine agency. According to legend, God dictated the form of the church to Bishop Oliver King in a dream; this story has been immortalized in the carvings on the west front. The bishop began work in 1499, rebuilding a church that had been founded in the 8th century. The interior nave has impressive fan vaulting, an addition made by Sir George Gilbert Scott in 1874.

▥ National Trust Assembly Rooms and Fashion Museum

Bennett St. **Tel** 01225 477789. **Open** Jan–Feb & Nov–Dec: 10:30am–4pm daily; Mar–Oct: 10:30am–5pm daily. **Closed** 25 & 26 Dec. 🔊 ♿ 🏠 **W fashionmuseum.co.uk**

The Assembly Rooms, built by Wood the Younger in 1769, were a meeting place for the elite and

a backdrop for glittering balls. Jane Austen's novel *Northanger Abbey* (1818) describes the gossip and flirtation that went on here. In the basement there is a superb display of costumes from the 1500s to the present day.

▥ Jane Austen Centre

40 Gay St. **Tel** 01225 443000. **Open** 10am–4pm daily (Apr–Oct: to 5:30pm). **Closed** 1 Jan, 25 & 26 Dec. 🔊 ♿ limited. 🖥 🏠 **W janeausten.co.uk**

From 1801 to 1806, Bath was Austen's *(see p92)* home. This lovely museum explores how the author's experiences here affected her work.

▥ No. 1 Royal Crescent

Royal Crescent. **Tel** 01225 428126. **Open** Feb–mid-Dec: noon–5:30pm Mon, 10:30am–5:30pm Tue–Sun. **Closed** 25 & 26 Dec. 🔊 ♿ limited. 🖉 🏠 **W no1royalcrescent.org.uk**

This museum offers a glimpse of what life was like for 18th-century aristocrats, such as the Duke of York, who stayed here. Visitors can see Georgian mousetraps and a spit turned by a dog wheel.

▥ Holburne Museum of Art

Great Pulteney St. **Tel** 01225 388569. **Open** 10am–5pm Mon–Sat, 11am–5pm Sun. **Closed** 1 Jan & 24–26 Dec. 🔊 ♿ 🖥 🏠 **W holburne.org**

This building is named after William Holburne of Menstrie (1793–1874), whose collections form the nucleus of the display of fine and decorative arts, including superb silver and porcelain. Paintings by Gainsborough and Stubbs are on show.

▦ Thermae Bath Spa

Hot Bath St. **Tel** 01225 331234. **Open** 9am–9:30pm daily. **Closed** 1 Jan, 25 & 26 Dec. 🔊 under-16s not permitted. ♿ 🖥 🏠 **W thermaebathspa.com**

People have bathed in the warm, mineral-rich waters of the spa town of Bath since Roman times, and the opening of the Thermae Bath Spa in 2006 once again made Bath a popular day-spa destination. There are three pools fed by natural thermal waters: the New Royal Bath has two baths, including an open-air rooftop pool with views over the city. Across the road, the oval Cross Bath is a more intimate open-air bath, ideal for shorter sessions. The spa offers an array of treatments that need to be booked in advance. The signature therapy is *watsu*, a water-based version of the shiatsu massage.

▥ American Museum

Claverton Manor, Claverton Down. **Tel** 01225 460503. **Open** mid-Mar–Oct: noon–4:30pm Tue–Sun (daily in Aug). **Closed** Nov–mid-Mar. 🔊 ♿ limited. 🖥 🏠 **W americanmuseum.org**

Founded in 1961, this was the first American museum in Britain. Its founders, psychiatrist Dr Dallas Pratt and antiques dealer John Judkyn, bought Claverton Manor

Spectacular fan vaulting over the nave in Bath Abbey

to showcase US arts and crafts and promote Anglo-American understanding. The rooms in the 1820 manor house are decorated in many different styles, from the rudimentary dwellings of the first settlers to the opulent style of 19th-century homes. The museum has special sections on Shaker furniture, quilts and Native American art, and a replica of George Washington's Mount Vernon garden of 1785.

Richard "Beau" Nash (1674–1762)

Elected in 1704 as Master of Ceremonies, "Beau" Nash played a crucial role in transforming Bath into a fashionable centre of Georgian society. During his career, he devised an endless selection of games, balls and entertainment (including gambling), which kept the idle rich amused and ensured a constant flow of visitors.

Portrait of Richard "Beau" Nash

The Great Bath

According to legend, Bath owes its origin to the Celtic King Bladud, who discovered the curative properties of its natural hot springs in 860 BC. In the 1st century, the Romans built baths and a temple around the therapeutic waters. Bath Abbey's medieval monks also later exploited the spring's properties, and Bath became a fashionable hub of high society after Queen Anne bathed here in 1702–3. Work began on the present structure in the 18th century, and further building work in the 19th-century revealed the remains of the Roman Bath chambers.

VISITORS' CHECKLIST

Practical Information
Entrance in Abbey Churchyard.
Tel 01225 477785. **Open** 9:30am–5pm daily (Jul & Aug: to 9pm).
Closed 25 & 26 Dec. 🅿 🚻 limited. 🖪 ⓦ **romanbaths.co.uk**

The dome (1897) is based on St Stephen Walbrook Church in London.

Roman Influences
Steps, column bases and paving stones around the edge of the bath date from Roman times.

York Street

A late 19th-century terrace bears statues of famous Romans.

The sacred spring was a focal point for worship in the Roman period, and offerings to the goddess Sulis Minerva were thrown into the water. The reservoir was later named the King's Bath, and niches were added for bathers to sit in.

The water flows from the spring into the corner of the bath at a constant temperature of 46° C (115° F).

Piers
Around the edges of the bath are the bases of piers that once supported a barrel-vaulted roof.

DEVON

A county of lush pasture divided into a patchwork of tiny fields, Devon is threaded with narrow lanes whose banks support a mass of wildflowers, from the primroses of early spring to summer's colourful tangle of foxglove and cornflower. On its coastline are dramatic beetling cliffs and long sandy beaches, along with some of the country's most famous seaside resorts. Historic cities, idyllic villages, sheltered rivers, bustling ports and the vast moors of Dartmoor only add to the mix.

Prehistoric Devon may have had a warmer climate than much of Britain, and it is the earliest known place in England to have been settled after the end of the last Ice Age – a jawbone discovered at Kents Cavern, near Torquay, is thought to belong to the earliest modern human in northwest Europe. By 6000 BC, Dartmoor seems to have played a key role in Mesolithic and Neolithic culture – the bleak moorland holds the remains of the oldest surviving buildings in the country, although this could be because the moor was infertile and never ploughed.

Only a few parts of Devon fell under Roman rule, and the county continued to play a marginal role in history until Tudor times, when the natural harbour at Plymouth became the point of departure for explorers and adventurers such as Sir Walter Raleigh and Sir Francis Drake.

Plymouth was also the point of arrival for the first exotic imports from the Americas, including spices, wine, corn, potatoes and tobacco. Devon's central role during the Age of Discovery also left it with some remarkable Tudor houses and villages.

Devon became an important destination again during the Victorian era, as new train lines and a vogue for sea air and swimming saw the development of many seaside towns. Most famous were the resort towns on the South Coast – Torquay, Paignton and Brixham – which became known as the English Riviera for their relatively balmy climate, subtropical vegetation and palm-lined promenades. These towns continue to draw the crowds, and today tourism has overtaken agriculture as Devon's main source of income, but the two traditions still unite in the county's most famous delicacy – the Devonshire Cream Tea.

The iconic Burgh Island Hotel, as seen from the coastal village of Bantham

◀ View of Dartmoor National Park from Bel Tor, a granite outcrop

Exploring Devon

With a network of waymarked paths winding through picturesque villages, wild moorland and stunning coastlines, Devon is a fantastic region for walkers. More gentle pursuits include pottering about in the villages or touring the tranquil waters of the Dart Estuary. There are classic seaside resorts on both the north and south coasts, such as Torquay, Sidmouth and Ilfracombe, while country villages and towns range from vibrant Totnes to idyllic Clovelly and Dittisham. Devon's rich history can be explored in its charming cities, ranging from the magnificent cathedral city of Exeter to the lively port of Plymouth.

Sights at a Glance

1. Beer
2. Exeter
3. Torquay
4. Tor Bay
5. Totnes
6. Dittisham
7. *Dart Estuary p139*
8. Dartmouth
9. Salcombe and the South Hams
10. Burgh Island
11. Buckfastleigh
12. Buckland Abbey
13. *Dartmoor National Park pp142–3*
14. Plymouth
15. Morwellham Quay
16. Cotehele
17. Lynton and Lynmouth
18. Ilfracombe
19. Barnstaple
20. Broomhill Sculpture Gardens
21. Appledore
22. Bideford
23. Clovelly
24. Hartland Point
25. *Lundy Island pp150–51*

The South Lighthouse, set on picturesque Lundy Island

Getting Around

During summer and on bank holiday weekends, progress can be slow along the M5 motorway and A38 trunk road, as large numbers of drivers, many towing caravans (trailers), take to the road. Once in Devon, allow plenty of time if travelling by car along the region's narrow lanes. Regular train services from Paddington run along Brunel's historic Great Western Railway, with stops at most major towns. Devon's airport is in Exeter, with flights from London and major regional airports. There are also flights onward to the Isles of Scilly.

Key

— Motorway

— Dual carriageway

— Main road

⋯ Other road

⋯ Railway

— County border

△ Peak

For hotels and restaurants in this region see p178 and pp189–90

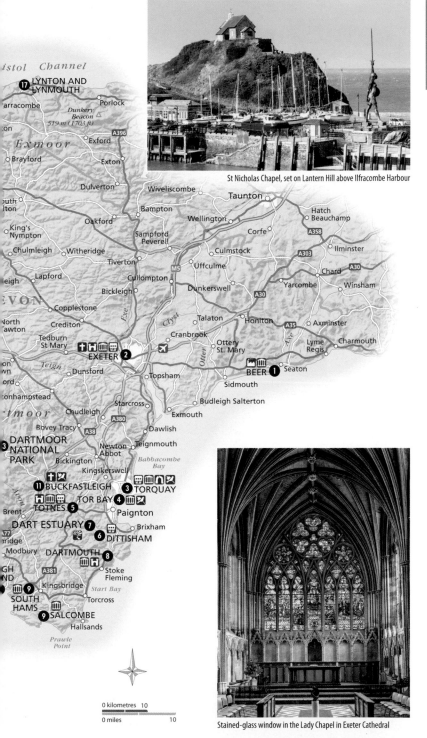

St Nicholas Chapel, set on Lantern Hill above Ilfracombe Harbour

Bristol *Channel*

17 LYNTON AND LYNMOUTH

arracombe ○ Porlock

Dunkery Beacon 519 m (1703 ft)

○ Exford

Exmoor

○ Brayford ○ Exton

○ Wiveliscombe

Taunton ○

○ Dulverton

outh lton

○ Bampton Wellington ○

Hatch ○ Beauchamp

King's ○ Nympton

Oakford ○ Corfe ○

A358

○ Chulmleigh ○ Witheridge

Sampford Peverell ○ Culmstock ○

A303

○ Ilminster

Tiverton ○ Uffculme ○

Chard A30

leigh ○ Lapford

Cullompton ○

Yarcombe ○ Winsham

○ Bickleigh

Dunkerswell ○

A30

Exe

DEVON

North ○ Copplestone ○

M5

○ Crediton *Clyst* ○ Talaton Honiton ○

A35

○ Axminster

Tedburn St Mary

Cranbrook ○ Ottery St. Mary ○

Lyme Regis ○ Charmouth

Axe

on wn ord

✝ 🏠 🏛 **2** EXETER

Teign ○ Dunsford ○ Topsham

🏠🏛 BEER **1** ○ Seaton

Sidmouth ○

onhampstead ○ Starcross

Otter

tmoor

Chudleigh ○ Exmouth ○ Budleigh Salterton

3 DARTMOOR NATIONAL PARK

Bovey Tracy ○ A380 ○ Dawlish

A38 Newton Abbot ○ Teignmouth ○

○ Bickington

Babbacombe Bay

✝ 🏂 ○ Kingskerswell

11 BUCKFASTLEIGH 🏠🏛🏛 **3** TORQUAY

Brent ○ 🏠🏛🏛 **5** TOTNES TOR BAY **4** 🏛🏂 ○ Paignton

A77 ridge DART ESTUARY **7** 🏂 **6** 🏛 ○ Brixham DITTISHAM

○ Modbury DARTMOUTH 🏛🏠 **8**

GH ND A381 ○ Stoke Fleming

🏛 **9** ○ Kingsbridge *Start Bay*

SOUTH HAMS ○ Torcross

🏛 **9** SALCOMBE

○ Hallsands

Prawle Point

0 kilometres 10

0 miles 10

Stained-glass window in the Lady Chapel in Exeter Cathedral

For additional map symbols *see back flap*

Dramatic limestone cliffs abutting the scenic shingle beach at Beer in Lyme Bay

❶ Beer

Devon. **Map** E5. 🚠 1,300. 🚌 Beer Cross. 🛈 The Underfleet, Seaton; 01297 21660.

Set on a fine shingle beach backed by white limestone cliffs, this fishing village derives its name from the old Anglo-Saxon word *bearu*, which referred to the woodland that once surrounded the settlement. It is one of the few fishing villages without a harbour; boats are winched out of the sea over oiled logs to ease their passage.

Beer is famous for its local stone, which has been used in many cathedrals, including St Paul's and Westminster Abbey. The vast underground complex of **Beer Quarry Caves** was mined from Roman times until the 1920s. It also provided a place of refuge for Catholics at times of persecution, and an ideal hiding place for smugglers.

A key attraction for children is **Pecorama**, the home of the iconic model railway manufacturers, Peco. The highlight here is a ride on a miniature steam train.

Thomas II locomotive, built in 1979 by Roger Marsh, at Pecorama

🎪 Beer Quarry Caves
Quarry Ln. **Tel** 01297 680282. **Open** Apr–Sep: 10am–4pm daily, Oct: 10am–3pm daily. 🎟 🎥 every 30 mins. 🚻 🅿 🌐 **beerquarrycaves.co.uk**

🏛 Pecorama
Underleys, Seaton. **Tel** 01297 21542. **Open** Apr–Oct: 10am–5pm daily; Nov–Mar: 10am–5:30pm Mon–Fri, 10am–1pm Sat. 🦽 partial. 🚻 🅿 🌐 **pecorama.co.uk**

❷ Exeter

Devon's capital, Exeter, is a lively city with a great deal of character, despite the World War II bombing that destroyed much of its centre. Built high on a plateau above the River Exe, the city is encircled by substantial sections of Roman and medieval wall, and the street plan has not changed much since the Romans first laid out what is now the High Street. Cathedral Close has one of the country's finest Gothic churches, and there are atmospheric cobbled streets which invite leisurely exploration. For shoppers there is a wide selection of big stores and smaller speciality shops.

🏰 Exeter Cathedral
1 The Cloisters. **Tel** 01392 285973. **Open** 9am–5pm daily. 🎟 🦽 🎁 🚻 🅿 🌐 **exeter-cathedral.org.uk**

Completed around 1400, the majestic Cathedral Church of St Peter is one of the most gloriously ornamented cathedrals in Britain. Its West Front is intricately carved with tier upon tier of kings, angels, apostles and prophets – 66 in all, the largest single collection of medieval figure sculptures in England. Inside, breathtaking Gothic fan vaulting sweeps from one end of the church to the other, each join decorated with a unique gilded boss – the most famous depicts the assassination of Thomas Becket. The intricately carved misericords, dating from 1220–30 and 1250–60, are the oldest complete set in England. The elephant is especially well known. A catflap in the door by the clock dates back to when the cathedral cat was paid a penny a week to catch mice.

Full of relaxed crowds listening to buskers perform on the green, the close surrounding the cathedral contains a variety of architectural styles. One of the finest buildings here is Mol's Coffee House, built in 1596.

🏛 The Guildhall
High St. **Tel** 01392 665500. **Open** daily; times vary, call ahead. 🦽 🌐 **exeter.gov.uk**

Among the many historic buildings that survived World War II is the magnificent Guildhall (1330) on the High Street. It is one of Britain's oldest civic buildings and has functioned as a prison, a court-house, a police station and a place for civic functions and celebrations. It still serves as the meeting place for the Mayor and the City Council.

🏛 St Nicholas Priory
Fore St. **Tel** 01392 271732. **Closed** for restoration. 🌐 **exeter.gov.uk**

Visitors can trace the fascinating history of this 12th-century Benedictine priory from its austere monastic beginnings

The impressive West Front of the Cathedral Church of St Peter

Historic industrial buildings and warehouses lining the picturesque quayside in Exeter

VISITORS' CHECKLIST

Practical Information
Devon. **Map** D5. 125,000.
Dix's Field; 01392 665700.
visitexeter.com

Transport
Exeter St David's. Paris St.

to its post-Dissolution use as a residence for wealthy Protestant merchants. It is now decorated as a typical Elizabethan townhouse, with oak panelling and elaborate plasterwork ceilings.

Underground Passages
Paris St. **Tel** 01392 665887. **Open** daily; times vary, call ahead. exeter.gov.uk

Under the city centre lie the remains of Exeter's medieval water-supply system. An excellent video and guided tour explain how the tunnels were built in the 14th and 15th centuries on a slight gradient in order to bring in fresh water from springs outside the town.

Exeter Castle
Castle St. **Tel** 01392 420703. **Open** for events only. exetercastle.co.uk

Built by William the Conqueror after his invasion of England, the Norman castle was badly damaged in 1497, and most of the remaining structures were demolished in 1773. Little remains of the original fortress except for the tall gatehouse, which can be found in the gardens of Rougemont House, an 18th-century courthouse that is now used for private events.

The Quay
Custom House: 46 The Quay. **Tel** 01392 271611. **Open** Apr–Oct: 10am–5pm daily; Nov–Mar: 11am–4pm Sat & Sun. exeter.gov.uk

Exeter's historic quay has been restored, with early 19th-century warehouses now home to interesting crafts and antique shops, as well as an eclectic mix of delightful cafés, pubs and restaurants. Boats can be hired for cruising down the canal.

Located in the heart of the quayside is the opulent Custom House. Built in 1680, it now has a visitor centre with lively displays and audiovisual presentations highlighting Exeter's rich history from Roman times until today.

Royal Albert Memorial Museum and Art Gallery
Queen St. **Tel** 01392 265858. **Open** 10am–5pm Tue–Sun.

This museum has a wonderfully varied collection, including Roman remains, an Egyptian mummy, samurai armour and a stuffed Bengal tiger shot by George V. Interactive displays bring Exeter's long history to life.

Environs
South of Exeter on the A376, **A La Ronde** is a 16-sided house built in 1796 by two cousins, designed so that they could follow the course of the sun through the day. The interior is decorated with shells, feathers and souvenirs they gathered on their ten-year Grand Tour of Europe.

A short drive away is Exmouth, a typical British seaside town. A popular Regency sea bathing spot, it still has some Georgian terraces and Victorian villas.

Bird's-eye view of the unique, 16-sided A La Ronde, located near Exmouth

Further east along the coast, the unspoiled seaside town of Sidmouth lies in a sheltered bay. It boasts an eclectic array of architecture, the earliest buildings dating from the 1820s when Sidmouth became a popular summer resort. In the first week of August the town hosts Folk Week, a festival of music and dance (see p29).

North of Sidmouth lies the magnificent church at Ottery St Mary. Built in 1338–42, under the supervision of Bishop Grandisson, it is a scaled-down version of Exeter Cathedral, which he had helped build. In the churchyard wall is a memorial to the poet Samuel Taylor Coleridge, who was born in the town in 1772.

To the north of Exeter, **Killerton** is home to the National Trust's costume collection. Here, displays of bustles and corsets and vivid tableaux illustrate aristocratic fashions from the 18th century to the present day.

Further north, near Tiverton, is **Knightshayes Court**, a Victorian Gothic mansion designed by William Burges. The grounds feature a series of fine formal gardens.

A La Ronde
Summer Lane, Exmouth. **Tel** 01395 265514. **Open** Feb–Oct: 10:30am–5:30pm daily. nationaltrust.org.uk

Killerton
Broadclyst. **Tel** 01392 881345. **Open** House: mid-Feb–mid-Mar: 11am–4pm daily; mid-Mar–Oct: 11am–5pm daily. Garden: 10am–5:30pm daily (from 9am Sat). **Closed** 25 & 26 Dec. nationaltrust.org.uk

Knightshayes Court
Tiverton, Bolham. **Tel** 01884 254665. **Open** House: 11am–5pm daily. Garden: 10am–5pm daily. **Closed** 24 & 25 Dec. nationaltrust.org.uk

❸ Torquay

Devon. **Map** D5. 🏔 65,000. 🚲 🚌
Lymington Rd. 🛈 English Riviera
Tourism Company, 5 Vaughan Parade;
01803 211211. **W** englishriviera.co.uk

This town has been popular since
the 1850s. The opening of the
railway in the 1840s saw droves of
Victorians arriving. The wealthiest
built Italianate villas, which can
still be seen today. Torquay's
most famous resident was crime
writer Agatha Christie, and the
garden of **Torre Abbey** has a
Potent Plants collection inspired
by the poisons in her books. The
Torquay Museum also has a
room evoking her life in the town.
   The marina has a pedestrian
bridge that links to the **Living
Coasts**, a coastal zoo. About 2 km
(1 mile) to the east, **Kents Cavern**
is a significant prehistoric site.
Stone Age living is now brought
to life here with guided tours.

Children dressed in 16th-century costumes exploring the Totnes Elizabethan Museum

🏛 Torre Abbey

King's Dr. **Tel** 01803 293593. **Open**
Mar–May & Oct–Dec: 10am–5pm
Wed–Sun; Jun–Sep: 10am–5pm daily.
Closed 24–26 Dec & Jan–Feb. 🅿 ♿
🖥 📷 **W** torre-abbey.org.uk

🏛 Torquay Museum

529 Babbacombe Rd. **Tel** 01803
293975. **Open** 10am–4pm Mon–Sat
(also Sun in summer). ♿ 🖥 📷
W torquaymuseum.org

🐧 Living Coasts

Torquay Harbourside, Beacon Hill. **Tel**
01803 202470. **Open** 10am–4pm daily.
🅿 ♿ 🖥 📷 **W** livingcoasts.org.uk

🦅 Kents Cavern

91 Ilsham Rd. **Tel** 01803 215136. **Open**
Apr–Oct: 9:30am–4pm; Nov–Mar:
10am–3:30pm. **Closed** 25 Dec. 🅿 📷
🖥 📷 **W** kents-cavern.co.uk

❹ Tor Bay

Devon. **Map** D5. 🏔 49,000 (Paignton),
17,000 (Brixham). 🚲 Paignton. 🚌
Dartmouth Rd, Paignton and Brixham
Town Sq. **W** englishriviera.co.uk

The seaside towns of Paignton
and Brixham merge with Torquay
to form an almost continuous
resort around the great sweep
of Tor Bay. Due to its mild climate,
semitropical gardens and
Victorian hotel architecture,
this coastline has been dubbed
the English Riviera. Today, there
are plenty of sights, including
Babbacombe Model Village,
the Tudor village of Cockington,
and **Paignton Zoo**, from where a
steam railway runs to Dartmouth.

🏛 Babbacombe Model Village

Hampton Ave, Torquay. **Tel** 01803
315315. **Open** mid-Mar–Jul & Sep–
Oct: 10am–4pm daily (to 8pm Thu);
Aug: 10am–9pm daily; Nov–mid-Mar:
10am–3pm daily. **Closed** 25 Dec.
🅿 ♿ limited. 🖥 📷
W model-village.co.uk

🦒 Paignton Zoo

Totnes Rd, Paignton. **Tel** 01803 697500.
Open 10am–4:30pm daily (Apr–Oct: to
5pm). **Closed** 25 Dec. 🅿 ♿ 🅿 🖥
📷 **W** paigntonzoo.org.uk

❺ Totnes

Devon. **Map** D5. 🏔 8,000. 🚲 🚌
🚲 to Dartmouth. 🚌 Fri & Sat
(also Tue in summer).
W englishriviera.co.uk

One of the most ecologically
minded towns in the UK,
vibrant Totnes is committed to
sustainable food, energy and
buildings. It is set at the highest
navigable point on the River
Dart, with the Norman **Totnes
Castle** perched high on the hill
above. Linking the two is the
steep High Street, lined with
bow-windowed Elizabethan
houses and lots of independent
shops. Bridging the street is the
Eastgate, part of the medieval
town wall. Life in the town's
heyday is explored in the **Totnes
Elizabethan Museum**, which
also has a room devoted to
the renowned mathematician
Charles Babbage (1791–1871),
who is regarded as the pioneer
of modern computers. Nearby is
the **Guildhall** and a church with
a delicately carved and gilded
rood screen. On Tuesdays in the
summer, market stallholders
dress in Elizabethan costume.

🚩 Totnes Castle

Castle St. **Tel** 01803 864406.
Open Apr–Sep: 10am–6pm daily;
Oct: 10am–5pm daily; Nov–Mar:
10am–4pm Sat & Sun. **Closed** 24–
26 Dec & 1 Jan. 🅿 ♿ limited. 📷
🇪🇭 **W** english-heritage.org.uk

🏛 Totnes Elizabethan Museum

70 Fore St. **Tel** 01803 863821.
Open mid-Mar–Sep: 10am–4pm Tue–
Fri. 🅿 **W** totnesmuseum.org

🏛 Guildhall

5 Ramparts Walk. **Tel** 01803 862147.
Open 11am–3pm Mon–Fri.
Closed public hols. **W** totnestown
council.gov.uk

Agatha Christie (1890–1976)

The best-selling author of all time, Agatha
Christie spent much of her childhood in Torquay,
and later bought a home near Dittisham.
Her first novel, *The Mysterious Affair at Styles*,
featuring the detective Hercule Poirot, was
published in 1920. Poirot's character was
inspired by Belgian refugees living in Torquay
after the invasion of Belgium during World
War I. Several attractions in Torquay celebrate
the author, including the Agatha Christie
Mile, which explores her connections with
the town, and the Agatha Christie Trail, which
traces some of the locations of her novels.

Plaque, Agatha Christie Mile

For hotels and restaurants in this region see p178 and pp189–90

❻ Dittisham

Devon. **Map** D6. 🏕 420. 🚊 Dittisham, Dartmouth, Brixham or Torquay.

Dittisham (pronounced "ditsum") is a pretty riverside village with pastel-painted cottages over-looking the quayside. Scattered around the village are cottages built by villagers who returned from the New Zealand gold rush in the 1860s.

Immediately upstream from the village, the Dart widens into a glassy expanse known as Dittisham Lake, the best area on the river for sailing and boating. Visible from the river path back to Dartmouth are a number of local landmarks, including the Scolding Stone, to which unfaithful women were tied, and Harmblyn's Coombe, where Sir Walter Raleigh is believed to have experimented with growing potatoes.

A red ferry shuttles across the river from Dittisham to **Greenway**, a lovely cream stucco Georgian mansion, which was bought by Agatha Christie in 1938. The house appears in several of her novels, most prominently in *Dead Man's Folly* (1956). Now owned by the National Trust, Greenway offers a packed programme of family-friendly activities, from croquet on the lawn to murder-mystery trails.

🏠 Greenway

Greenway Rd, Galmpton. 🚊 Greenway Ferry Service; 01803 882811. **Open** mid-Feb–Oct: 10:30am–5pm daily. 🚫 👜 limited. 📷 🏠 NT W **nationaltrust.org.uk**

❼ Dart Estuary

The tidal estuary of the River Dart, stretching for 19 km (12 miles) from Totnes to the sea, has been designated an Area of Outstanding Natural Beauty. Dotted with unspoiled waterside villages and beaches, the estuary is home to a variety of wildlife, including seals. The river can be explored along the waymarked footpaths of the Dart Valley Trail and by river cruiser, paddle steamer or kayak. The area is also a paradise for foodies, with a vineyard, a cider press, cheesemakers and an oyster farm.

VISITORS' CHECKLIST

Practical Information
Between Dartmouth and Totnes, Devon. **Map** D5–6.
W **southdevonaonb.org.uk**
W **dartmouthrailriver.co.uk**

Transport
🚆 to Totnes; Dartmouth Steam Railway. 🚊 from Totnes to Dartmouth.

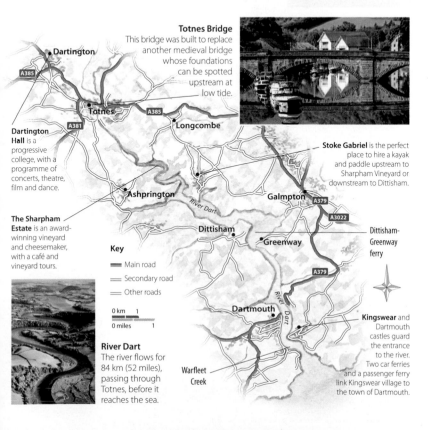

Totnes Bridge
This bridge was built to replace another medieval bridge whose foundations can be spotted upstream at low tide.

Dartington Hall is a progressive college, with a programme of concerts, theatre, film and dance.

Stoke Gabriel is the perfect place to hire a kayak and paddle upstream to Sharpham Vineyard or downstream to Dittisham.

The Sharpham Estate is an award-winning vineyard and cheesemaker, with a café and vineyard tours.

Dittisham-Greenway ferry

Key
▬ Main road
═ Secondary road
═ Other roads

0 km 1
0 miles 1

River Dart
The river flows for 84 km (52 miles), passing through Totnes, before it reaches the sea.

Kingswear and Dartmouth castles guard the entrance to the river. Two car ferries and a passenger ferry link Kingswear village to the town of Dartmouth.

Dartington
A385
Totnes
A385
Longcombe
A381
Ashprington
River Dart
Galmpton
A379
A3022
Dittisham
Greenway
A379
Dartmouth
Warfleet Creek
River Dart

❽ Dartmouth

Devon. **Map** D6. 🔝 5,000.
ℹ️ Mayor's Ave; 01803 834224.
🌐 **discoverdartmouth.com**

The town of Dartmouth has long been a vital naval port. English fleets used to set sail from here to join the Second and Third Crusades. Sitting high on the hill above the River Dart is the Royal Naval College, where British naval officers have trained since 1905.

The town's medieval origins can be seen in the hilly, stepped alleyways around Browns Hill, and in the 13th-century Church of St Saviour, whose wooden carved altar screen includes a depiction of a pagan Green Man.

Several 18th-century houses adorn the cobbled quay of Bayards Cove, while carved-timber buildings line the 17th-century Butterwalk, home to the **Dartmouth Museum**. To the south is the imposing **Dartmouth Castle**, built in 1388 to protect Dartmouth from French attack.

🏛️ Dartmouth Museum
The Butterwalk, Duke St. **Tel** 01803 832923. **Open** Apr–Oct: 10am–4pm Tue–Sat, 1–4pm Sun & Mon; Nov–Mar: noon–3pm daily. **Closed** 1 Jan, 25 & 26 Dec. 📷 🌐 **dartmouthmuseum.org**

🏰 Dartmouth Castle
Castle Rd. **Tel** 01803 833588. **Open** Apr–Oct: 10am–5pm daily; Nov–Mar: 10am–4pm Sat & Sun. **Closed** 1 Jan & 24–26 Dec. ♿ limited. 🖥️ 📷 EH 🌐 **english-heritage.org.uk**

Salcombe Bay, Devon's southernmost port, at the mouth of the Kingsbridge Estuary

❾ Salcombe and the South Hams

Devon. **Map** D6. 🔝 1,900. 🚂 Plymouth, Totnes. 🚌 from Plymouth and Totnes. 🚢 timetable from information centre and at Ferry Pier.
ℹ️ Market St; 01548 843927.
🌐 **visitsouthdevon.co.uk**

Magnificently set on a steep hill at the mouth of the Kingsland Estuary, Salcombe is Devon's most exclusive resort, with the most expensive seaside real estate in the country. Once a humble port, where the main industries were sail-making and boat-building, it is now full of high-end boutiques, delis and restaurants, and is the birthplace of the yacht clothing chains Crew Clothing and Jack Wills. The small, volunteer-run **Maritime Museum** below the tourist information centre beautifully evokes Salcombe's past, with a collection of model boats, nautical paraphernalia, paintings, photographs and finds from the numerous ships wrecked on the coast nearby.

🏛️ Maritime Museum
The Old Council Hall, Market St. **Tel** 01548 843080. **Open** Apr–Oct: 10:30am–12:30pm, 2:30–4:30pm daily. **Closed** Nov–Mar. 📷 ♿ 🌐 **salcombemuseum.org.uk**

Environs
Salcombe is the perfect base for exploring the numerous villages, beaches and coves of the South Hams, an Area of Outstanding Natural Beauty. Highlights include the quaint fishing villages of Inner and Outer Hope, Burgh Island and Kingsbridge, a town at the head of the estuary that is famous for its quayside farmers' market (held on the first and third Saturday of each month). Also of interest at nearby Wigford Cross is the **South Devon Chilli Farm**, which grows around 200 varieties of chilli.

There are two sheltered sandy beaches just a short walk south of Salcombe. For those who do not want to walk, there is a passenger ferry to South Sands, and both beaches have car parks. Beaches on the far side

The Mayflower

In August 1620, a group of 40 English Protestants seeking religious freedom joined a larger group of economic migrants seeking a better life, and set sail from Southampton in two ships, the *Mayflower* and the *Speedwell*, bound for the east coast of America. The *Speedwell* sprang a leak and both the ships pulled into Dartmouth for repairs, sheltering in Bayard's Cove. The ships made another

Painting depicting the *Mayflower* in 1620

emergency stop at Plymouth before setting sail again on 6 September. After the *Speedwell* sprang another leak and was forced to return, the *Mayflower* continued alone, with 102 passengers and about 30 crew members. Two months later, the ship reached the New World. Although the boat originally set out for Virginia, it landed in Cape Cod and the pilgrims founded a colony there, which they named Plymouth.

of the peninsula are also served by passenger ferries. For fantastic coastal views, continue along the South West Coast Path to the rocky headland of Bolt Head.

🔆 South Devon Chilli Farm
Wigford Cross, Loddiswell, Kingsbridge. **Tel** 01548 550782. **Open** 10am–4:30pm daily. 🌿 🔆 limited. ▯ 🏠 🆆 **southdevon chillifarm.co.uk**

⑩ Burgh Island

Devon. **Map** D6. 🚢 Plymouth then bus to Bigbury-on-Sea. ℹ️ The Quay, Kingsbridge; 01548 853195. 🆆 **visitsouthdevon.co.uk**

The short walk across the sands at low tide from Bigbury-on-Sea to Burgh Island takes visitors back to the era of the 1920s and 1930s. It was here that the millionaire Archibald Nettlefold built the glamorous Burgh Island Hotel *(see p178)* in 1929. Art Deco in style, with a natural rock sea-bathing pool, it was known as the "smartest hotel west of the Ritz" and, in its heyday, was the exclusive retreat of figures such as the Duke of Windsor and English playwright Sir Noël Peirce Coward. It also served as the setting for two novels by Agatha Christie: *And Then There were None* and *Evil Under the Sun*. The restored hotel is the island's star attraction, and the restaurant is open to non-residents.

Visitors can also explore Burgh Island. Highlights include the Pilchard Inn (1336), reputed to be haunted by the ghost of a smuggler, and Huer's Hut,

up the hill from here. Until the early 19th century, a lookout was posted at this hut throughout the pilchard season, warning fishermen when a new shoal was spotted arriving.

A sea tractor heading to the famous Art Deco Burgh Island hotel

⑪ Buckfastleigh

Devon. **Map** D5. 🖼️ 3,400. ℹ️ Fore St, Buckfastleigh; 01364 644522. 🆆 **visitsouthdevon.co.uk**

This market town, situated on the edge of Dartmoor *(see pp142–3)*, is dominated by **Buckfast Abbey**. The original abbey, founded by King Cnut in 1018, fell into ruin after the Dissolution of the Monasteries *(see p36)* and it was not until 1882 that a small group of French Benedictine monks set up a new abbey here. Work on the present building was financed by donations and carried out by the monks. The

abbey was completed in 1938 and has gardens, a restaurant and a shop selling tonic wine, honey and other products. The mosaics and stained-glass window are also the work of the monks.

Nearby is the **Buckfast Butterfly Farm and Dartmoor Otter Sanctuary**, and the **South Devon Steam Railway** terminus, where steam trains leave for Totnes *(see p138)*.

🏛️ Buckfast Abbey
Just off Grange Rd. **Tel** 01364 645500. **Open** 9am–6pm Mon–Sat & noon–6pm Sun. **Closed** Good Fri & 25–27 Dec. 🚻 🆆 **buckfasttourism.org.uk**

🦋 Buckfast Butterfly Farm and Dartmoor Otter Sanctuary
The Station. **Tel** 01364 642916. **Open** Mar–Oct: 10am–5pm daily; Nov Feb: 11am–3pm daily. 🆆 **otters andbutterflies.co.uk**

🚂 South Devon Steam Railway
🆆 **southdevonrailway.co.uk**

⑫ Buckland Abbey

Yelverton. **Map** C5. **Tel** 01822 853607. **Open** Abbey: mid-Feb–Oct: 11am–5pm daily; Nov, 1–23 Dec & 27–31 Dec: open for guided tours only. Garden: mid-Feb–Oct: 10am–5pm daily. **Closed** Jan, early Feb & 24–26 Dec. 🍽️ 🔆 NT 🆆 **nationaltrust.org.uk**

Founded by Cistercian monks in 1278, Buckland Abbey was converted to a house after the Dissolution and became the home of Sir Francis Drake *(see p144)* from 1581. Drake's life is recalled through memorabilia in the house. Many of the monastic buildings survive in the grounds of the estate, notably the 14th-century tithe barn.

The striking exterior of Buckfast Abbey, reconstructed from the ruins of an abbey founded in the reign of King Cnut

⓲ Dartmoor National Park

The dramatic landscape of central Dartmoor is one of contrasts, providing an impressive variety of striking vistas. The high, open moorland served as the eerie backdrop for the Sherlock Holmes tale *The Hound of the Baskervilles* (1902), while one of Britain's most famous prisons, Dartmoor Prison, is surrounded by weathered outcrops of stone tors in Princetown. Also dotting the landscape are scores of ancient remains that have survived thanks to the durability of granite. Creating pockets of tranquility, streams tumble through wooded and boulder-strewn ravines forming waterfalls, and thatched cottages nestle in the sheltered valleys and villages around the margins of the moor.

Lydford Gorge
There is a circular 5-km (3-mile) walk through this remote ravine.

St Michael de Rupe
Legend has it that the Devil tried to prevent the construction of this church, perched atop Brent Tor, by moving the stones. Whatever the truth, there has been a church here since the 12th century. Reached by a footpath, there are stunning views over Dartmoor from here.

KEY

① **Dartmoor Prison**

② **The Ministry of Defence** uses much of this area for training, but access is available on non-firing days (call 0800 458 4868 to check).

③ **Okehampton** is home to the Museum of Dartmoor Life and a ruined 14th-century castle.

④ **Grimspound** is the impressive remains of a Bronze Age settlement.

⑤ **Dartmeet** marks the confluence of the East and West Dart rivers.

⑥ **Becky Falls** is a 22-m- (72-ft-) high waterfall set in delightful woodlands.

⑦ **Haytor Rocks** is one of the most remarkable of Dartmoor's many tors.

⑧ **Bovey Tracey** is a small town close to an extensive woodland reserve.

⑨ **Buckfast Abbey** was founded by King Cnut in 1018 *(see p141)*.

⑩ **Buckfast Butterfly Farm and Dartmoor Otter Sanctuary** *(see p141)*.

⑪ **South Devon Steam Railway** runs between Buckfastleigh and Totnes *(see p141)*.

0 kilometres 5
0 miles 5

Postbridge
In the centre of the moor and set on the River Dart, the village of Postbridge is a good starting point for walks on the moor. There is a medieval "clapper" bridge here, built to enable pack horses to carry mined tin across the river.

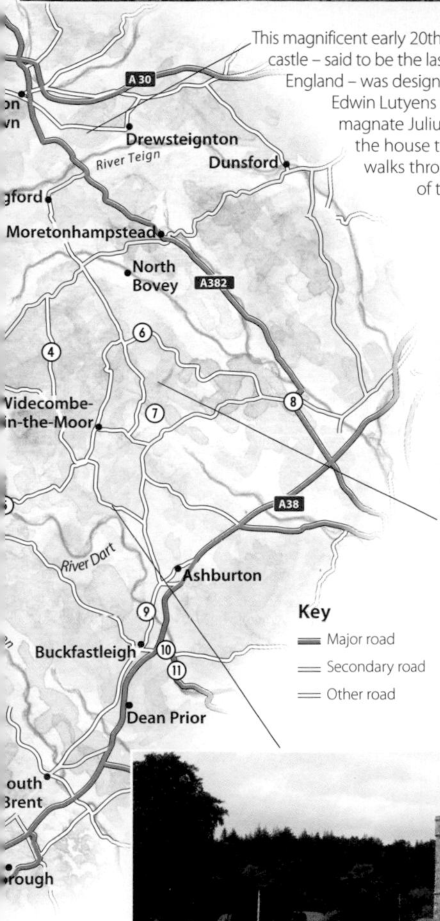

Castle Drogo

This magnificent early 20th-century mock castle – said to be the last castle built in England – was designed by architect Edwin Lutyens for the grocery magnate Julius Drewe. From the house there are lovely walks through the gorge of the River Teign.

VISITORS' CHECKLIST

Practical Information
Devon. **Map** D5. 🛈 Princetown Visitor Centre; Tavistock Rd. Dartmoor National Park Authority Visitor Centre; 01822 890 414. 🅦 **dartmoor.gov.uk**. Okehampton Castle: Castle Lane. **Tel** 01837 52844. **Open** Apr–Nov: 10am–5pm daily. 🚻 EH Museum of Dartmoor Life: West St, Okehampton. **Tel** 01837 52295. **Open** Apr–mid-Dec: 10am–3pm Mon–Fri, 10am–1pm Sat. 🚻 ♿ Castle Drogo: Drewsteignton. **Tel** 01647 433306. **Open** Castle: Mar–Oct: 11am–5pm daily; Nov–mid-Dec: 11am–4pm Sat & Sun. Gardens: Mar–Oct: 10am–5:30pm daily; Nov–mid-Dec: 11am–4pm Sat & Sun. 🚻 ♿ gardens only. 🅿 🛒 NT

Transport
🚆 🚌 Exeter, Plymouth, Totnes, then bus.

Drewsteignton
River Teign
Dunsford

A 30

Moretonhampstead

North Bovey A382

④

Widecombe-in-the-Moor

⑥

⑦

⑧

A38

River Dart

Ashburton

Key

━━━ Major road
═══ Secondary road
─── Other road

⑨

Buckfastleigh ⑩

⑪

Dean Prior

outh Brent

rough

Hound Tor

The remains of this village lie on the eastern edge of Dartmoor. The settlement consists of a cluster of 13th-century stone longhouses – in which the family lived at one end and the animals at the other – on land that was originally farmed in the Bronze Age. It was probably deserted in the early 15th century.

Buckland-in-the-Moor

One of the many picturesque villages on the southeastern side of Dartmoor, Buckland-in-the-Moor features a cluster of pretty thatched stone cottages and a small granite church.

⑭ Plymouth

Plymouth. **Map** C6. ▨ 255,000.
🚆 🚌 🚢 *i* 3–5 The Barbican;
01752 306330. 🏛 Mon–Sat.
w visitplymouth.co.uk

The most iconic of all English ports, Plymouth is the place from which several explorers, discoverers and adventurers, including Sir Francis Drake, Sir Walter Raleigh, James Cook and the Pilgrim Fathers, set sail and changed the history of the world.

The city was heavily bombed during World War II, and its Victorian centre was almost completely destroyed. Seen from a distance, it is the post-war redevelopments that dominate Plymouth. The hills above the vast reach of its natural harbour, Plymouth Sound, are covered with triangular-roofed houses, a resonant testimony to the social optimism of the 1950s and 1960s. The city is now being rapidly regenerated, with the waterfront areas Millbay and Devonport being redeveloped.

What has survived of Old Plymouth clusters around the historic Barbican quarter and Sutton Harbour. Several of the Tudor and Jacobean buildings and waterfront structures here escaped wartime bombing, including the spot from which the Pilgrim Fathers set sail for the New World in 1620 (a story told through interactive graphics at the **Plymouth Mayflower Exhibition**). Plymouth Hoe, the legendary patch of turf on which Drake is said to have insisted on finishing his game of bowls as the Spanish Armada approached

Sir Francis Drake (c.1540–96)

Sir Francis Drake was the first Englishman to circumnavigate the globe for which he was knighted by Elizabeth I in 1580. Four years later he introduced tobacco and potatoes to England, after bringing home 190 colonists who had tried to

establish a settlement in Virginia. To many, however, Drake was no more than an opportunistic rogue, renowned for his exploits as a "privateer", the polite name for a pirate. Catholic Spain was England's bitter rival for supremacy on the seas and Drake further endeared himself to the queen and the people by his part in the famous victory over King Philip II's Armada (*see p36*), which was defeated by bad weather and the buccaneering spirit of the English.

Elizabethan explorer Francis Drake

the port in 1588, can also be found in this area of the city. Until the early 17th century, there were images of the giants Gog and Magog cut into the turf exposing the white limestone beneath. Sadly, no trace of them remains. Today, the Hoe is a pleasant park and parade ground surrounded by memorials to naval heroes, including Drake. Overlooking the Hoe is the **Royal Citadel**, built in 1660 by Charles II to guard the harbour. Dominating the skyline is the red-and-white-striped upper portion of the 18th-century Eddystone Lighthouse, moved stone by stone from its original site on the Eddystone Rocks and re-erected here in 1877.

The **Plymouth Gin Distillery** is on the west side of Sutton Harbour. Established in 1793, and occupying a former Dominican monastery, this is the oldest working gin distillery in the UK, and can be explored on

a 40-minute tour that includes tastings and a complimentary gin and tonic. True aficionados should book in advance for the Master Distillers Tour, which allows guests to create their own handmade gin.

Just across the harbour (and reached by a swing footbridge), stands the fascinating **National Marine Aquarium**, the largest public aquarium in the UK, set in a state-of-the-art glass building. In replicated habitats, ranging from the Eddystone Reef to the Great Barrier Reef, are ten species of shark, seahorses, jellyfish and Miss Squishy – a giant Pacific octopus that can change colour.

Further west is the Royal William Yard, a former Royal Navy victualing yard. Stunning early 19th-century buildings designed by Sir John Rennie (1794–1874) are set right on the waterfront. Abandoned for years, the yard has been beautifully restored

Colourful boats docked in Sutton Harbour in the historic Barbican quarter, Plymouth

and revived, with art galleries, shops, restaurants, bars, luxury apartments and a Sunday morning food market. The most dramatic way to arrive is on one of the hourly ferries that connect the yard with the Barbican.

🏛 Plymouth Mayflower Exhibition
3–5 The Barbican. **Tel** 01752 306330. **Open** Apr–Oct: 9am–5pm Mon–Sat, 10am–4pm Sun; Nov–Mar: 9am–5pm Mon–Fri, 10am–4pm Sat.

🏰 Royal Citadel
The Hoe. **Tel** 01752 306330. **Open** for guided tours only. 🎫 May–Sep: 2:30pm Tue, Thu & Sun. **EH** 🆆 english-heritage.org.uk

🏛 Plymouth Gin Distillery
60 Southside St, Barbican. **Tel** 01752 665292. **Open** 10am–5pm Mon–Sat, 11am–5pm Sun. **Closed** 25 & 26 Dec. 🖥 📷 🆆 plymouthdistillery.com

🐟 National Marine Aquarium
Rope Walk, Coxside. **Tel** 08448 937938. **Open** 10am–5pm daily. 🅿 🎫 ♿ 🖥 📷 🆆 national-aquarium.co.uk

The Atlantic Ocean exhibit at the National Marine Aquarium, Plymouth

⑮ Morwellham Quay

Morwellham, Tavistock. **Map** C5. **Tel** 01822 832766. 🚂 Gunnislake. **Open** Mar–May, Sep & Oct: 10am–5pm daily; Jun–Aug: 10am–6pm daily; Nov–Feb: 10am–4pm daily. **Closed** 25 & 26 Dec. ♿ limited. 🖥 📷 🆆 morwellham-quay.co.uk

This area was a neglected and overgrown industrial site until 1970, when members of a local village trust began restoring its abandoned cottages, farmyards, schoolhouse, quay and copper

Visitors enjoy a horse-drawn carriage ride at the industrial museum, Morwellham Quay

mines to their original condition. Today, Morwellham Quay is a thriving and fascinating industrial museum, where a whole day can easily be spent partaking in the typical activities of a Victorian village, from preparing the shire horses for a day's work to riding a tramway deep into a copper mine in the hillside behind the village. Costumed characters give demonstrations through the day, bringing the museum to life. Visitors can watch or lend a hand to the cooper while he builds a barrel, attend a lesson in the schoolroom, take part in Victorian playground games or dress up in 19th-century hooped skirts, bonnets, top hats and jackets. The staff, who convincingly play the part of villagers, offer a glimpse of Victorian life and impart a huge amount of information about the history of this small copper-mining community.

⑯ Cotehele

St Dominick, near Saltash. **Map** C5. **Tel** 01579 351346. 🚂 Saltash. 🚢 seasonal trips. **Open** House & Mill: mid-Mar–Oct: 11am–4pm daily. Grounds: dawn–dusk daily. **Closed** 25 & 26 Dec. 🅿 🎫 ♿ limited. 🎫 🖥 📷 NT 🆆 nationaltrust.org.uk

Magnificent woodland and lush river scenery make the grand estate of Cotehele (pronounced "coteal") one of the most lovely spots on the River Tamar, and an enjoyable day can be spent exploring the grounds here.

Far from civilization and tucked into a wooded fold in the east Cornish countryside, the estate has slumbered for 500 years.

Built mainly between 1489 and 1520, Cotehele is a rare example of a Tudor manor house, and is set around three courtyards with a magnificent open hall, kitchen, chapel and a warren of private parlours and chambers. The romance of the house is enhanced by colourful terraced gardens to the east, leading via a tunnel into a richly planted valley garden. The path through this garden passes a domed medieval dovecote and descends to Cotehele Quay, where lime and coal were once shipped.

The quay is now home to the *Shamrock*, a restored sailing barge. In summer there are trips upriver in the *Shamrock* support boat, with a guide to explain the history, flora and fauna of the Tamar Valley.

The estate includes Cotehele Mill, a working mill producing wholemeal flour. Visitors can also explore wheelwright, saddler and blacksmith workshops, and there is a traditional furniture-maker and a working potter.

Boat moored at the picturesque Cotehele Quay on the River Tamar

Whitewashed cottages and fishing boats lining the harbour in the historic fishing village of Clovelly ▶

⑰ Lynton and Lynmouth

Devon. **Map** D4. 1,600. Town Hall, Lee Rd, Lynton; 01598 752225.
lynton-lynmouth-tourism.co.uk

Situated at the point where the East and West Lyn rivers meet the sea, Lynmouth is a picturesque, though rather commercialized, fishing village. The pedestrianized main street, lined with shops selling seaside souvenirs, runs parallel to the Lyn, now a canal with high embankments to protect against flash floods. One flood devastated the town at the height of the holiday season in 1952, fuelled by heavy rain on Exmoor *(see pp122–3)*. The worst affected area was not rebuilt and is now overgrown with trees in the pretty Glen Lyn Gorge, which leads north out of the village.

Sister to Lynmouth is Lynton, a Victorian town perched on the clifftop at a height of 130 m (427 ft), offering views across the Bristol Channel to the Welsh coast. It can be reached from the harbourfront by the **Lynton & Lynmouth Cliff Railway** (open mid-Feb–Oct), by road or a steep walking path.

Lynton & Lynmouth Cliff Railway
cliffrailwaylynton.co.uk

Environs
Lynmouth makes an excellent starting point for walks on Exmoor. There is a 3-km (2-mile) trail that leads southeast to

The cliff railway connecting Lynmouth at the foot of the cliff with Lynton at the top

Watersmeet. On the western edge of Exmoor, the village of Combe Martin lies in a sheltered valley. Its main street is lined with Victorian villas and is home to the 18th-century **Pack O' Cards Inn**, which was built by a gambler and has 52 windows – one for each card in the pack.

Pack O' Cards Inn
High St, Combe Martin. **Tel** 01271 882300. **packocards.co.uk**

⑱ Ilfracombe

Devon. **Map** C4. 13,000. Barnstaple then bus. Landmark Theatre, Promenade; 01271 863001.
visitilfracombe.co.uk

Flanked by rugged cliffs, hilly Ilfracombe is a Victorian seaside resort built around a natural harbour. Since 2012 the town has been dominated by *Verity*, a 20-m- (65-ft-) high stainless steel, fibreglass and bronze statue by artist Damien Hirst, who lives in nearby Combe Martin. It features the internal anatomy of a naked pregnant woman with her foetus and womb clearly visible. There is more work by Hirst in his fashionable quayside restaurant 11 The Quay, which features several of his "Medicine Cabinet" installations of empty packets of pharmaceuticals, designed to call into question society's faith in modern medicine.

The nearby Tunnels Beaches provide a more reassuring diversion. A sheltered beach with natural and man-made tidal swimming pools can be accessed through four tunnels that were carved into the bare rock by Welsh miners in 1823. Lively information boards evoke the history of the beaches (originally men and women were segregated for swimming). There is a lovely café bar and a children's play hut, and kayaks are also available for hire.

Environs
With their sweeping sandy beaches and some of the most challenging waves in the country, Croyde and Woolacombe are popular with both families and surfers. Croyde, a picturesque village of thatched houses in a crescent-shaped bay, is prettier. The resort of Woolacombe

Picturesque view of Ilfracombe harbour, seen from Capstone Hill on the South West Coast Path

For hotels and restaurants in this region see p178 and pp189–90

The interior of Barnstaple's glass-roofed Victorian Pannier Market, with a range of stalls

retains some elegant Regency houses among its many bungalows and holiday homes.

🟢 Barnstaple

Devon. **Map** C4. 🚶 24,000.
ℹ The Square; 01271 375000.
W staynorthdevon.co.uk

Although Barnstaple is an important distribution centre for the whole region, its town centre remains quiet and tranquil due to the exclusion of traffic. The glass-roofed **Pannier Market** (1855) has stalls of organic food, much of it produced on local farms. Nearby stands St Peter's Church, with its twisted spire, said to have been caused by a lightning strike warping the timbers in 1810.

On the Strand is a wonderful arcade topped with a statue of Queen Anne. It was originally built as an exchange where merchants traded the contents of their cargo boats moored on the River Taw.

Nearby is the 15th-century bridge and the **Museum of Barnstaple and North Devon**, where displays cover the rich history of the surrounding area, including the 700-year-old pottery industry, as well as otters and other local wildlife in the Tarka Room. The 290-km-(180-mile-) long Tarka Trail circuits around Barnstaple and offers lovely views; 56 km (35 miles) of it can be cycled.

📷 Pannier Market
Butchers Row. **Tel** 01271 379084.
Open 9am–4pm Mon–Sat.
W barnstaplepanniermarket.co.uk

🏛 Museum of Barnstaple and North Devon
The Square. **Tel** 01271 346747. **Open** 10am–4pm Mon–Sat (mid-Mar–Oct: to 5pm). **Closed** 24 Dec–1 Jan. 🚻 limited. 🖥 W devonmuseums.net

Environs
West of Barnstaple, Braunton "Great Field" covers approximately 140 ha (350 acres) and is a well-preserved relic of medieval open-field cultivation. Beyond it lies Braunton Burrows, one of the most extensive wild dune reserves in Britain. It is a must for plant enthusiasts, who can admire sea kale, sea holly, sea lavender and horned poppies growing in their natural habitat. **Arlington Court and National Trust Carriage Museum**, north of Barnstaple, is packed with

treasures. It has a collection of model ships and horse-drawn vehicles, including over 50 carriages; rides are available most days. The museum is set on a grand estate with grounds featuring magnificent perennial borders and a lake.

🏛 Arlington Court and National Trust Carriage Museum
Arlington. **Tel** 01271 850296. **Open** House & Museum: mid-Feb–Oct: 11am–5pm daily; Nov–mid-Dec: 11am–4pm daily. Grounds: dawn–dusk daily. 🚻 🚻
🖥 📷 NT W nationaltrust.org.uk

🟢 Broomhill Sculpture Gardens

Muddiford Rd, Barnstaple. **Map** C4.
Tel 01271 850262. **Open** 11am–4pm daily. **Closed** late Dec–mid-Jan. 🚻
🖥 📷 W broomhillart.co.uk

This mesmerizing sculpture garden lies in the enchanting grounds of a Victorian country house, with paths twisting through rhododendrons and woodland to a pretty river. There are 300 sculptures in all, both abstract and figurative, by over 60 contemporary artists. The pieces have been artfully placed within the woodland by Dutch owners Rinus and Aniet van de Sande. Among the most striking of the sculptures is a giant red stiletto shoe by Greta Berlin, who has been involved with Broomhill since it was founded in 1997.

Every year the gardens host the Broomhill National Sculpture competition, with works by the ten finalists exhibited in the meadow. The house is a hotel, and has a café and restaurant open to non-residents (see p178).

A typical cream tea with jam, clotted cream and scones

Devonshire Cream Teas
Devonians claim all other versions of a cream tea are inferior to their own, much to the indignation of the Cornish. The essential ingredient is Devonshire clotted cream, made by heating double cream (from Jersey cattle fed on rich Devonshire pasture) in order to evaporate some of the excess liquid. The cream is spread thickly on freshly baked scones, with lashings of delicious home-made strawberry jam. Disputes about whether cream (Devon) or jam (Cornwall) should be smeared on first can get very passionate.

Georgian cottages lining the riverside quay in the pretty town of Appledore

㉑ Appledore

Devon. **Map** C4. 🏠 2,800. 🛈 Bideford.

This town's remote position at the tip of the Torridge Estuary has helped to keep its charms intact. Busy boatyards line the riverside quay, the departure point for fishing trips and ferries to the beaches of Braunton Burrows on the opposite shore. Regency houses line the main street, which runs parallel to the quay, and behind is a network of cobbled lanes with 18th-century fishermen's cottages. Shops retain their original bow windows and sell antiques and souvenirs. Uphill from the quay is the **North Devon Maritime Museum**, with an exhibition on the experiences of Devon emigrants to Australia and displays explaining the work of local shipyards. The Victorian Schoolroom, affiliated with the museum, shows documentary videos on local trades such as fishing and shipbuilding.

🏛 **North Devon Maritime Museum** Odun Rd. **Tel** 01237 422064. **Open** Apr–Oct: 10:30am–5pm daily. ♿ limited. 🖥 **northdevon maritimemuseum.co.uk**

㉒ Bideford

Devon. **Map** C4. 🏠 17,000. 🛈 Burton Art Gallery, Kingsley Rd; 01237 477676. 🖥 **northdevon.com**

Strung out along the estuary of the River Torridge, Bideford thrived on importing tobacco from the New World. A few 17th-century merchants' houses survive on Bridgeland Street, including the house at No. 28 (1693). Beyond is Mill Street, leading to the parish church and the fine medieval bridge. The quay stretches from here to a park and a statue of 19th-century social reformer and writer, Charles Kingsley (1819–75), famous for his classic novel *The Water Babies* (1863).

Environs
To the west of Bideford, the village of Westward Ho! was built in the late 19th century and named after Kingsley's popular novel, published in

㉕ Lundy Island

Jointly owned and managed by the National Trust and the Landmark Trust, Lundy Island is a 5-km- (3-mile-) long sliver of granite lying 19 km (12 miles) off the North Devon coast. Once important for its stone quarries and copper mine, it is now abundant in birdlife, including puffins. One of the most remote places in England, it can be visited as a day trip from Ilfracombe, but it is also possible to rent holiday houses for a longer stay.

Battery Point
The Battery operated as a fog signal station between 1863 and 1897.

Old Light
Built in 1819, the Old Light has the highest base of any lighthouse in the UK. Abandoned in 1897, it can now be rented as a holiday home.

The cemetery is an ancient burial ground with several gravestones dating to the 5th or 6th century AD.

Marisco Tavern
Opened as a village shop for quarrymen in the 1860s, Lundy's sole pub is decorated with relics of local shipwrecks.

For hotels and restaurants in this region see p178 and pp189–90

1855. In the Torridge Valley is the 290-km (180-mile) Tarka Trail. Part of the walking and cycling trail runs along a disused railway line beside the Torridge, close to the Royal Horticultural Society's (RHS) lovely **Rosemoor Garden**.

 Rosemoor Garden
Great Torrington. **Tel** 0845 2658072. **Open** 10am–5pm daily. **Closed** 25 Dec.
limited. rhs.org.uk

⑳ Clovelly

Devon. **Map** C4. 440. Clovelly Visitor Centre, just off Hobby Drive; 01237 431781. **clovelly.co.uk**

A famous beauty spot since novelist Kingsley wrote about it in *Westward Ho!*, Clovelly village has been privately owned by the same family since 1738, with little trace of the fishing industry to which it owed its birth. It is an idyllic place, with whitewashed houses and cobbled streets rising

up the cliff from the harbourside. Until the 1990s, deliveries were made by donkeys – sledges are now used instead. There are superb views from the lookout points and paths from the quay.

Hobby Drive is a 5-km (3-mile) walk from the village through woodland along the coast. The road was constructed in 1811–29 to provide employment at the end of the Napoleonic Wars.

Charming cottages lining a steep, narrow cobbled street in the village of Clovelly

㉔ Hartland Point

Devon. **Map** C4.

This is Devon's wildest, most unspoiled stretch of coastline. The coast and the inland village of Hartland featured in the 2016 BBC TV series *The Night Manager*. The rugged landscape is best appreciated by walking the 5 km (3 miles) of coastal path from the lighthouse at Hartland Point to the Hartland Quay harbour, with its Shipwreck Museum. There are great views from the platform to the west of the lighthouse.

Environs
Inland is stately **Hartland Abbey**, built as a monastery in around 1157. Now a family home, some of the interior can be visited.

Hartland Abbey
Hartland, Bideford. **Tel** 01237 441496. **Open** late Mar–Sep: 11:30am–5pm Sun–Thu. limited.
hartlandabbey.com

The Lundy Granite Company's abandoned buildings lie along the north coast. The company was founded in 1863 and went into liquidation just six years later.

North Lighthouse

Devil's Slide

MS Oldenberg
From late March to late October, the MS *Oldenburg* brings visitors and supplies to the island, and ships Lundy lambs and pigs back to the mainland.

South Lighthouse

VISITORS' CHECKLIST

Practical Information
Bristol Channel, Devon.
Map B4. NT nationaltrust.org.uk

Transport
Barnstaple. Barnstaple. from Bideford or Ilfracombe.

Puffins
Lundy's unique ecosystem supports rare wildlife, including puffins and Manx shearwaters. The island also attracts many migrating birds in spring and autumn.

CORNWALL

With a magnificent coastline encompassing spectacular rock formations, secluded coves and sandy beaches interspersed with seaside resorts, picturesque fishing villages and smugglers' caves, Cornwall is one of the most enticing regions of the country. Inland is Bodmin Moor, peppered with enigmatic standing stones, while ancient woodland and subtropical gardens lie in the beautiful, sheltered Fowey, Fal and Helford river valleys of the south.

Cornwall occupies the extreme tip of the southwest peninsula, jutting out between the wild Atlantic Ocean and the calmer waters of the English Channel. Its remote position has kept the county cut off from the rest of Britain; when dinosaurs roamed the Jurassic Coast, Cornwall was actually an island. Its volcanic past has also left it richer in minerals – including gold, copper and tin – than anywhere else in Britain. Although mining continues, many pits have been abandoned – the famous Eden Project was created within a disused clay quarry.

Cornwall remains in many ways a land apart. For centuries, harbours such as Falmouth were part of an international network of ports, safe havens and anchorages, linked more by sea trade (and piracy) than any loyalty to state or Crown. Its isolation and natural beauty have fostered a distinct culture and mythology, and the region is rich in folk tradition and legends. King Arthur is believed to have been born in Tintagel, while the arrival of Celtic missionaries from Wales, Ireland and Brittany gave rise to a plethora of legends and holy sites where Christian mythology merged with popular ideas of magic. Folk tradition remains a vibrant part of contemporary culture, with ancient festivals such as Helston's Furry Dance and Mousehole's Tom Bawcock's Eve involving entire communities.

The region has a long history of attracting non-conformists, artists and exiles from metropolitan life, including the artists whose work forms the core of the renowned Tate St Ives. The area's wild, dramatically rugged landscape and romantic history have inspired several novels, by authors ranging from Daphne du Maurier to Patrick Gale.

Sea thrift clinging to the cliffs overlooking Bedruthan Steps, between Padstow and Newquay

◀ Bacchanalian sculptures inside the fascinating Mediterranean Biome at the Eden Project

Exploring Cornwall

Cornwall's few major roads – forced to remain inland by the rugged serrated coastline of the north, and the deep river valleys and rolling peninsulas of the south – reveal little of the country's beauty or character. Inland attractions include the Eden Project and Bodmin Moor, while along the coast and river estuaries of the south are the Lost Gardens of Heligan, the scenic villages of Fowey and St Mawes, and numerous sandy beaches. On the northern coast are arty St Ives, food mecca Padstow, and Arthurian Tintagel, along with surfers' paradises Bude and Newquay. Every nook and cranny of the 483-km (300-mile) coast can be accessed by the South West Coast Path.

Portheras Cove, a beach on one of the wildest stretches of Cornish Coast in Penwith

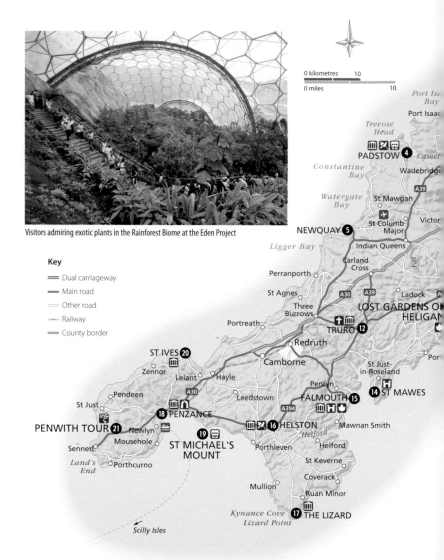

Visitors admiring exotic plants in the Rainforest Biome at the Eden Project

Key

━━ Dual carriageway
━━ Main road
┅┅ Other road
╌╌ Railway
━━ County border

0 kilometres   10
0 miles   10

Port Isaac Bay
Port Isaac
Trevose Head
PADSTOW ④
Camel
Constantine Bay
Wadebridge
Watergate Bay
St Mawgan
St Columb Major
Victor
NEWQUAY ⑤
Ligger Bay
Indian Queens
Carland Cross
Perranporth
St Agnes
Ladock
Three Burrows
LOST GARDENS OF HELIGAN
Portreath
TRURO ⑫
Redruth
Camborne
St Just-in-Roseland
Por
Penryn
ST IVES ⑳
FALMOUTH ⑮
Zennor
Lelant
Hayle
⑭ ST MAWES
St Just
Pendeen
Leedstown
Mawnan Smith
PENZANCE ⑱
HELSTON ⑯
PENWITH TOUR ㉑
Newlyn
Helford
Mousehole
ST MICHAEL'S MOUNT ⑲
Porthleven
Helford
Sennen
St Keverne
Land's End
Porthcurno
Coverack
Mullion
Ruan Minor
Kynance Cove
Lizard Point
⑰ THE LIZARD
Scilly Isles

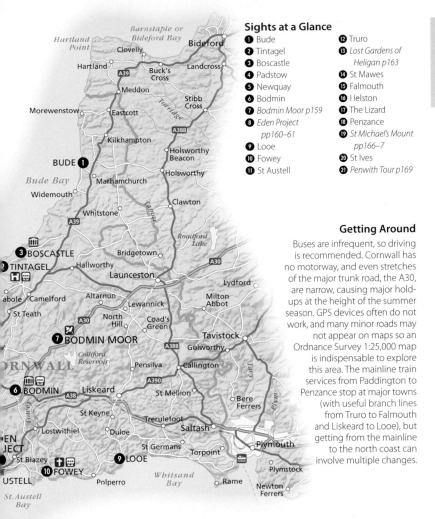

Sights at a Glance

Getting Around

Buses are infrequent, so driving is recommended. Cornwall has no motorway, and even stretches of the major trunk road, the A30, are narrow, causing major hold-ups at the height of the summer season. GPS devices often do not work, and many minor roads may not appear on maps so an Ordnance Survey 1:25,000 map is indispensable to explore this area. The mainline train services from Paddington to Penzance stop at major towns (with useful branch lines from Truro to Falmouth and Liskeard to Looe), but getting from the mainline to the north coast can involve multiple changes.

Colourful boats moored side by side in Newquay's picturesque harbour

For additional map symbols see back flap

Ruins of the medieval castle of Tintagel, on the north coast of Cornwall

❶ Bude

Cornwall. **Map** C5. 🏔 9,000.
ℹ️ Crescent Car Park; 01288 354240.
🚌 Easter–Sep: Fri. **W** visitbude.info

Once a bustling port, Bude has become a popular resort due to its wonderful golden beaches. In the 18th century, lime-rich sand from the beaches was transported along a canal to inland farms, where it was used to neutralize the acidic soil. The canal was abandoned in 1880 but a short stretch survives, providing a haven for birds.

❷ Tintagel

Cornwall. **Map** B5. 🏔 1,800.
🚌 Opp. Visitor Centre. ℹ️ Bossiney Rd; 01840 779084. **W** visitboscastle andtintagel.com

The ruins of **Tintagel Castle**, built around 1240 by Richard, Earl of Cornwall, sit on a hilltop. Visitors can reach the castle via two staircases along the cliffside.

The earl was persuaded to build the castle in this isolated spot by the popular belief that this was the birthplace of the legendary King Arthur.

Fine Mediterranean pottery from the 5th century has been discovered here, indicating that the site was a trading centre long before the castle was built.

A clifftop path leads from the castle to Tintagel's church, which has Norman and Saxon masonry. In the village, the **Old Post Office** is a rare example of a restored 14th-century Cornish manor house.

🏛 Tintagel Castle
Tintagel Head. **Tel** 01840 770328.
Open Apr–Sep: 10am–6pm daily;
Oct: 10am–5pm daily; Nov–Feb:
10am–4pm Sat & Sun. 🚯 🏛 EH
W english-heritage.org.uk

🏛 Old Post Office
Fore St. **Tel** 01840 770024.
Open Apr–Sep: 10:30am–5:30pm
daily; Mar & Oct: 11am–4pm daily.
🚯 🏛 NT **W** nationaltrust.org.uk

A painting showing King Arthur in conversation with court dignitaries

King Arthur

Historians think the legendary figure of King Arthur was probably inspired by a Romano-British chieftain or warrior who led British resistance to the Saxon invasion of the 6th century (see p34). Geoffrey of Monmouth's *History of the Kings of Britain* (1139) is the source of many legends connected with him – how he became king by removing the sword Excalibur from a stone, his final battle with the treacherous Mordred, and the story of the Knights of the Round Table.

❸ Boscastle

Cornwall. **Map** B5. 🏔 670.
🚌 Boscastle Bridge. **W** visit boscastleandtintagel.com

Squeezed into a narrow natural inlet between the ominously rugged headlands of Willapark and Penally Point, tiny Boscastle was almost destroyed in 2004 when the River Valency burst its banks. About 2,000 million litres (440 million gal) of water poured at a rate of 64 kmph (40 mph) through the village in a single day, and several people had to be airlifted out. The village has now been restored, and a flood defence warning system installed. The story of the flood, along with the rest of the village's history, is related in the **Boscastle Visitor Centre**, which had to be rebuilt after the original was washed away.

Boscastle was North Cornwall's main commercial port until 1893, when the railway arrived at Camelford. In its heyday, it was visited by up to 200 ships a year, mostly from Bristol and Wales, but some from as far away as Canada. It was the only safe harbour for 64 km (40 miles) or more, though navigating the small inlet, especially in a storm, was so hazardous that ships had to be towed in by 8-man "hobbler" rowing boats. Once the ships were docked, goods were carried by teams of horses up the steep village street to the main road.

By the harbour is the **Museum of Witchcraft and Magic**, the UK's largest public collection of items related to the occult.

Founder Cecil Williamson chose Boscastle because of its proximity to the sacred prehistoric site of Rocky Valley, where an 18-m (59-ft) waterfall plunges into a natural basin, and where ancient occult rock carvings, including two taking the form of circular labyrinths, have been found. The museum has informative displays, and also organizes workshops, candlelit visits and folklore and magic walks.

The novelist Thomas Hardy worked briefly as an architect in Boscastle. He met his wife Emma in 1870 while working on the restoration of St Juliot church. *A Pair of Blue Eyes* is set here, and the poem "Castle Boterel" records a visit he made to the village as an old man. A 5-km- (3-mile-) long path leads from Boscastle to the church through the beautiful Valency Valley.

To fully appreciate the stunning beauty of this stretch of coast, follow the South West Coast Path 5 km (3 miles) along the clifftops to Crackington Haven. At low tide, look out for the blowhole beneath Penally Point, known as the Devil's Bellows, which can shoot water right across the harbour entrance.

Ⅲ Boscastle Visitor Centre
The Harbour. **Tel** 01840 250010.
Open 10am–4pm daily.
Closed 25 & 26 Dec.

Ⅲ Museum of Witchcraft and Magic
The Harbour. **Tel** 01840 250111.
Open 10:30am–6pm Mon–Sat, 11:30am–6pm Sun (last adm: 5:30pm). **Closed** 5 Nov–26 Dec.
🚹 📷 🅦 **museumofwitchcraft andmagic.co.uk**

The exterior of the Museum of Witchcraft and Magic in Boscastle

Ornate furnishings in the Grenville Room at the Elizabethan manor Prideaux Place

❹ Padstow
Cornwall. **Map** B5. 🚶 3,000. 🚌
🛈 North Quay; 01841 533449.
🅦 **padstowlive.com**

A picturesque little fishing port on the sheltered estuary of the River Camel, chic Padstow is a magnet for foodies, as well as having several wonderful sandy beaches nearby. The gastronomic revolution was triggered by celebrity chef Rick Stein, who opened his first restaurant in the village over 40 years ago *(see p191)* and has since devoted much energy to shining the spotlight on Cornish produce. He now has five eateries here, as well as a cooking school. Other chefs have followed in his wake, making Padstow the undisputed gourmet capital of Cornwall.

The heart and soul of the village is the quayside, where the daily catch is landed, while the photogenic, labyrinthine cobbled streets are studded with boutiques, art galleries and delicatessens. At the **National Lobster Hatchery**, you can see lobsters, crabs and crustaceans up close – and even adopt a baby lobster. The little **Padstow Museum** displays a range of artifacts, including archaeological finds, items recovered from shipwrecks, historic shipbuilding and fishing equipment, and costumes from the annual Obby Oss (Hobby Horse) celebration, an ancient May Day ritual with pagan origins *(see p28)*.

The Elizabethan manor house **Prideaux Place** has been home to the Prideaux-Brune family since 1592. The family's ancestors include famous figures such as William the Conqueror and Jane Austen *(see p92)*. The house, with its richly furnished rooms and superb plasterwork, has been used as a location for many films and TV series, ranging from adaptations of Rosamunde Pilcher to Trevor Nunn's *Twelfth Night* (1996). The dramatic headland of Stepper Point, on the Prideaux estate, also featured prominently in the popular TV series *Poldark* (2015).

⊠ National Lobster Hatchery
South Quay. **Tel** 01841 533877.
Open 10am–4pm daily (to 7pm in summer). **Closed** 25 Dec.
🅦 **nationallobsterhatchery.co.uk**

Ⅲ Padstow Museum
Market Pl. **Tel** 01841 532752.
Open Easter–Oct: 10:30am–4:30pm Mon–Fri, 10:30am–1pm Sat.
🅦 **padstowmuseum.co.uk**

🏛 Prideaux Place
Padstow. **Tel** 01841 532411.
Open House: 1:30–4pm Sun–Thu. Grounds & Tearoom: 12:30–5pm Sun–Thu. 🚹 📷 🖼
🅦 **prideauxplace.co.uk**

Environs
From Padstow, a bike and walking trail follows the route of a disused railway (much admired by the celebrated English poet Sir John Betjeman). The trail runs for 27 km (17 miles) across vast tidal mudflats, and then through wooded valleys, following the River Camel to St Breward on the edge of Bodmin Moor.

A passenger ferry crosses the estuary to the village of Rock – even more upmarket than Padstow, with regular visitors such as Prince Harry and Hugh Grant.

Wine connoisseurs should visit the award-winning **Camel Valley Vineyard** for guided tours with wine-tastings.

🍇 Camel Valley Vineyard
Nanstallon, Bodmin. **Tel** 01208 77959.
Open Easter–Sep: 10am–5pm Mon–Sat; Oct–Easter: 10am–5pm Mon–Fri.
🅦 **camelvalley.com**

The church on the Lanhydrock estate, located south of Bodmin

❺ Newquay

Cornwall. **Map** B5. 🚉 20,000.
✈ Newquay, Cornwall. 🚂 Cliff Rd.
🚌 Marcus Hill. **ℹ** Marcus Hill; 01637
838516. 🏪 daily. 🏄 Boardmasters:
Aug; Fish Festival: Sep. **W** **visit
newquay.org**

Beginning life as an Elizabethan
sailing port, Newquay quickly
became one of Cornwall's biggest
pilchard fisheries. After the arrival
of the railway in the 1870s, it
also became the county's most
popular beach resort. Today, the
proximity of Newquay airport has
helped maintain its popularity.

Traditionally downmarket, with
its huge sandy beaches attracting
a budget-conscious crowd of
backpackers, surfers, clubbers,
pensioners and families, parts of
Newquay are now showing signs
of gentrification. Jamie Oliver and
Rick Stein eateries have opened
in the town, along with boutique
hotels and two sustainable
living projects, sponsored by
the Duchy of Cornwall.

❻ Bodmin

Cornwall. **Map** B5. 🚉 15,000.
🚂 Bodmin Parkway. 🚌 Bodmin.
ℹ Mount Folly Sq; 01208 76616.
W **bodminlive.com**

Cornwall's ancient county town
lies on the sheltered western
edge of Bodmin Moor. The
history and archaeology of the
town and moor are covered by
Bodmin Town Museum, while
Bodmin Jail was built in 1779 by
prisoners of war, forced to lug
20,000 tonnes of granite from
Bodmin's Cuckoo Quarry. Public
executions took place until 1862,
and among the exhibits are the
execution blocks and hanging pit.

The waters of a holy spring
gush out of the mouths of two
gargoyles at the foot of the
St Petroc churchyard. It was by
the original site of these waters –
diverted from their natural
location in the 16th-century –
that St Petroc discovered the
hermit St Guron living in a cell,
and established a monastery in

the 6th century. The monastery
has disappeared, but the bones
of St Petroc remain, housed in
a splendid 12th-century ivory
casket in the church. A stained-
glass window shows St Petroc
with a wolf – according to legend
he lived on an island in the Indian
Ocean for seven years, and when
he returned to Cornwall he
brought a tame wolf with him.

For a pleasant day out, ride on
the **Bodmin & Wenford Railway**,
or take part in a Victorian murder
trial at the Courtroom Experience,
run by the tourist office.

Located south of Bodmin, also
accessible along a 3-km (2-mile)
path from Bodmin Station, is the
famous National Trust-owned
Lanhydrock estate. The lovely
main house dates from the 17th
century, but only parts of the
original structure still exist; the
east wing was demolished in
the 18th century and most of
the rest of the house was rebuilt
following a fire in 1881. Visits
give an insight into the life of
a country house, covering the
kitchens, nurseries and servants'
rooms as well as the quarters of
the family that lived here. Exhibits
also examine the impact of
World War I on the estate.

The house is child-friendly, with
plenty of hands-on activities,
toys and a Victorian schoolroom.
The grounds include a formal
parterre *(see p24)* with displays
of rhododendrons and camellias.
There are acres of woodland,
with riverside walks and cycle
trails, including routes for families.

🏛 **Bodmin Town Museum**
Mt Folly Sq. **Tel** 01208 77067.
Open Easter–Oct: Mon–Sat & Good Fri.
Closed public hols. 🚻 limited. 📷

🏛 **Bodmin Jail**
Berrycombe Rd. **Tel** 01208 76292.
Open 9:30am–6pm daily.
Closed 25 Dec. 🍴 🚻 limited. 🚫
🍽 📷 **W** **bodminjail.org**

🚂 **Bodmin & Wenford Railway**
Bodmin General Station. **Tel** 01208
73555. **W** **bodminrailway.co.uk**

🏡 **Lanhydrock**
Bodmin. **Tel** 01208 265950.
Open House: Mar–Oct: 11am–5pm
daily. Gardens: mid-Feb–Oct: 10am–
5:30pm daily. **Closed** 25 Dec. 🍴 🚻
🚫 📷 **NT** **W** **nationaltrust.org.uk**

Surfing Around Newquay

Newquay is the UK's self-styled
surfing capital, attracting surfers
from all over Europe and hosting
several competitions. It is also
an ideal place for novices. Long,
straight Fistral Beach, with regular,
consistent waves, is a good place
to start. Small and quieter, Mawgan
Porth (to the north of Newquay)
faces the same direction as Fistral,
so it has great waves but without
the crowds. Adventure-seekers
should target Watergate Bay,
which offers bodyboarding, SUP,
wave-skiing, kitesurfing and other
sports, plus traditional surfing.

Surfers in action on Fistral Beach

❼ Bodmin Moor

Bodmin Moor is a huge expanse of bleak moorland and dramatic granite tors at the heart of Cornwall. This great inland wilderness lies over an outcrop of the granite batholith that runs from Dartmoor through the Cornish peninsula and under the sea to the Scilly Isles and beyond. Covering 207 sq km (80 sq miles), it is a landscape of mystery and legend, with sacred prehistoric sites, a history of smuggling and many associations with King Arthur.

Tips for Drivers

Tour length: 48 km (30 miles). **Stopping-off points:** Jamaica Inn, or, for a more authentic experience, the Blisland Inn. To hike to Rough Tor and Brown Willy, park at the convenient car park north of Rough Tor (the turn-off is at Camelford). The walk from Bolventor village is much longer.

⑤ Brown Willy
At 420 m (1,378 ft), this is the highest point in Cornwall. Its name is a corruption of *bronn wennili*, Cornish for "hill of swallows". The most spectacular walk takes in the summits of Rough Tor and Brown Willy.

① Altarnun
The village is home to the 15th-century Church of St Nonna, known as the Cathedral of the Moor. Nearby at Five Lanes is Wesley's Cottage, where the Methodist preacher John Wesley (1703–91) often stayed.

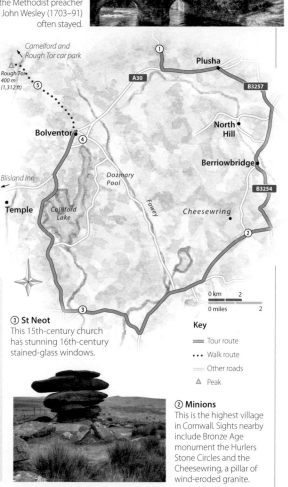

④ Jamaica Inn
A staging inn on the old turnpike road, this 1750 inn inspired Du Maurier's eponymous novel, and is also home to a small museum.

Daphne du Maurier

The period romances of Daphne du Maurier (1907–89) are inextricably linked with the stunning wild Cornish landscape where she grew up. *Jamaica Inn* established her reputation in 1936, and with the publication of *Rebecca* two years later she found herself one of the most popular authors of her day. *Rebecca* was later made into a cult film by Alfred Hitchcock, starring Joan Fontaine and Laurence Olivier.

③ St Neot
This 15th-century church has stunning 16th-century stained-glass windows.

Key
━━━ Tour route
••• Walk route
═══ Other roads
△ Peak

② Minions
This is the highest village in Cornwall. Sights nearby include Bronze Age monument the Hurlers Stone Circles and the Cheesewring, a pillar of wind-eroded granite.

Map labels:
Camelford and Rough Tor car park
Rough Tor 400 m (1,312 ft)
Plusha
A30
B3257
North Hill
Bolventor
Berriowbridge
B3254
Blisland Inn
Dozmary Pool
Temple
Colliford Lake
Fowey
Cheesewring
0 km 2
0 miles 2

❽ Eden Project

The Eden Project is a global garden for the 21st century, and a dramatic setting in which to tell the fascinating story of plants, people and places. Two futuristic conservatories mimic the conditions of warmer climes, the Rainforest Biome (hot and humid) and the Mediterranean Biome (warm and dry). The outdoor gardens are planted with species that thrive naturally in the Cornish climate. The relationship between humans and nature is interpreted by artists throughout the site. The Core education centre is used for exhibitions, films and workshops. For an aerial view of the biomes, visitors can ride over them on a 660-m (2,165-ft) zip wire, the longest in England.

Tropical South America
A huge waterfall crashes through this lush green rainforest.

West Africa
Made from timber recycled from Falmouth Docks, traditional West African totem sculptures loom over plants in the Rainforest Biome.

Malaysia
This display features a Malaysian house with a vegetable plot and a paddy field. The star attraction here is the titan arum flower, which grows to 3 m (8 ft) and smells of rotting flesh.

Tropical islands
These islands have many fascinating plants, such as the rare Madagascar periwinkle (*Catharanthus roseus*), which is used in the treatment of leukaemia.

For hotels and restaurants in this region see pp178–9 and pp190–91

Building Eden
Cornwall's declining china clay industry left behind many disused pits, and the Eden Project made ingenious use of this industrial landscape. After partly infilling a pit, the massive biomes were constructed using a record 370 km (230 miles) of scaffolding.

Transparent hexagons made of ultralight high-tech plastic

Crops and cultivation
The banana (*Musa acuminata*) is one of the many plants on display that are used in our everyday lives.

Rainforest Biome

This vast conservatory has a treetop-level viewing platform and aerial walkway.

The entrance to both the Rainforest and Mediterranean Biomes is via the Link, where the Eden Bakery is located.

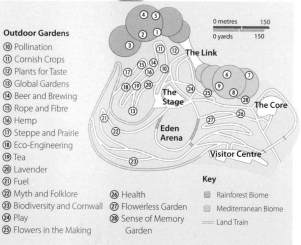

The Site

Access to the site, with its outdoor and covered biomes, is via the Visitor Centre.

Rainforest Biome
① Tropical Islands
② Malaysia
③ West Africa
④ Tropical South America
⑤ Crops and Cultivation

Mediterranean Biome
⑥ The Mediterranean
⑦ South Africa
⑧ California
⑨ Crops and Cultivation

Outdoor Gardens
⑩ Pollination
⑪ Cornish Crops
⑫ Plants for Taste
⑬ Global Gardens
⑭ Beer and Brewing
⑮ Rope and Fibre
⑯ Hemp
⑰ Steppe and Prairie
⑱ Eco-Engineering
⑲ Tea
⑳ Lavender
㉑ Fuel
㉒ Myth and Folklore
㉓ Biodiversity and Cornwall
㉔ Play
㉕ Flowers in the Making
㉖ Health
㉗ Flowerless Garden
㉘ Sense of Memory Garden

The Link

The Stage

The Core

Eden Arena

Visitor Centre

0 metres 150
0 yards 150

Key
▪ Rainforest Biome
▪ Mediterranean Biome
═══ Land Train

Colourful buildings lining the busy harbour in the Cornish seaside town of Fowey

❾ Looe

Cornwall. **Map** C6. 🏔 5,500. � 🚌 🚋 **i** Fore St; 01503 262072. 🛒 daily. 🎭 Looe Music Festival: Sep; Polperro Music and Arts Festival: Jun. **W** looeguide.co.uk

A down-to-earth fishing village and seaside resort, Looe straddles the mouth of its homonymous river, the two sides connected by a seven-arched bridge. In Victorian times, Looe was one of Cornwall's major ports, exporting tin, copper and arsenic. With the opening of the railway in 1860, the village rapidly became a popular holiday resort.

Just 32 km (20 miles) from Plymouth, Looe continues to attract the crowds, who come for an old-fashioned British seaside holiday, to pick up the latest catches from the famous daily harbourside fish market, or to enjoy the summertime Looe Music Festival, when rock concerts are held on the beach.

Looe is the UK's headquarters for sharking – the sharks are attracted to the boats by bags of smelly, mashed-up fish and, once caught, are measured, tagged and returned to the sea unharmed.

Environs

There is a lovely coastal walk to Polperro, which was a famous smuggling port in the 19th century. Another attraction is the **Monkey Sanctuary**, a flagship of the UK conservation movement.

🐒 **Monkey Sanctuary**
Murrayton House, St Martins. **Tel** 01503 262532. **Open** Apr–Sep: 11am–4:30pm daily; Oct: 11am–4:30pm Sat & Sun. ♿ limited. 📷 📷 **W** monkeysanctuary.org

❿ Fowey

Cornwall. **Map** B6. 🏔 2,500. **i** 5 South St; 01726 833616. **W** fowey.co.uk

The river, creeks and gentle waters of the Fowey Estuary were most likely the inspiration for *The Wind in the Willows*, whose author Kenneth Grahame regularly visited this pretty village. With its tangle of flower-filled streets and seafood restaurants, Fowey can get busy in the summer.

The church of St Fimbarrus marks the end of the ancient Saint's Way footpath from Padstow, a reminder of the Celtic missionaries who arrived on the shores of Cornwall to convert people to Christianity. A flower-lined path leads to a majestic porch and carved tower. Within, there are some fine 17th-century memorials to the Rashleigh family, whose seat, Menabilly, became Du Maurier's home and featured as Manderley in *Rebecca* (1938).

⓫ St Austell

Cornwall. **Map** B6. 🏔 20,000. 🚋 🚌 **i** Behind Texaco Service Station, Southbourne Rd; 01726 879500. 🛒 Wed, Sat & Sun. **W** staustellbay. co.uk

The busy industrial town of St Austell is the capital of the local china clay industry, which rose to importance in the 18th century. China was the only other place where clay of such quality and quantity could be found, and it was in Cornwall that William Cookworthy (1705–80) succeeded in replicating fine Chinese porcelain in the

18th century. At the **Wheal Martyn China Clay Museum**, displays evoke the history and human impact of clay and clay quarrying, while nature trails weave through abandoned clay works – and give eerie views of a vast working clay pit.

🏛 **Wheal Martyn China Clay Museum**
Carthew. **Tel** 01726 850362. **Open** 10am–4pm daily. **Closed** 24 Dec– mid-Jan. 📷 ♿ limited. 📷 📷 **W** wheal-martyn.com

⓬ Truro

Cornwall. **Map** B6. 🏔 20,000. 🚌 Green St. 🚋 Trelissick Gardens, St Mawes and Falmouth. **i** Boscawen St; 01872 274555. 🛒 Wed & Sat (farmers' market). 🎭 Truro Arts Festival: Apr; Great Cornwall Food Festival: Sep; City of Lights: Nov. **W** visittruro.org.uk

A historic city and one-time port, Truro is now the administrative capital of Cornwall. Truro's Victorian cathedral of 1876 was the first to be built since St Paul's (*see pp58–9*) in London. With its central tower, lancet windows and spires, the cathedral looks more French than English.

The **Royal Cornwall Museum** gives an introduction to the history of the county, and features displays on tin mining, Methodism and smuggling.

🏛 **Royal Cornwall Museum**
River St. **Tel** 01872 272205. **Open** 10am–4:45pm Mon–Sat (also Sun in Aug). **Closed** 25 Dec & 1 Jan. ♿ 📷 📷 **W** royalcornwallmuseum.org.uk

Interior of Truro Cathedral, designed by J L Pearson and completed in 1910

For hotels and restaurants in this region see pp178–9 and pp190–91

⓭ Lost Gardens of Heligan

These enchanting gardens formed part of an estate owned by the Tremayne family, who lived at Heligan House for over 400 years. When 16 of the 22 gardeners were killed during World War I, the gardens began to run wild and lay forgotten until Tim Smit (who went on to develop the Eden Project) rediscovered them in the 1990s. Inspired by the story of the lost gardeners, Smit set about not simply restoring the gardens, but reviving the traditional low-impact farming and cultivation methods that had evolved here over the centuries.

VISITORS' CHECKLIST

Practical Information
Pentewan, St Austell, Cornwall.
Map B6. **Tel** 01726 845100.
Open Gardens & Estate: Apr–Sep: 10am–6pm daily; Oct–Mar: 10am–5pm daily. **Closed** 25 Dec. 🅿 ♿ limited. 🅰 🆆 **heligan.com**

Transport
🚆 🚌

Vegetable Garden
Fruit, vegetables and herbs – many of them rare heritage varieties – are grown here for the Heligan café kitchen.

Locator Map
▪ Area illustrated

The Melon Yard and Pineapple Pit
is a walled garden where the Victorian trend for growing exotic fruits has been revived.

The Poultry Orchard
is home to rare-breed chickens, ducks and geese, which roam freely in the orchard.

The Thunderbox Room is where the gardeners signed their names on the eve of their departure for World War I.

Jungle

Ancient Sikkim rhododendrons
have been left to grow wild, just as they were when first discovered by Tim Smit.

Woodland Walk
Sculptures here are made of natural materials and emerge from the earth, including the *Mud Maid* and *Grey Lady*.

Pleasure Grounds
Landscaped in the early 1800s and designed for leisurely strolls, these grounds include a Mediterranean-inspired Italian Garden, set around a rectangular lily pond, and a historic collection of camellias and rhododendrons.

St Mawes Castle, built by Henry VIII to guard the harbour at Falmouth

⓮ St Mawes

Cornwall. **Map** B6. 🏛 850. 🚐 🚢 to Falmouth, Trelissick Gardens, Truro & Place Creek. 🛈 Roseland Visitor Centre; The Square; 01326 270440. 🎭 Roseland Arts Festival: Apr/May; Classic Car Festival: May. 🖥 **stmawesandtheroseland.co.uk**

An idyllic village of whitewashed cottages and townhouses with gleaming slate roofs, St Mawes has been an exclusive holiday retreat since Edwardian times. The village is set on the lush, rolling Roseland Peninsula in a sheltered, south-facing corner of the Fal Estuary. Often described as England's answer to St Tropez, St Mawes may be chic, but it is also the perfect place to enjoy muddy walks along the river.

Much of the area can be explored by ferry and on foot. The tiny Place Ferry connects the village to one of the most beautiful stretches of the South West Coast Path, with walks to the St Anthony headland, whose lighthouse appeared as "Fraggle Rock" in the famous 1980s TV series, and to Portscatho, passing pristine sandy beaches such as Towan. There is also a 1.5-km (1-mile) walk along the river to the church of St Just-in-Roseland, set within subtropical gardens and deemed by John Betjeman to be "the loveliest churchyard on earth". To the west of the village is St Mawes Castle, the best preserved of Henry VIII's coastal fortresses. Ferry services operate to Falmouth, Trelissick Gardens and Truro (see p162).

⓯ Falmouth

Cornwall. **Map** B6. 🏛 22,000. 🚉 🚐 🚢 opposite Visitor Centre. 🛈 11 Market Strand; 01326 741194. 🛒 Tue. 🖥 **falmouth.co.uk**

A vibrant university town, with a clutch of fine sandy beaches, Falmouth owes its existence to having the third deepest natural harbour in the world.

The liveliest of Cornwall's towns, Falmouth has a packed calendar of festivals – celebrating everything from sea shanties to oysters – which bring visitors in all year round. The town is a fine sight, its hilly core stacked with multihued Victorian and Georgian cottages and townhouses, and topped by the distinctive tower of a meteorological observatory built in 1868.

Falmouth's main street, lined with shops and cafés, follows the river. From the Prince of Wales pier, ferries operate across the

Sailing crafts displayed at the National Maritime Museum Cornwall

river to the villages of Flushing and St Mawes. Towards the town centre is the **Falmouth Art Gallery**, which has rotating exhibitions showcasing its permanent collection and the work of contemporary artists.

On the waterfront, the **National Maritime Museum Cornwall** dominates Discovery Quay, a waterside complex with shops, cafés and apartments. The museum features Britain's finest public collection of historic and contemporary watercraft. Exhibits look at maritime themes and the social impact of the sea on those whose lives have depended on it.

From Discovery Quay, the South West Coast Path heads uphill to **Pendennis Castle**, built by King Henry VIII. From the castle the path continues along the coast to a series of long sandy beaches. The most popular are Gyllyngvase Beach, with a lovely café-restaurant, and Swanpool, named after the swans on the pool behind it.

🖼 Falmouth Art Gallery
The Moor. **Tel** 01326 313863. **Open** 10am–5pm Mon–Sat. **Closed** 1 Jan, 25 & 26 Dec. 🖥 **falmouthartgallery.com**

🖼 National Maritime Museum Cornwall
Discovery Quay. **Tel** 01326 313388. **Open** 10am–5pm daily. **Closed** 25 & 26 Dec. 🎭 ♿ 🅿 📷 🖥 **nmmc.co.uk**

🏰 Pendennis Castle
The Headland. **Tel** 01326 316594. **Open** Apr–Oct: 10am–5pm daily; Nov–Mar: 10am–4pm Sat & Sun. **Closed** 1 Jan & 24–26 Dec. 🎭 📷 ♿ limited. 🅿 📷 EH 🖥 **english-heritage.org.uk**

Environs
To the south, **Glendurgan** and **Trebah** gardens are both set in sheltered valleys leading down to sandy coves on the Helford.

🌳 Glendurgan
Mawnan Smith. **Tel** 01326 252020. **Open** mid-Feb–Oct: 10:30am–5:30pm Tue–Sun & public hols; Aug: 10:30am–5:30pm daily. **Closed** Good Fri. 🎭 🅿 📷 NT 🖥 **nationaltrust.org.uk**

🌳 Trebah
Mawnan Smith. **Tel** 01326 252200. **Open** 10am–5pm daily. **Closed** 25 & 26 Dec. 🎭 ♿ 🅿 📷 🖥 **trebahgarden.co.uk**

🔟 Helston

Cornwall. **Map** B6. 🗠 12,000. 🚉
from Penzance. 🚏 Market Pl;
01326 564027. 🎭 Furry Dance: May.
W visithelston.com

The attractive town of Helston
is famous for its annual Furry
Dance (also called Flora Dance),
which welcomes spring with
plenty of revelry, including
dancing through the streets;
Helston Museum explains the
history of this ancient custom.

The Georgian houses and
inns of Coinagehall Street are
a reminder that Helston was
once a thriving stannary town,
where tin ingots were brought
for weighing and stamping
before being sold. Until the
13th century, locally mined tin
was brought downriver to a
harbour at the bottom of this
street, but access to the sea
was blocked when a shingle
bar formed across the River Loe
creating the freshwater lake,
Loe Pool. A lovely walk skirts
its wooded shores.

In 1880, Helston's trade was
taken over by a new harbour
created to the east on the River
Helford, at Gweek. Today, Gweek
is the home of the **Cornish Seal
Sanctuary**, where sick seals are
nursed back to health before
being returned to the sea.

The **Poldark Mine** covers the
history of Cornwall's tin mining
industry, from Roman to recent
times. The mine has underground
guided tours, which showcase
the difficult working conditions
of 18th-century miners.

Children dressed in white participating
in the annual Furry Dance, Helston

🏛 **Helston Museum**
Market Pl. **Tel** 01326 564027.
Open 10am–4pm Mon–Sat.
Closed Christmas week. 🖼 ♿ 🖼
W helstonmuseum.co.uk

🦭 **Cornish Seal Sanctuary**
Gweek. **Tel** 01326 221361. **Open**
10am–dusk daily. **Closed** 25 Dec. 🖼
♿ 💻 🖼 **W** sealsanctuary.co.uk

🏛 **Poldark Mine**
Wendron. **Tel** 01326 573173.
Open 10:30am–3pm daily. 🎫 11am &
12:30pm Tue, Thu & Sat. 💻 🖼
W poldarkmine.org.uk

🔟 The Lizard

Cornwall. **Map** B6. ✈ Newquay.
✈ Newquay. 🚌 🚌 🚌
W lizard-peninsula.co.uk

The southernmost peninsula on
the British mainland, the Lizard is
an area of extreme and beautiful
contrasts, stretching from the
quaint villages, dense woodland
and labyrinthine route of the
River Helford to serpentine cliffs
and dramatic sea-sculpted coves.

From the whitewashed village
of Helford – with a picturesque
waterside pub – a circular walk
runs through the oak woodland
to Frenchman's Creek, named
after the novel by Du Maurier,
which was later adapted for a
film and a TV series. En route is
Kestle Barton, a cultural centre
which stages exhibitions and
has a self-service café.

On the southwest edge of
Goonhilly Downs, Kynance Cove
is the Lizard's most stunning spot,
with golden sands, fractured
cliffs and huge, giant shards of
rock surging from the sea. To
the south (accessible by road
or the coastal footpath) is Lizard
Point, the most southerly point
in Britain, where a tour of the
restored lighthouse – which
includes climbing to the top –
is highly recommended.

At Poldhu Cove, around
2 km (1 mile) north of Mullion,
the **Marconi Centre** marks the
spot where, in 1901, Guglielmo
Marconi transmitted the first
transatlantic radio signal all
the way to Newfoundland
on Canada's east coast.

🏛 **Kestle Barton**
Manaccan, Helston. **Tel** 01326 231811.
Open Apr–end Oct: 10:30am–5pm
Tue–Sun. **W** kestlebarton.co.uk

🏛 **Marconi Centre**
Poldhu Rd, Mullion. **Tel** 01326 241656.
Open May, Jun & Sep: 1:30–4:30pm Sun
& Wed, 7–9pm Tue & Fri; Jul & Aug:
1:30–4:30pm Sun, Wed & Thu, 7–9pm
Tue & Fri; Oct–Apr: 1:30–4:30pm Sun,
7–9pm Tue & Fri. **W** marconi-centre-
poldhu.org.uk

Pretty white cottages on the banks of the river in the charming village of Helford on the Lizard peninsula

Fishing and sailing boats at the port of Penzance

⑱ Penzance

Cornwall. **Map** A6. 🔼 38,000. 🚆 🚌 🚢 **i** Station Approach; 01736 335530. **W** lovepenzance.co.uk

Penzance is a bustling town and port with a climate so mild that palm trees and subtropical plants grow happily in the lush Morrab Gardens. The town offers fine views of St Michael's Mount and Marazion Beach, a great sweep of golden sands across the bay.

The main road through the town is Market Jew Street, at the top of which stands the domed Market House (1837), fronted by a statue of Sir Humphrey Davy

(1778–1829). Davy invented the miner's safety lamp, which detected lethal gases in mines.

Chapel Street is lined with curious buildings, none more striking than the flamboyant Egyptian House (1835), with its richly painted façade and lotus bud decoration. Just as curious is Admiral Benbow Inn (1696) on the same street, which has a pirate perched on the roof looking out to sea. The **Penlee House Gallery and Museum** has works by the Newlyn School of artists.

🏛 Penlee House Gallery and Museum
Morrab Rd. **Tel** 01736 363625. **Open** Apr–Oct: 10am–5pm Mon–Sat; Nov–Mar: 10am–4:30pm Mon–Sat. **Closed** 1 Jan, 25 & 26 Dec. 🅿 ♿ 🖥 📷
W penleehouse.org.uk

⑲ St Michael's Mount

A craggy island that emerges dramatically from the waters of Mounts Bay, the mount was an important centre for the Cornish tin trade during the Iron Age and was later known to the Romans as the island of Ictis. It is dedicated to the archangel St Michael who, it is said, appeared here in 495. When the Normans conquered England in 1066, they were struck by the island's resemblance to Mont-St-Michel and invited Benedictine monks to build an abbey here. The abbey was absorbed into a fortress during the Dissolution, when Henry VIII set up coastal defences. In 1659, St Michael's Mount was bought by Colonel John St Aubyn, whose descendants turned the fortress into a magnificent house.

Rocky Slopes
These slopes were planted with subtropical trees and shrubs by the St Aubyn family.

Access to the island is by boat from Marazion or on foot by a cobbled causeway at low tide.

Harbourside village

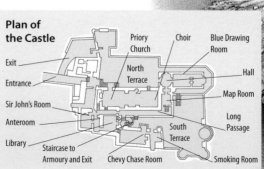

Plan of the Castle

Exit
Entrance
Sir John's Room
Anteroom
Library
Staircase to Armoury and Exit
Priory Church
North Terrace
Chevy Chase Room
Choir
South Terrace
Blue Drawing Room
Hall
Map Room
Long Passage
Smoking Room

Environs

A short distance south of Penzance, Newlyn *(see p169)* is Cornwall's largest fishing port and has given its name to the local school of artists founded by Stanhope Forbes (1857–1947). They painted outdoors, aiming to capture the fleeting impressions of wind, sun and the sea. North of Penzance, overlooking the beautiful Cornish coast, **Chysauster** is a fine example of a Romano-British village. The site has remained almost undisturbed since it was abandoned during the 3rd century.

From Penzance, regular boat services depart for the Isles of Scilly, an enchanting archipelago forming part of the same granite mass as Land's End *(see p169)*, Bodmin Moor *(see p159)* and

Dartmoor *(see pp142–3)*. Along with tourism, flower-growing is the main source of income on the islands – fields of scented narcissi and pinks only add to the exceptional wild beauty of the Isles of Scilly.

Cornish Smugglers

In the days before income tax, the main form of government income came from tax on imported luxury goods, such as brandy and perfume. Huge profits were to be made by evading these taxes, which were at their height during the Napoleonic Wars (1780–1815). Cornwall, with its rivers penetrating deep into the mainland, was prime smuggling territory. Some notorious families resorted to

Smugglers with their cargo

deliberate wrecking – setting up deceptive lights to lure vessels onto the sharp rocks in the hope of plundering the wreckage – inspiring many stories, including Du Maurier's 1936 novel *Jamaica Inn*.

Chysauster
Newmill, off B3311. **Tel** 07831 757934.
Open Apr–Jun & Oct: 10am–5pm daily; Jul & Aug: 10am–6pm daily; Sep, Nov–Mar: 10am–4pm daily.
Closed 1 Jan & 24–26 Dec. 🅿 📷 EH
🆆 **english-heritage.org.uk**

Priory Church
Rebuilt in the late 14th century, this church at the summit of the island has fine stained glass.

Castle entrance

The Armoury displays military trophies brought back by the St Aubyn family from various wars.

The Chevy Chase Room takes its name from a plaster frieze (1641) that depicts hunting scenes.

The South Terrace forms the roof of the large Victorian wing.

VISITORS' CHECKLIST

Practical Information
Marazion. **Map** A6. 🚉 30. **Tel** 01736 710507; 01736 710265 (tide and ferry information). **Open** Castle: mid-Mar–Oct: 10:30am–5pm Sun–Fri. Garden: mid-Apr–Jun: 10:30am–5pm Mon–Fri; Jul–Sep: 10:30am–5:30pm Thu & Fri. 🅿 📷 of castle by appt. 📷 📷 NT 🆆 **nationaltrust.org.uk**

Transport
🚤 from Marazion (Mar–Oct) or on foot at low tide.

Blue Drawing Room
This room is decorated in Rococo Gothic style and features fine plasterwork and furniture, as well as paintings by Thomas Gainsborough and Thomas Hudson.

Panoramic view of Porthminster Beach and the picturesque town of St Ives

⑳ St Ives

Cornwall. **Map** A6. 🏯 11,000. 🚂
🚌 ℹ️ Street-an-Pol; 09052 522250.
🆆 **visitstives.org.uk**

With its dazzling whitewashed cottages, flower-filled gardens and golden sandy beaches, St Ives combines the traditional pleasures of a seaside holiday with the more refined delights of its prestigious artistic heritage. The town is famous for the clarity of its light, which attracted a group of artists to set up a seaside art colony here in the 1930s. Their work is celebrated at the **Barbara Hepworth Museum and Sculpture Garden** and **Tate St Ives**. The former presents the sculptor's work in the house and garden where she lived for many years. Tate St Ives displays the work of modern British artists who have worked in the area. The building was designed to frame a panoramic view of Porthmeor Beach, reminding visitors of the natural surroundings that inspired the art on display.

The best beaches in the town include Porthgwidden, which is sheltered and great for children, and Porthmeor, which is good for surfing. The star, though, is sweeping Porthminster.

🏛️ Barbara Hepworth Museum and Sculpture Garden
Barnoon Hill. **Tel** 01736 796226. **Open** Mar–Oct: 10am–5:20pm daily; Nov–Feb: 10am–4:20pm Tue–Sun. **Closed** 24–26 Dec. 🐾 ♿ by appt. 📷

🏛️ Tate St Ives
Porthmeor Beach. **Tel** 01736 796226. **Open** Mar–Oct: 10am–5:20pm daily; Nov–Feb: 10am–4:20pm Tue–Sun. **Closed** 24–26 Dec. 🐾 ♿ 📷 📷
🆆 **tate.org.uk**

St Ives Artists of the 20th Century

In the 19th and 20th centuries, St Ives, together with Newlyn (see p167), became a magnet for aspiring artists. In 1939, Ben Nicholson and Barbara Hepworth arrived in St Ives. They formed the nucleus of a group of artists that made a major contribution to the development of abstract art in Europe. Other prolific artists associated with the area include the potter Bernard Leach and the painter Patrick Heron, whose Coloured Glass Window dominates the Tate St Ives entrance. Much of the art on display at Tate St Ives is abstract and illustrates new responses to the rugged Cornish landscape, the human figure and the ever-changing patterns of sunlight on sea.

Bernard Leach (1887–1979) became fascinated with raku pottery while living in Japan. On his return to England in 1920, he founded the Leach Pottery, a ceramic studio. A small museum at the studio celebrates his life and work.

Barbara Hepworth (1903–75) was one of the foremost abstract sculptors of the 20th century. Two Forms (Divided Circle) (1969), a bronze sculpture created just six years before her death, is considered one of her most famous works.

Patrick Heron (1920–99) was an abstract and figurative artist who met Ben Nicholson, Barbara Hepworth and other St Ives artists while working at the Leach Pottery from 1944 to 1945. St Ives Harbour (1948) is typical of his earlier figurative works.

㉑ Penwith Tour

This tour passes through a spectacular, remote Cornish landscape, dotted with relics of the tin-mining industry, picturesque fishing villages and many prehistoric remains. The magnificent coastline varies between gentle rolling moorland in the north and the rugged, windswept cliffs that characterize the dramatic coast to the south. The beauty of the area, combined with the clarity of light, has attracted artists since the 19th century. Their work can be seen in Newlyn, St Ives and Penzance.

Tips for Drivers

Tour length: 50 km (31 miles)
Stopping-off points: There are pubs and cafés in most villages. The coastal village of Sennen Cove also makes for a pleasant stop.

② **Lanyon Quoit**
One of many prehistoric monuments, this chambered tomb is visible on the left from the road to Madron.

① **Zennor**
The carved mermaid in the church in this pretty village recalls the legend of the mermaid who lured the local squire's son to her ocean lair.

⑨ **Botallack Mine**
Derelict engine houses clinging to the cliffside are a vivid reminder of the region's former industry of tin mining.

③ **Trengwainton**
These gardens are noted for their exotic plants and trees.

④ **Newlyn**
Cornwall's largest fishing port gave its name to a school of artists founded in the 1880s (see p167). Examples of their work can be seen in the art gallery here.

⑧ **Land's End**
England's most westerly point is noted for its dramatic and wild landscape. A local exhibition reveals its history, geology and wildlife.

Key
━━ Tour route
═══ Other roads

⑦ **Minack Theatre**
This Ancient Greek-style theatre (1923) overlooks the spectacular bay of Porthcurno. It forms a wonderful backdrop for productions in summer.

⑥ **Merry Maidens**
This Bronze Age stone circle is said to be made up of 19 girls that were turned to stone for dancing on a Sunday.

⑤ **Mousehole**
This tiny fishing village (pronounced "mowzel") is set above a sheltered harbour. A fishermen's legend inspired Tom Bawcock's Eve on 23 December, which ends with the entire village eating stargazy pie (see p182).

Map labels: St Ives, B3306, Morvah, B3306, Trewellard, B3318, St Just, B3306, Madron, A30, A3071, Penzance, B3283, B3315, Sennen Cove, A30, B3283, Lamorna, B3315, B3315, Porthcurno

0 km 2
0 miles 2

TRAVELLERS' NEEDS

WHERE TO STAY

Visitors are spoiled for choice with the variety of accommodation on offer across England's South Coast. This section suggests places to stay throughout the area and across a range of prices, from a hotel filled with Regency splendour in the centre of Bath to a quirky base in Brighton, a slick London hotel, a modest B&B in Kent, a pub deep in cider country, or a family hotel on the Cornish Riviera. The area has plenty of cozy rural inns with excellent restaurants, luxurious country houses, as well as chic seaside hotels and ones geared to families on bucket-and-spade holidays. Whatever the price bracket, these hotels are among the best of their kind, selected for their distinctive character, their exceptional hospitality, facilities, great location or value for money.

Country-House Hotels

Quintessentially English, country-house hotels occupy buildings of architectural or historic interest. They usually have extensive grounds, classic decoration and antique furniture, and many have first-rate dining rooms, spas and gym facilities. Comfort, even luxury, is assured. Service is often outstanding, but rates tend to be high. Some of these hotels are still privately owned and personally managed; others belong to groups.

Seating area in the lobby at The Goring, a luxury hotel in London

Boutique Hotels

Luxurious but cutting-edge, design-conscious hotels revel in ground-breaking architecture with minimalist decoration and high-tech gadgets. Some of them have excellent restaurants. Chains such as **ABode**, **Hotel du Vin**, **Pig Hotels** and **hub by Premier Inn** are included in this category. Popular with budget-conscious travellers, the boutique B&B is a spin-off of the trend.

Historic and Character Hotels

Historic hotels have a connection with the history of their area, while character hotels have charm and appeal. Character hotels may have cozy rooms, exposed beams and open fires, though they may also be more striking and contemporary.

Hotel Groups

Although chain hotels lack individuality, they are almost always efficiently run and conveniently placed. They represent good value for money, and often have reduced rates in low season. Budget chains with no-frills accommodation include **Ibis**, **Mercure**, **Travelodge** and **Premier Inn**; among the mid-market chains are **Holiday Inn**, **Novotel**, **Marriott** and **Hilton**. Independently owned franchise hotels are also found in the South Coast, including **Best Western** and **Pride of Britain**.

Inns and Pubs with Rooms

Coaching inns, dating from the 17th and 18th centuries, are a familiar sight in the south of England. Most have traditional decor and a warm and friendly atmosphere. Other types of pubs or inns also offer comfortable accommodation and good food; many are family friendly. The best offer facilities and services that rival most hotels.

Guesthouses and B&Bs

The seaside guesthouse may have been consigned to history, but the B&B (bed-and-breakfast) is a popular form of low-cost accommodation in England. There are two types: small hotels with no restaurant and few communal amenities, and family-owned private homes.

Regional tourist offices have lists of local registered B&Bs. The **VisitBritain** (see p202) and **London Bed and Breakfast Agency** websites are also good resources.

Rates and Bookings

Check whether the advertised rate includes just the room, B&B or half-board (dinner and bed-and-breakfast) per person. Rates generally include Value Added Tax (VAT) and service charges, but most hotels charge hefty single-person supplements. Prices in London are elevated, while those in the rural areas

Picturesque setting of the Art Deco-inspired Burgh Island Hotel in Devon

◀ Pots and plants for sale at the flower market on Columbia Road in London represent good value, particularly for mid-week stays. Many hotels outside London insist on a two-night minimum stay at weekends. The summer, Christmas and key events tend to hike up prices.

Most hotels have an online booking facility. Bargains can be found by booking through websites such as **LateRooms**, **lastminute.com**, **Expedia**, **Kayak** or **Travelocity**.

Self-Catering

Self-catering has a number of advantages, especially for families and those on a budget. Sites such as **Airbnb** and **onefinestay** offer homes to rent directly from their owners. There are a range of places available to rent, from luxury apartments to log cabins. Properties with character can be rented from organizations such as the **Landmark Trust**, **English Heritage** *(see p202)* and the **National Trust** *(see p202)*. Other good sources of rental properties are **Sawday's** and local tourist offices, which may also offer a booking service. Be sure to confirm what is included in the price before you book.

Caravanning, Camping and Motor Homes

Most of England's South Coast campsites and caravan parks are only open in the summer months, but you need to book in advance. Helpful organizations include the **Camping and Caravanning Club** and the **Caravan Club**, which publish lists of their member parks.

The cost of camping or caravanning pitches depends on the facilities and the number of people. For a list of sites, check the websites **Just Go, Pitch Up, Cool Camping** or **South Coast Campsites**. Motor homes are more flexible, with a wider choice of places to stay. Check **LandCruise** for more information.

Travellers with Disabilities

Tourist boards provide information about disabled access in their accommodation and sightseeing guides. The VisitBritain website has an Accessible Britain section detailing nearby attractions and transport, and runs the National Accessible Scheme for accommodation. The scheme grades properties approved by the **Tourism for All** initiative. The **Disability Rights UK** website provides links to holidays and activities. Before booking accommodation, be sure to check that it meets your needs.

Recommended Hotels

The following places to stay have been selected for their excellent facilities, location and value. England's South Coast

Sign for The Pig on the Beach hotel in Dorset

has a wide range of accommodation options. From country-house retreats to pubs with rooms, there is something to suit every visitor's preference and budget. For the best in each area, look out for hotels designated as DK Choice. These offer something unique: a striking location, spectacular views, fascinating history or a distinctive atmosphere.

DIRECTORY

Boutique Hotels

ABode
W brownswordhotels.co.uk

Hotel du Vin
W hotelduvin.com

hub by Premier Inn
W premierinn.com/gb/en/hub.html

Pig Hotels
W thepighotel.com

Hotel Groups

Best Western
W bestwestern.co.uk

Hilton
W hilton.com

Holiday Inn
W holidayinn.com

Ibis
W ibis.com

Marriott
W marriott.com

Mercure
W mercure.com

Novotel
W novotel.com

Premier Inn
W premierinn.com

Pride of Britain
W prideofbritainhotels.com

Travelodge
W travelodge.co.uk

Guesthouses and B&Bs

London Bed and Breakfast Agency
W londonbb.com

Rates and Bookings

Expedia
W expedia.co.uk

Kayak
W kayak.co.uk

lastminute.com
W lastminute.com

LateRooms
W laterooms.com

Travelocity
W travelocity.co.uk

Self-Catering

Airbnb
W airbnb.co.uk

Landmark Trust
W landmarktrust.org.uk

onefinestay
W onefinestay.com

Sawday's
W sawdays.co.uk

Caravanning, Camping and Motor Homes

Camping and Caravanning Club
W campingandcaravanningclub.co.uk

Caravan Club
W caravanclub.co.uk

Cool Camping
W coolcamping.co.uk

Just Go
W justgo.uk.com

LandCruise
W landcruise.uk.com

Pitch Up
W pitchup.com

South Coast Campsites
W southcoastcampsites.com

Travellers with Disabilities

Disability Rights UK
W disabilityrightsuk.org

Tourism for All
W tourismforall.org.uk

Where to Stay

London

hub by Premier Inn Spitalfields £
Boutique   City Map F2
86 Brick Lane, E1 6RL
Tel *03330 030025*
🅦 hubhotels.co.uk
Expect smart TVs and comfortable beds in cleverly designed rooms at this high-tech budget hotel. There is no restaurant, but the in-house deli offers tempting goodies.

Andaz Liverpool Street ££
Boutique   City Map F2
40 Liverpool St, EC2M 7QN
Tel *020 7961 1234*
🅦 londonliverpoolstreet.
andaz.hyatt.com
There are three bars and four restaurants in this hotel, which is located close to the station. There is also a hidden Masonic temple.

The Hoxton ££
Boutique
81 Great Eastern St, EC2A 3HU
Tel *020 7550 1000*
🅦 thehoxton.com
The vast open-plan lobby of this hip hotel has a real buzz. It offers distinctive rooms, fair prices and a destination restaurant.

Kennington B&B ££
B&B
103 Kennington Park Rd, SE11 4JJ
Tel *020 7735 7669*
🅦 kenningtonbandb.com
A family-run B&B in a lovingly restored Georgian townhouse with contemporary decor.

Lime Tree ££
B&B
135–137 Ebury St, SW1W 9QU
Tel *020 7730 8191*
🅦 limetreehotel.co.uk
You get real value for money at this welcoming family-run B&B. The delightful garden is a bonus.

Artist Residence London £££
Boutique
52 Cambridge St, SW1V 4QQ
Tel *020 7931 8946*
🅦 artistresidencelondon.co.uk
This former pub has been transformed into a charming hotel with quirky decor. It has a basement bar and restaurant.

Batty Langley's £££
Character   City Map F2
12 Folgate St, E1 6BX
Tel *020 7377 4390*
🅦 battylangleys.com
Set in the heart of lively Spitalfields, the inviting panelled rooms

here are inspired by the famous 18th-century architect and landscape gardener Batty Langley.

The Beaumont Mayfair £££
Boutique   City Map C3
Brown Hart Gardens, W1K 6TF
Tel *020 7499 1001*
🅦 thebeaumont.com
From the popular restaurateurs who set up The Wolseley and The Delaunay, this fabulously chic hotel features an Antony Gormley sculpture-suite and Art Deco-style rooms.

The Capital £££
Luxury   City Map B4
22–24 Basil St, SW3 1AT
Tel *020 7589 5171*
🅦 capitalhotel.co.uk
All the luxury and service of a grand hotel, but in a much more intimate and personal setting. The location – just a short walk from Harrods – is excellent.

The Goring £££
Historic   City Map C4
15 Beeston Pl, SW1W 0JW
Tel *020 7396 9000*
🅦 thegoring.com
A great English institution with liveried doormen, private gardens and crackling fires on winter days. The Duchess of Cambridge stayed here before her wedding.

The Grazing Goat £££
Pub with rooms   City Map B3
6 New Quebec St, W1H 7RQ
Tel *020 7724 7243*
🅦 thegrazinggoat.co.uk
This Marylebone gastro-pub has eight rustic-chic rooms. Guests can take a rainforest shower and sleep in a sleigh bed.

Luxurious bedroom with silk-lined walls and a chandelier at the Goring, London

---

Price Guide
Prices are based on one night's stay in high season for a standard double room, inclusive of service charges and taxes.

£	up to £100
££	£100–200
£££	over £200

DK Choice

Ham Yard £££
Boutique   City Map C3
1 Ham Yard, W1D 7DT
Tel *020 3642 2000*
🅦 firmdalehotels.com
The latest hotel from the vibrant Firmdale collection has an urban village feel. Kit Kemp's interiors – including a library, theatre and 1950s-style bowling alley – are colourful and contemporary. Alongside the 91 rooms are 24 stunning apartments. It has a pretty rooftop terrace, with show-stopping views.

The Kensington £££
Luxury   City Map A4
109–113 Queen's Gate, SW7 5LR
Tel *020 7589 6300*
🅦 doylecollection.com
This is a captivating new address from Irish hoteliers the Doyles. Rooms are elegant, with fine art. There's also a sleek bar.

The Ritz £££
Luxury   City Map C3
150 Piccadilly, W1J 9BR
Tel *020 7493 8181*
🅦 theritzlondon.com
Perfectly preserved with its original Louis XVI-style decor, this place has glamour and glitz all rolled into one. Don't miss the famous afternoon tea.

The Stafford £££
Character   City Map C3
16–18 St James's Pl, SW1A 1NJ
Tel *020 7493 0111*
🅦 thestaffordlondon.com
An elegant hotel decorated in country-house style and set in the heart of the West End. It is home to the American Bar, a highlight of London's cocktail scene.

Kent and Sussex

BRIGHTON: Artist Residence ££
Boutique   Road Map D2
33 Regency Sq, East Sussex, BN1 2GG
Tel *01273 324302*
🅦 artistresidencebrighton.co.uk
Set in a listed townhouse, this hotel has sea views, and is

Retro decor and fantastic views at Belle Tout Lighthouse on Beachy Head, Eastbourne

decorated by artists and furnished with vintage finds. There's a café, restaurant and a cocktail shack.

CANTERBURY: Canterbury Cathedral Lodge £
Boutique　　　　Road Map F1
The Precincts, Kent, CT1 2EH
Tel *01227 865350*
Ⓦ canterburycathedrallodge.org
A modern hotel with smart, airy rooms in the peaceful grounds of Canterbury Cathedral.

CHICHESTER: Crab and Lobster £££
Rooms with a view　　Road Map C2
Mill Lane, Sidlesham, West Sussex, PO20 7NB
Tel *01243 641233*
Ⓦ crab-lobster.co.uk
This 350-year-old pub has a good selection of stylishly simple rooms, each with stunning views over salt marshes and woods to the sea.

CLIMPING: Bailiffscourt £££
Character　　　　Road Map C2
Climping St, West Sussex, BN17 5RW
Tel *01903 723511*
Ⓦ hshotels.co.uk/bailiffscourt
Although built in the 1920s, this place has medieval and traditional furnishings, such as tapestries, oak chests and four-poster beds.

DK Choice

EASTBOURNE: Belle Tout Lighthouse £££
Character　　　　Road Map D2
Beachy Head, East Sussex, BN20 0AE
Tel *01323 423185*
Ⓦ belletout.co.uk
Have you ever longed to stay in a lighthouse? Belle Tout is the real McCoy. It was built in 1832, decommissioned in 1902, and opened in 2010 as an unusual B&B with a retro seaside feel and 360° views. Nostalgics can sleep in the original lighthouse-keeper's bunk room. There is a minimum stay of two nights.

HASTINGS: Swan House ££
B&B　　　　　　Road Map E2
Hill St, East Sussex, TN34 3HU
Tel *01424 430014*
Ⓦ swanhousehastings.co.uk
A half-timbered 1490s guesthouse with tastefully furnished rooms. The gourmet breakfasts are sourced from local suppliers, and the owners are very helpful.

HEVER: Hever Castle B&B ££
Character　　　　Road Map D1
The Astor Wing, Hever Castle, Edenbridge, Kent, TN8 7NG
Tel *01732 861800*
Ⓦ hevercastle.co.uk
The childhood home of Queen Anne Boleyn has now been converted into a luxury B&B, with access to the wonderful castle and its fabulous grounds, as well as a golf course.

LEWES: Berkeley House £
B&B　　　　　　Road Map D2
2 Albion St, East Sussex, BN7 2ND
Tel *01273 476057*
Ⓦ berkeleyhouselewes.com
This pristine Grade II-listed Regency townhouse, close to Glyndebourne, is a real home away from home.

MARGATE: Sands Hotel ££
Boutique　　　　Road Map F1
16 Marine Dr, Kent, CT9 1DH
Tel *01843 228228*
Ⓦ sandshotelmargate.co.uk
A stunningly restored beachside hotel in tune with the revived town. The pretty interiors feature fresh, subtle decoration inspired by sun, sand and sea.

MIDHURST: Park House ££
Country House　　Road Map C2
Bepton, West Sussex, GU29 0JB
Tel *01730 819020*
Ⓦ parkhousehotel.com
Relaxed and comfortable, this place is more a family home than a hotel. Guests can swim, play croquet or grass-court tennis, take a walk on the downs or relax in the excellent spa.

PETWORTH: Old Railway Station ££
Character　　　　Road Map C2
Station Rd, West Sussex, GU28 0JF
Tel *01798 342346*
Ⓦ old-station.co.uk
Stay in a Pullman carriage parked in the sidings or in the clapboard station itself at this romantic hotel. Continue the theme with your breakfast in the waiting room.

RAMSGATE: Albion House ££
Character　　　　Road Map F1
Albion Pl, Kent, CT11 8HQ
Tel *01843 606630*
Ⓦ albionhouseramsgate.co.uk
This stunning hotel in a Georgian building has sophisticated rooms and breathtaking views.

RYE: Jeake's House £
B&B　　　　　　Road Map E2
Mermaid St, East Sussex, TN31 7ET
Tel *01797 222828*
Ⓦ jeakeshouse.com
An ivy-covered traditional 16th-century house with an honesty bar and a galleried breakfast room. Some rooms have four-poster beds.

ST LEONARDS-ON-SEA: Zanzibar International ££
Boutique　　　　Road Map E2
9 Eversfield Pl, East Sussex, TN37 6BY
Tel *01424 460109*
Ⓦ zanzibarhotel.co.uk
A fun seafront hotel with eight lovely bedrooms, each attractively themed around a different country or continent.

SISSINGHURST: The Milk House ££
Pub with rooms　　Road Map E2
The Street, Kent, TN17 2JG
Tel *01580 720200*
Ⓦ themilkhouse.co.uk
This trendy all-day dining pub has elegant rooms and a dairy theme. It is right on the doorstep of the castle and its garden.

WEST HOATHLY: Gravetye Manor £££
Country House　　Road Map D2
Vowels Lane, West Sussex, RH19 4LJ
Tel *01342 810567*
Ⓦ gravetyemanor.co.uk
Beautifully restored Elizabethan manor with William Robinson gardens, charming staff and Michelin-starred food.

WHITSTABLE: Sleeperzzz £
B&B　　　　　　Road Map F1
30 Railway Ave, Kent, CT5 1LH
Tel *01227 636975*
Ⓦ sleeperzzz.net
Close to the town centre, this simple and pleasant B&B serves hearty English breakfasts.

For more information on types of hotels *see pages 172–3*

Trendy furnishings and decor at the Pig, a stylish country hotel in Brockenhurst

Hampshire and Salisbury Plain

BEAULIEU: Montagu Arms £££
Character   **Road Map** B2
New Forest, Hampshire, SO42 7ZL
Tel *01590 624467*
ⓦ montaguarmshotel.co.uk
A wisteria-clad traditional hotel
set in the heart of a picturesque
village. There are lovely gardens,
log fires and 22 inviting bedrooms
and comfortable suites.

BROCKENHURST: The Pig ££
Boutique   **Road Map** B2
Beaulieu Rd, Hampshire, SO42 7QL
Tel *01590 622354*
ⓦ thepighotel.com
The original Pig hotel – now one
of a chain of five – occupies a
Georgian shooting lodge, with
shabby-chic rooms, tennis courts
and prolific kitchen gardens.

CHIPPENHAM: Lucknam Park £££
Country House   **Road Map** A1
Colerne, Wiltshire, SN14 8AZ
Tel *01225 742777*
ⓦ lucknampark.co.uk
This gorgeous Palladian mansion
in parkland offers Michelin-starred
cuisine. There's a cookery school,
a spa and an equestrian centre.

HINDON: The Lamb ££
Historic   **Road Map** A2
High St, Salisbury, Wiltshire, SP3 6DP
Tel *01747 820573*
ⓦ lambhindon.co.uk
A modernized Young's pub with
12th-century origins. There's a mix
of historic panelling, flagstones
and contemporary bedrooms.

LACOCK: Sign of the Angel ££
Character   **Road Map** A1
6 Church St, Wiltshire, SN15 2LB
Tel *01249 730230*
ⓦ signoftheangel.co.uk
This half-timbered 15th-century
inn serves up delicious home-
cooked food. It has antique beds
and inviting, roaring fires.

LONGLEAT: The Bath Arms ££
Character   **Road Map** A2
*Horningsham, Warminster, Wiltshire,
BA12 7LY*
Tel *01985 844308*
ⓦ batharms.co.uk
This comfortable but quirky pub
has 17 rooms in the heart of the
Longleat estate. It makes a great
base for parties, and is dog- and
family-friendly.

LYMINGTON: East End Arms ££
Pub with rooms   **Road Map** B3
Main Rd, Hampshire, SO41 5SY
Tel *01590 626223*
ⓦ eastendarms.co.uk
There are smart, modern rooms
at this good-value New Forest pub
with a no-nonsense restaurant.
The place is owned by John
Illsley, Dire Straits' bass guitarist.

LYNDHURST: Lime Wood £££
Luxury   **Road Map** B2
Beaulieu Rd, Hampshire, SO43 7FZ
Tel *02380 287177*
ⓦ limewoodhotel.co.uk
An opulent New Forest bolthole
that's glamorous yet informal.
Pamper yourself in the Herb
House Spa or take yoga classes
on the roof garden.

**MALMESBURY: Whatley
Manor** £££
Country House   **Road Map** A1
Easton Grey, Wiltshire, SN16 0RB
Tel *01666 822888*
ⓦ whatleymanor.com
The perfect choice for a hedonistic
weekend away. It has extensive
gardens, a spa, a cinema, and
casual or more formal dining.

**PEWSEY: Red Lion Freehouse &
Troutbeck Guest House** ££
Boutique   **Road Map** A1
East Chisenbury, Wiltshire, SN9 6AQ
Tel *01980 671124*
ⓦ redlionfreehouse.com
Eat in the stylish, low-key pub and
sleep at the guesthouse down the
road. There are five comfortable
rooms with bespoke beds.

PORTSMOUTH: Number Four ££
Boutique   **Road Map** B2
*69 Festing Rd, Southsea, Hampshire,
PO4 0NQ*
Tel *02392 008444*
ⓦ number4hotel.co.uk
This plush designer hotel close to
the sea has smart, stylish rooms
and a high-quality restaurant.

SALISBURY: Howard's House ££
Boutique   **Road Map** A2
Teffont Evias, Wiltshire, SP3 5RJ
Tel *01722 716392*
ⓦ howardshousehotel.co.uk
Great for country pursuits, this
honey-stone house in the Nadder
Valley has gardens and open fires,
which add to the unpretentious
charm of the place.

SOUTHAMPTON: TerraVina ££
Boutique   **Road Map** B2
*174 Woodlands Rd, Woodlands,
Hampshire, SO40 7GL*
Tel *02380 293784*
ⓦ hotelterravina.co.uk
Expect high standards at this
chic hotel. There are handmade
toiletries and rain showers in
every room. There's also a heated
outdoor swimming pool and an
exceptional wine cellar.

DK Choice

TISBURY: The Beckford Arms £
Pub with rooms   **Road Map** A2
Fonthill Gifford, Wiltshire, SP3 6PX
Tel *01747 870385*
ⓦ beckfordarms.com
A welcoming traditional pub
close to historic Stonehenge,
with eight rooms upstairs. A
15-minute stroll away are two
"Splendens Pavilions," luxurious
split-level lodges with their
own sitting rooms and kitchens.
Guests want for nothing, with
a range of amenities from iPod
docks and woolly-covered hot-
water bottles to outstandingly
delicious pub food.

TOLLARD ROYAL: King John Inn £
Boutique   **Road Map** A2
Tollard Royal, Wiltshire, SP5 5PS
Tel *01725 516207*
ⓦ kingjohninn.co.uk
This wonderful Victorian inn
has an open-plan ground floor,
a lovely tiered garden, and
comfortable rooms.

VENTNOR: Hillside ££
Boutique   **Road Map** B3
*151 Mitchell Ave, Isle of Wight,
PO38 1DR*
Tel *01983 852271*
ⓦ hillsideventnor.co.uk
An all-white Scandi-inspired
guesthouse. Rooms boast

designer furniture and abstract art. There's a great dining room with a daily changing menu.

WINCHESTER: The Old Vine ££
Character   **Road Map** B2
8 Great Minster St, Hampshire, SO23 9HA
Tel *01962 854616*
W oldvinewinchester.com
This Grade II-listed 18th-century inn is a stone's throw from the cathedral. There's a beamed bar, six antique-filled rooms and a family-friendly apartment.

YARMOUTH: The George ££
Rooms with a view   **Road Map** B3
Quay St, Isle of Wight, PO41 0PE
Tel *01983 760331*
W thegeorge.co.uk
A 1670s seafront house. Ask for one of the Prestige rooms, which each have an iroko-wood terrace from which to enjoy the view.

Dorset and Somerset

ABBOTSBURY: The Abbey House £
B&B   **Road Map** F5
Church St, Dorset, DT3 4JJ
Tel *01305 871330*
W theabbeyhouse.co.uk
This small and friendly B&B has pretty, traditional rooms (including one suite) and a picturesque garden. No children under 12.

BATH: Grays ££
Boutique   **Road Map** F3
9 Upper Oldfield Park, Somerset, BA2 3JX
Tel *01225 403020*
W graysbath.co.uk
Away from the bustle, this Victorian villa is a quietly sophisticated B&B, with superb bed linen, fluffy towels and delicious breakfasts served in an airy sunroom.

DK Choice

BATH: The Royal Crescent £££
Luxury   **Road Map** F3
16 Royal Crescent, Somerset, BA1 2LS
Tel *01225 823333*
W royalcrescent.co.uk
A sumptuous Relais & Châteaux hotel, this occupies a historic house in the city's most iconic terrace. Inside, there are high-ceilinged rooms, an impressive spa, lovely walled gardens, a fashionable bar and a gourmet restaurant. Step into the very best of the Georgian era while enjoying the outstanding modern amenities.

BOURNEMOUTH: Urban Beach ££
Boutique   **Road Map** A3
23 Argyll Rd, Dorset, BH5 1EB
Tel *01202 301509*
W urbanbeach.co.uk
Family-friendly accommodation with a lively bistro. It is close to the beach, and offers free membership of a local health club to guests.

BRIDPORT: The Seaside Boarding House ££
Boutique   **Road Map** E5
Cliff Rd, Burton Bradstock, Dorset, DT6 4RB
Tel *01308 897205*
W theseasideboardinghouse.com
This grown-up retreat is a newer version of an old-fashioned seaside boarding house. It boasts magnificent views of the Channel.

BRISTOL: Brooks Guesthouse £
B&B   **Road Map** F3
St Nicholas St, BS1 1UB
Tel *01179 300066*
W brooksguesthousebristol.com
This bright B&B behind St Nicholas market is a real find. Guests have the option of staying in pretty rooms or in one of the two rooftop retro caravans.

BRISTOL: Hotel du Vin ££
Boutique   **Road Map** F3
The Sugar House, Narrow Lewins Mead, BS1 2NU
Tel *01174 032979*
W hotelduvin.com/bristol
A classy hotel in a restored 18th-century sugar warehouse, with a bar, a popular brasserie and romantic, modern rooms.

BRUTON: At the Chapel ££
Boutique   **Road Map** F4
High St, Somerset, BA10 0AE
Tel *01749 814070*
W atthechapel.co.uk
Eight rooms are available in this former chapel. The all-day restaurant serves freshly made dishes from an open kitchen.

LYME REGIS: Hix Townhouse ££
B&B   **Road Map** E5
1 Pound St, Dorset, DT7 3HZ
Tel *01297 442499*
W hixrestaurants.co.uk
This boutique B&B has luxurious touches and breakfast hampers filled with delicious local produce.

LYME REGIS: Hotel Alexandra ££
Boutique   **Road Map** E5
Pound St, Dorset, DT7 3HT
Tel *01297 442010*
W hotelalexandra.co.uk
Enjoy lovely views of the beach and the Cobb *(see p117)* at this hotel. Two self-catering family cottages are also available.

MELLS: Talbot Inn £
Pub with rooms   **Road Map** F4
Selwood St, Somerset, BA11 3PN
Tel *01373 812254*
W talbotinn.com
A younger sister of the Beckford Arms in Tisbury, this hotel is set in a stone building with a cobbled courtyard. Expect a series of snug dining areas and attractive rooms.

STUDLAND: The Pig on the Beach ££
Boutique   **Road Map** A3
Manor House, Manor Rd, Dorset, BH19 3AU
Tel *01929 450288*
W thepighotel.com
Another Pig hotel, this fairy-tale house bristles with turrets and chimneys. Highlights here include the conservatory restaurant and a kitchen garden. The bedrooms are delightfully eccentric and each comes with a bucket and spade.

TAUNTON: Langford Fivehead ££
Historic   **Road Map** E4
Lower Swell, Fivehead, Somerset, TA3 6PH
Tel *01460 282020*
W langfordfivehead.co.uk
This fabulous 15th-century manor, furnished with fine antiques, is home to a first-rate restaurant with rooms, which is open for dinner from Tuesday to Saturday. No children under 12.

YEOVIL: Little Barwick House ££
Boutique   **Road Map** F4
Barwick, Somerset, BA22 9TD
Tel *01935 423902*
W littlebarwick.co.uk
Set in a white-painted early 18th-century house, this hotel is unpretentious and smoothly run. It has an outstanding restaurant and quiet, comfortable rooms.

The lovely Brinsley Sheridan drawing room at the Royal Crescent in Bath

For more information on types of hotels *see pages 172–3*

Devon

BARNSTAPLE: Broomhill Art Hotel £
Boutique   Road Map C4
Muddiford Rd, EX31 4EX
Tel *01271 850262*
W broomhillart.co.uk
This hotel is a haven in a superb modern sculpture park. From Wednesday to Saturday rates include dinner as well as breakfast.

DK Choice

BIGBURY-ON-SEA: Burgh Island £££
Luxury   Road Map D6
TQ7 4BG
Tel *01548 810514*
W burghisland.com
Accessible on foot at low tide and otherwise only by water tractor, this peaceful, faithfully restored Art Deco hotel is set on its own private island. It was a favourite of Agatha Christie, who set two novels here, and it now stages popular murder-mystery parties, with guests wearing 1930s-style costumes.

CHAGFORD: Gidleigh Park £££
Country House   Road Map D5
Newton Abbot, TQ13 8HH
Tel *01647 432367*
W gidleigh.co.uk
This lovely half-timbered hotel is famed for fine dining and features luxurious interiors and beautiful grounds. Spa suites are available.

DARTMOOR: Bovey Castle £££
Luxury   Road Map D5
North Bovey, TQ13 8RE
Tel *01647 445000*
W boveycastle.com
A lavishly furnished castle hotel with a golf course, spa and some self-catering cottages. Watch out for midweek bargains.

DARTMOUTH: Nonsuch House ££
B&B   Road Map D6
Church Hill, Kingswear, TQ6 0BX
Tel *01803 752829*
W hoteldartmouth.co.uk
This place has four bedrooms, a warm sitting room and a sunny breakfast space with splendid views. The dedicated owners are helpful and knowledgable.

HONITON: The Pig at Combe ££
Boutique   Road Map E5
Gittisham, EX14 3AD
Tel *01404 540400*
W thepighotel.com
The newest – and arguably the most glamorous – Pig hotel. Set in a splendid Elizabethan manor, it

Inviting drawing room with oversized sofas and a fireplace at the Pig at Combe, Honiton

boasts a relaxed, wood-panelled restaurant and spacious rooms with far-reaching views.

LIFTON: The Arundell Arms ££
Character   Road Map C5
1 Fore St, PL16 0AA
Tel *01566 784666*
W arundellarms.com
This welcoming hotel is ideal for fishing and walking holidays. A selection of 25 comfortable bedrooms, decorated in country-house style, and self-catering cottages is available.

MILTON ABBOT: Hotel Endsleigh £££
Luxury   Road Map C5
PL19 0PQ
Tel *01822 870000*
W hotelendsleigh.com
This former hunting and fishing lodge, with country-chic interiors, is set in Repton-designed gardens. The hotel has two gorgeous new stable suites and is welcoming of children and younger guests.

SALCOMBE: South Sands £££
Rooms with a view   Road Map D6
Bolt Head, TQ8 8LL
Tel *01548 845900*
W southsands.com
A boutique hotel on the water's edge with fine views of the estuary. There are 22 beautifully decorated bedrooms, each named after sailing boats. It is very well placed for exploring South Devon.

TAVISTOCK: Horn of Plenty ££
Rooms with a view   Road Map C5
Gulworthy, PL19 8JD
Tel *01822 832528*
W thehornofplenty.co.uk
Picture windows make the most of spectacular views at this peaceful country-house hotel set in lovely gardens. It offers a combination of classic and glossy modern rooms.

TORQUAY: Orestone Manor ££
Country House   Road Map D5
Rock House Lane, Maidencombe, TQ1 4SX
Tel *01803 897511*
W orestonemanor.com
There are vintage-style bedrooms at this family-run hotel with an award-winning restaurant.

Cornwall

BOSCASTLE: The Old Rectory £
Historic   Road Map B5
St Juliot, PL35 0BT
Tel *01840 250225*
W stjuliot.com
A Victorian house where famous writer Thomas Hardy once stayed. There are glorious gardens, and breakfast is made with locally sourced produce, including eggs from their own free-range hens.

BUDE: The Beach at Bude ££
Boutique   Road Map C5
Summerleaze Crescent, EX23 8HJ
Tel *01288 389800*
W thebeachatbude.co.uk
The last word in seaside chic. Rooms are beautifully decorated in New England style, and there's also an uber cool bar.

DK Choice

CAMELFORD: Belle Tents £££
Camping   Road Map B5
Owl's Gate, Davidstow, PL32 9XY
Tel *01840 261556*
W belletentscamping.co.uk
This cluster of candy-coloured luxury tents in a private dell near Tintagel is great for a family holiday with a twist. The tents have beds and kitchen areas, and there is a fire pit and shared bar tent for the evening. A good base for exploring Bodmin Moor.

FOWEY: Fowey Hall ££
Country House **Road Map** B6
Hanson Dr, PL23 1ET
Tel *01726 833866*
W foweyhallhotel.co.uk
An excellent hotel in a fine-looking
country house that was the original
model for Toad Hall in Kenneth
Grahame's *The Wind in the Willows*.

FOWEY: The Old Ferry Inn ££
Rooms with a view **Road Map** B6
Bodinnick, PL23 1LX
Tel *01726 870237*
W oldferryinn.co.uk
A traditional 17th-century inn
at the Bodinnick and Fowey
ferry crossing. Expect a cheerful
welcome and delicious hearty
meals in the restaurant.

FOWEY: The Old Quay House ££
Rooms with a view **Road Map** B6
28 Fore St, PL23 1AQ
Tel *01726 833302*
W theoldquayhouse.com
This modern boutique hotel
is in a Victorian building full of
character. It boasts a fantastic
location overlooking the estuary,
with a sunny terrace where guests
can enjoy the view *(see p190)*.

MAWGAN PORTH: Bedruthan ££
Rooms with a view **Road Map** B5
Trenance, TR8 4BU
Tel *01637 861200*
W bedruthan.com
A bright and colourful hotel
with a beach and superb family
facilities. There are two pools, a spa
and a typically Cornish restaurant.

**MAWGAN PORTH:
The Scarlet** £££
Luxury **Road Map** B5
Trenance, TR8 4DQ
Tel *01637 861800*
W scarlethotel.co.uk
The UK's first five-star eco-hotel.
Expect super-luxury rooms and
relax in the Ayurvedic spa, which
offers baths and seaweed hot
tubs. It is strictly for adults only.

**MOUSEHOLE: The Old
Coastguard** £££
Rooms with a view **Road Map** A6
The Parade, TR19 6PR
Tel *01736 731222* **Closed** *Jan*
W oldcoastguardhotel.co.uk
Set in a charming fishing village,
this place has 14 traditionally
furnished rooms with Roberts
radios and beautiful sea views.

MULLION: Polurrian Bay ££
Boutique **Road Map** B6
Polurrian Rd, TR12 7EN
Tel *01326 240421*
W polurrianhotel.com
This family-friendly clifftop hotel
has it all: a crèche, spa, cinema

room, tennis court, indoor and
outdoor pools and, above all,
spectacular views.

NEWQUAY: Watergate Bay £££
Boutique **Road Map** B5
Watergate Bay, TR8 4AA
Tel *01637 860543*
W watergatebay.co.uk
This lavish hotel is set on a terrific
surf beach, perfect for an active
holiday with plenty of good food.

**PADSTOW: The Seafood
Restaurant** ££
Boutique **Road Map** B5
Riverside, PL28 8BY
Tel *01841 532700*
W rickstein.com/stay
Sixteen sophisticated rooms are
available above Rick Stein's
flagship restaurant *(see p191)*, a
couple with stunning roof terraces.
En suites come with fluffy towels
and Molton Brown toiletries.

**PADSTOW: Padstow
Townhouse** £££
Boutique **Road Map** B5
16–18 High St, PL28 8BB
Tel *01841 550950*
W paul-ainsworth.co.uk/padstow-
townhouse
An elegant guesthouse owned
by Michelin-starred culinary genius
Paul Ainsworth. There are six
distinctive suites and a generously
stocked honesty pantry, in case
you wake up hungry.

PENZANCE: Artist Residence ££
B&B **Road Map** A6
20 Chapel St, TR18 4AW
Tel *01736 365664*
W artistresidencecornwall.co.uk
This fun guesthouse is set near the
seafront in a Georgian mansion
with bold art on the walls.

PORTSCATHO: Driftwood £££
Rooms with a view **Road Map** B6
Rosevine, TR2 5EW
Tel *01872 580644*
W driftwoodhotel.co.uk
An unpretentious blue clapboard
house with a Michelin-starred

restaurant, beautiful grounds
(including a wildflower garden)
and a private beach.

ROCK: St Enodoc ££
Boutique **Road Map** B5
Cornwall, PL27 6LA
Tel *01208 863394*
W enodoc-hotel.co.uk
The emphasis is on comfort,
design and great food at this
stylish seaside hotel. Stunning
rooms and a fine restaurant
on the terrace.

ST IVES: Headland House ££
B&B **Road Map** A6
Headland Rd, Carbis Bay, TR26 2NS
Tel *01736 796647*
W headlandhousehotel.co.uk
Luxurious rooms with excellent
super-king-size beds and crisp bed
linen in an Edwardian house. The
afternoon cream teas are delicious.

ST MAWES: Hotel Tresanton £££
Luxury **Road Map** B6
27 Lower Castle Rd, TR2 5DR
Tel *01326 270055*
W tresanton.com
An effortlessly glamorous hotel
with impeccable service. Thirty
coastal-chic rooms plus two
cottages. It is in a class of its own.

TREBETHERICK: St Moritz ££
Boutique **Road Map** B5
Wadebridge, PL27 6SD
Tel *01208 862242*
W stmoritzhotel.co.uk
This smart, contemporary hotel
has excellent amenities and
a range of accommodation,
including penthouse apartments
and child-friendly garden villas.

ZENNOR: The Gurnard's Head ££
Boutique **Road Map** A6
St Ives, TR26 3DE
Tel *01736 796928*
W gurnardshead.co.uk
A gastro-pub with rooms in a
wild and picturesque spot. The
popular "Sunday Sleepover"
includes lunch, dinner and
breakfast on Monday.

Lounge chairs on the private sea-facing terrace at Driftwood, in the village of Portscatho

For more information on types of hotels *see pages 172–3*

WHERE TO EAT AND DRINK

England has a flourishing restaurant scene, particularly along the South Coast, which is home to a number of inspirational celebrity chefs and cookery writers, from Hugh Fearnley-Whittingstall in Dorset to Rick Stein in Cornwall. Food stalls, beach shacks, gastro-pubs and Michelin-starred restaurants make eating out an exciting prospect. Even at the simplest places, you can find fresh, seasonal produce prepared with a contemporary approach, inspired by international cuisines. Afternoon tea, a classic English tradition, is still popular, especially in the West Country, which is renowned for its cream teas. It is possible to eat well on any budget in larger towns and cities, where you will find places that serve food all day. Pub fare has perhaps undergone the greatest transformation, with good-quality food found in all kinds of establishments, particularly gastro-pubs. The restaurant listings in this guide have been carefully chosen and feature some of the very best places to eat and drink.

A selection of fresh, tempting salads on display at Ottolenghi, London

Cafés, brasseries and bars often stay open all day, serving coffee, snacks and simple dishes, along with a selection of wines and beers (see p183). Alcoholic drinks, however, may only be available at certain times. The atmosphere is usually young and urban, with decor to match.

Destination restaurants serve excellent food. They usually also offer a handful of bedrooms. These establishments tend to be expensive and are generally located out of town.

On the Menu

In London, you can sample a variety of cuisines, from the exotic – Ethiopian, Caribbean and Hawaiian – to the more usual – Mediterranean, Spanish, Mexican, Asian and Indian. You will also find an exciting range of culinary styles in other cosmopolitan southern English cities, such as Brighton and Bristol. In traditional country towns, the choices are usually more limited. However, inspired cooking can be found in the countryside at award-winning gastro-pubs, where you can expect beautifully presented food in a casual environment. It's always worth making a special trip to rural destination restaurants, such as Whatley Manor (see p176) and Gidleigh Park (see p178).

One of the common culinary terms used by various restaurants to describe their cuisine is "Modern European", which introduces international elements to traditional dishes, creating unusual but flavourful combinations, such as sea bass with ginger and mushrooms or crab linguine with chilli and lime. There is also "Modern British" cooking, which adopts a light, contemporary approach, in contrast to the hearty stews and pies that comprise "Traditional British" cookery. The best cooking employs fresh, high-quality, seasonal ingredients, cooked simply but creatively.

Places to Eat

Eateries across southern England are extremely varied, with brasseries, bistros, wine bars, pubs, tearooms, tapas bars and beach shacks competing with more conventional cafés and restaurants. Some of the finest restaurants are located in upscale hotels, which usually welcome non-residents. Dress codes can be stricter in these establishments and some restaurants may expect men to wear a jacket and tie.

Decadent champagne afternoon tea at the Royal Crescent in Bath

Vegetarian Food

Most restaurants offer a few vegetarian options on their menus, and there are an increasing number of places that only serve vegetarian food, particularly in London, Brighton, Bristol and Bath. Those who want a wider choice could seek out South Indian, Asian and other restaurants with a tradition of vegetarian cuisine.

Alcohol

Since 2003, England's licensing laws concerning the sale of alcohol have been relaxed, with some establishments extending their opening hours, especially on Friday and Saturday nights. Some restaurants only serve alcohol with food, and some unlicensed restaurants operate a "Bring Your Own" policy, when a corkage fee may be charged. It is illegal to sell alcohol to under-18s.

Fast-Food and Chain Restaurants

Fast food usually costs under £10. In addition to the ubiquitous fish and chip shops, there are many fast-food chains, including the more upmarket Pizza Express and Zizzi, the family-friendly ASK, Giraffe and Byron, as well as quick stops such as Pret A Manger, YO! Sushi and West Cornwall Pasty Co. Budget cafés, nicknamed "greasy spoons", serve inexpensive food – often endless variations of the classic English breakfast fry-up (see p182).

Prices and Service

All restaurants are required by law to display their prices clearly. These include Value Added Tax (VAT), currently at 20 per cent. Service and cover charges (if any) should be specified.

Set menus are often offered at lunchtime or in the early evening, and where available they offer better value than à la carte dishes.

Wine and extras, such as coffee or bottled water, can be expensive. A service charge (usually 10–15 per cent) is often added to the bill. You are entitled to subtract it if you feel that the service has been poor. If no service charge has been added and the service has been good, you are expected to add a 10–12 per cent tip to the bill. Most restaurants accept credit cards.

Children

English restaurants are generally welcoming to children. Some places actively encourage families, at least during the day and early evening. Formal restaurants tend to have a more adult ambience at dinnertime, and some impose age limits. If you want to take young children to a restaurant, it's advisable to check ahead.

Italian, Spanish, Indian and fast-food restaurants nearly always welcome children and sometimes provide special menus or high chairs for them. Even traditional English pubs generally accommodate families and may provide special rooms or play areas.

Disabled Access

Restaurant facilities for disabled visitors are slowly improving. Modern premises usually cater for mobility problems, but it is always best to check in advance if you have special needs. The **Open Britain** website (see p202) provides detailed information on accessible cafés and restaurants.

A plate of fresh Whitstable oysters with lemon

Picnics and Eating Outside

Eating outside is quite popular, especially during summer. Most pubs have beer gardens, and many restaurants and cafés offer alfresco dining.

The picturesque landscape of southern England features plenty of stunning picnic spots. Most towns have good delicatessens and bakeries where you can collect provisions. Look out for street or farmers' markets, or rural farm shops, to pick up fresh fruit and local cheeses. Pret A Manger, Marks & Spencer and most supermarkets sell excellent pre-packed sandwiches and snacks, or your hotel may be able to provide a packed lunch; ask at reception the night before.

Recommended Restaurants

The restaurants on the following pages have been chosen across a wide price range for their atmosphere, location and good food. They include no-frills seafood shacks, Japanese sushi places, Indian curry houses, cafés, Michelin-starred restaurants in beautiful country-house hotels and gastro-pubs. The very best places have been highlighted as a DK Choice. Each of these has one or more exceptional features, such as a celebrity chef, sensational food, good-value menus, family-friendly facilities, a remarkable or unusual location, or a distinctive atmosphere.

A branch of the popular sandwich chain Pret A Manger in London

The Flavours of England's South Coast

A food revolution has occurred in England in recent years, with a growing emphasis on locally grown produce. In the South, farmers' markets are thriving and hundreds of artisan growers specialize in all kinds of produce. The region's rich soil produces outstanding meat and dairy products as well as vegetables, fruit and cereals. With miles of coastline, fish and seafood always feature strongly. Although the cooked breakfast and other traditional English dishes are still popular in southern England, an exciting range of cuisine is now on offer.

The Dorset Naga chilli pepper

Stack of cheddar cheese roundels on display at the Bath & West Show, Somerset

Meat and Dairy

The moorlands of the southwest and the marshes of Kent and East Sussex provide excellent grazing for sheep. Lamb from the South Downs, Exmoor and Dartmoor, and Salt Marsh lamb from Romney, are all of superb quality and full of flavour. The lush countryside and rolling hills of the South are also ideal for grazing cows and keeping pigs, and pork from Hampshire and Wiltshire is renowned throughout the UK. Rural areas produce fresh game (more plentiful in the autumn and winter months).

Dairy cattle fare best in the southwest, the warmest part of the country. Somerset, Dorset, Devon and Cornwall all produce excellent cheeses, many hand-made by pioneering artisan cheese-makers. Devon and Cornwall are also well known for clotted cream, which is the basis of their famous cream teas when combined with scones and jam.

Fish and Seafood

Kent is famous for Whitstable oysters and Dover sole, which is also found off the coasts of

Oysters   Prawns   Lobster   Mackerel   Sea bass   Mussels

Selection of fresh fish and seafood typically found in southern English cuisine

South Coast Dishes and Specialities

The surge in popularity of tapas, curry, Asian street food and other world cuisines has sidelined traditional English dishes, but not entirely eclipsed them. Menus across southern England still feature classics such as fish and chips, shepherd's pie (minced lamb topped with mashed potatoes) and fish pie. As the area is famous for growing fruit, puddings made with apples or summer berries are popular; these include apple crumble, summer pudding (soft fruits encased in bread) and Eton mess (meringue, strawberries and cream). Fruit is also used in savoury dishes, such as Cornish mackerel with gooseberries. A "full English breakfast" is a fry-up of sausages, eggs, bacon, tomatoes, mushrooms and bread, sometimes with black pudding. Baked beans and fried potatoes may be included. Typical lunchtime snacks include a "ploughman's lunch" of cheese and pickles with a "doorstop" of bread or, one-time favourite of tin miners, a Cornish pasty (seasoned meat and vegetables in a thick pastry case).

Traditional Cornish pasty

Stargazy pie is a pastry-based Cornish dish with pilchards. The unique feature is the protruding fish heads gazing skyward.

Colourful fresh fruit and vegetable stall selling good-value produce

Sussex and Hampshire. Sea bass, cod, mackerel and bream are fished throughout the year from Kent to Cornwall. The warmer waters of the southwest attract red mullet, and the coasts of Devon and Cornwall are the preferred habitat of shellfish and crustaceans, including mussels and lobster.

Fruit and Vegetables

The South Coast's mild climate is ideal for the cultivation of fruit and vegetables. The county of Kent is known as the "Garden of England" for its glorious apple orchards and fields of hops and soft fruits. Apples also grow well in the fertile countryside of Sussex and Somerset.

A range of vegetables is grown throughout the region. Above average annual hours of sunshine make Isle of Wight tomatoes and garlic the best in the UK. Surprisingly, Dorset is responsible for producing the world's hottest chilli, the fiery Dorset Naga, while Hampshire has been the English centre of watercress cultivation since the 19th century.

What to Drink

Local pubs usually carry a good selection of local beers. There are some 230 breweries and microbreweries in southern England. The principal types of beer are ale (including bitter),

Flagons of scrumpy for sale at a local farm shop in Cornwall

lager and stout, differentiated by their fermentation and the hops and malt used. Almost 300 vineyards, producing red, white, rosé and sparkling wine, are planted along the South Coast. They include Cornwall's celebrated Camel Valley, responsible for an award-winning rosé. West Country cider-makers use sour cider apples and smaller producers sell scrumpy, which is an unfiltered, uncarbonated and particularly strong cider. Kent producers use sweeter dessert apples to make lighter cider. Long a favourite tipple, gin is now produced at nearly 250 English gin distilleries, including many craft gin-makers.

SOUTH COAST CHEESES

Beenleigh Blue Moist, crumbly Devon ewe's-milk cheese with bold green-blue veins.

Cheddar Firm, nutty and from Somerset, with a sting on the finish depending on maturity.

Cornish Yarg Creamy, semi-hard and fresh-tasting cow's-milk cheese with a mouldy nettle rind.

Dorset Blue Vinny Light and crumbly skimmed-milk cheese with fine blue veins.

Golden Cross Soft, raw Sussex goat's-milk cheese, log-shaped and covered in a velvety white rind.

Old Winchester Firm, dry and tasty with a washed rind, nicknamed "Old Smales".

Fish and chips consists of battered, deep-fried white fish and potato chips, traditionally served wrapped in newspaper.

Somerset honeyed pork stew is cooked in a sauce with apple juice and honey, which flavour and tenderize the pork.

Sussex pond pudding contains whole lemons, butter and sugar, which are encased in suet pastry and steamed for several hours.

Where to Eat and Drink

London

Ceviche Soho £
Peruvian **City Map** C3
17 Frith St, W1D 4RG
Tel *020 7292 2040*
Unpretentious *picantería*, serving tapas-style food from the Andes, with fresh ceviches (raw fish cured in citrus juice), meat skewers, salads and irresistible Pisco sours. Booking is advised.

Flat Iron Steak £
Steakhouse **City Map** D3
17–18 Henrietta St, WC2E 8QH
Tel *020 7683 0361*
Done out in wood and bare brick, this flagship restaurant of a small chain specializes in excellent steaks at affordable prices. The cut is the little-known "flat iron", which is juicy, tender and tasty.

On the Bab £
Korean
305 Old St, EC1V 9LA
Tel *020 3019 4212*
The capital's first Korean Anju restaurant serves street food accompanied by *soju* (a drink rather like saké) or exotic cocktails. Don't miss the mouthwatering fried chicken, *yangyum*.

Regency Café £
Traditional British **City Map** D4
17–19 Regency St, SW1P 4BY
Tel *020 7821 6596* **Closed** *Sun*
A no-frills 1950s-style "caff" that has featured in a couple of movie scenes. Opt for the set breakfast or try the heavenly hash browns and eggs Benedict.

Smoking Goat £
Thai **City Map** D3
7 Denmark St, WC2H 8LZ
Tel *none* **Closed** *Sun*
A tiny laid-back restaurant with scrubbed wood and exposed brick interiors. It serves delectable

street food – mostly slow-cooked or barbecued meat and fish. For a special experience, go in a group and pre-order one of the "Feasts".

Soho Joe £
Italian **City Map** C3
22–25 Dean St, W1D 3RY
Tel *07534 134398*
Thin-crust pizzas are the stars of the show at this all-day eatery. Fantastic pasta, burgers and salads are also on the menu.

Talli Joe £
Indian **City Map** D3
152–156 Shaftesbury Av, WC2H 8HL
Tel *020 7836 5400* **Closed** *Sun*
A buzzy bar and restaurant offering a range of cocktails and Indian street tapas with unusual, heady flavours. Don't miss the excellent Konkani seafood curry.

Tokyo Diner £
Japanese **City Map** D3
2 Newport Pl, WC2H 7JJ
Tel *020 7287 8777* **Closed** *Mon*
A modest diner that celebrates Japanese culture, with courteous service and complimentary tea. The authentic menu here includes *katsu* curry, sushi and bento boxes. There is strictly no tipping.

8 Hoxton Square ££
European
8 Hoxton Sq, N1 6NU
Tel *020 7729 4232*
An attractive terrace for alfresco dining, a well-priced wine list and a daily changing menu make this pleasingly understated restaurant a hit in vibrant Hoxton.

Al Duca ££
Italian **City Map** C3
4–5 Duke of York St, SW1Y 6LA
Tel *020 7839 3090* **Closed** *Sun*
Decorated in a simple, modern style, this popular eatery uses fresh ingredients to give classic Italian dishes a modern twist.

Price Guide

Prices are based on a three-course meal for one, with half a bottle of house wine, inclusive of tax and service charges.

£	under £35
££	£35–50
£££	over £50

Chisou ££
Japanese **City Map** C3
4 Princes St, W1B 2LE
Tel *020 7629 3931*
This reasonably priced bistro has a cozy atmosphere, delectable sushi and sashimi, plus an impressive selection of saké.

Clipstone ££
European **City Map** C2
5 Clipstone St, W1W 6BB
Tel *020 7637 0871* **Closed** *Sun*
Enjoy imaginative, attractively presented food, accompanied by pickles and flatbread, in an informal setting. It's a great spot for Saturday brunch.

The Duck & Rice ££
Chinese **City Map** C3
90 Berwick St, W1F 0QB
Tel *020 3327 7888*
Expect delicate and delicious street food paired with Asian cocktails at this imaginatively decorated Chinese gastro-pub.

J Sheekey Atlantic Bar ££
Seafood **City Map** D3
33–35 St Martin's Court, WC2N 4AL
Tel *020 7240 2565*
One of London's finest fish restaurants, this place offers a wonderfully varied menu of responsibly sourced seafood. You can sit at the horseshoe-shaped bar for the signature oysters and champagne or dine on the colourful terrace.

Mildreds ££
Vegetarian **City Map** C3
45 Lexington St, W1F 9AN
Tel *020 7494 1634* **Closed** *Sun*
The inspired organic vegetable dishes here will tempt even the most dedicated carnivores. Try the burritos and risotto cake. You can't book ahead, so arrive early.

Ottolenghi ££
Mediterranean
287 Upper St, N1 2TZ
Tel *020 7288 1454*
A deli-cum-restaurant in a chic yet relaxed designer space, complemented by daringly flavoured food. Highlights include the fabulous salads and pastries. The seating here is mostly at communal tables.

Seating on the lovely canopied terrace at J Sheekey Atlantic Bar, London

City Map *see pages 44–5;* **Road Map** *see inside back cover*

The Palomar ££
Israeli **City Map** C3
34 Rupert St, W1D 6DN
Tel *020 7439 8777*
A small slice of Jerusalem in Soho, this place is so popular that diners have to book months ahead. Try the mouthwatering polenta and something from the raw bar.

Chiltern Firehouse £££
American **City Map** B3
1 Chiltern St, W1U 7PA
Tel *020 7073 7676*
Rub shoulders with the A-List at London's hottest spot. The design makes imaginative use of space in this former fire station, where Portuguese chef Nuno Mendes has created an inspired, ingredient-driven menu.

DK Choice

Clos Maggiore £££
Modern European **City Map** D3
33 King St, WC2E 8JD
Tel *020 7379 9696*
Try for a table in the magical courtyard conservatory with blossom-laden branches. On balmy evenings the roof is opened to the stars, while a fire is lit when it's chilly. French regional food inspires the Modern European cooking. The set pre- and post-theatre menus are reasonably priced.

Dinner by Heston Blumenthal £££
Modern British **City Map** B4
Mandarin Oriental Hyde Park, 66 Knightsbridge, SW1X 7LA
Tel *020 7201 3833*
This famous restaurant showcases the celebrity chef's inspired take on classic cuisine. Be sure to try the signature Meat Fruit starter. The prices are exorbitant, but the experience is unforgettable.

The Ledbury £££
Modern British
127 Ledbury Rd, W11 2AQ
Tel *020 7792 9090*
One of London's most happening restaurants, the Ledbury is headed by the celebrated Australian chef Brett Graham. Expect two-Michelin-starred culinary fireworks, including an innovative vegetarian tasting menu, in stylish surroundings.

Rules £££
Traditional British **City Map** D3
35 Maiden Lane, WC2E 7LB
Tel *020 7836 5314*
Savour robust British food at London's oldest restaurant, established in 1798. With its

Bright, rustic interior of the Goods Shed in Canterbury, Kent

velvet chairs and pictures, it looks the part of a traditional chop-house. Try the steak and kidney pudding or game procured from Rules' own country estate.

Kent and Sussex

ARUNDEL: The Town House ££
European **Road Map** C2
65 High St, West Sussex, BN18 9AJ
Tel *01903 883847*
Set in a Georgian building with a stunning 16th-century Florentine ceiling, this restaurant boasts interesting, well-priced menus featuring local ingredients. There is also a wide-ranging wine list.

BODIAM: The Curlew ££
Modern British **Road Map** E2
Junction Rd, East Sussex, TN32 5UY
Tel *01580 861394* **Closed** Mon
Rooms in a clapboard-clad former coaching inn make a sophisticated yet informal setting for innovative dishes, such as mackerel ceviche and green-tea cake. Recipes are specially adapted for children.

BRIGHTON: Tookta's Café £
Thai **Road Map** D2
30 Spring St, East Sussex, BN1 3EF
Tel *01273 748071* **Closed** Sun
A modest café with charming cross-cultural decoration and a warm ambience. Perfectly spiced, well-presented dishes give traditional Thai cooking a contemporary twist. The restaurant only accepts cash.

BRIGHTON: The Gingerman ££
European **Road Map** D2
21A Norfolk Sq, East Sussex, BN1 2PD
Tel *01273 326688* **Closed** Mon
This small, intimate restaurant is the flagship and original site of Brighton's well-known Ginger group. It is delightfully

unpretentious, both in looks and cuisine. The food is full flavoured and created from fresh, high-quality ingredients.

BRIGHTON: Terre à Terre ££
Vegetarian **Road Map** D2
71 East St, East Sussex, BN1 1HQ
Tel *01273 729051*
An acclaimed restaurant serving refined vegetarian dishes. The flavour combinations will make your taste buds zing. There's a good selection of organic wines and a lovely sun terrace for alfresco dining.

CANTERBURY:
The Goods Shed ££
Traditional British **Road Map** F1
Station Rd West, Kent, CT2 8AN
Tel *01227 459153* **Closed** Mon
A unique all-day rustic restaurant and food hall, this place overlooks a farmers' market and all the tempting produce on display. A wide selection of outstanding local cheeses is also on offer.

CANTERBURY:
Kathton House £££
Modern British **Road Map** F1
6 High St, Sturry, Kent, CT2 0BD
Tel *01227 719999* **Closed** Sun & Mon
An upmarket, smartly decorated modern restaurant, with a menu that focuses on local and seasonal produce. Try the sea bream and scallops, loin fillet of Godmersham venison or rack of Kentish lamb.

CHICHESTER:
Field and Fork ££
Modern British **Road Map** C2
4 Guildhall St, West Sussex, PO19 1NJ
Tel *01243 789915* **Closed** Sun & Mon
If you have tickets for the Festival Theatre, this is the perfect spot for your pre-performance meal. The restaurant has an enticing, original menu, and tables in a smart dining room and a sunny conservatory.

For more information on types of restaurants *see pages 180–81*

CHICHESTER: The Royal Oak ££
Traditional British **Road Map** C2
*Pook Lane, East Lavant, West Sussex,
PO18 0AX*
Tel *01243 527434*
Fresh fish is delivered daily to this
restaurant set in an attractive
Georgian brick-and-flint inn.
There's a romantic beamed dining
room and an extensive wine list.

**CUCKFIELD:
Ockenden Manor** £££
French **Road Map** D2
Ockenden Lane, RH17 5LD
Tel *01444 416111*
This restaurant is located in an
Elizabethan manor with scenic
views of Cuckfield Park. Michelin-
starred chef Stephen Crane
creates classic French dishes with
fresh, locally sourced ingredients.

**DOVER: The Marquis
at Alkham** ££
Modern British **Road Map** F2
*Alkham Valley Rd, Alkham, Kent,
CT15 7DF*
Tel *01304 873410* **Closed** *Mon lunch*
This place is perfectly located for
the cross-Channel ferry. An airy,
stylish restaurant with first-rate
food and attentive service. Treat
yourself to afternoon tea or the
splendid six-course tasting menu.

**EASTBOURNE: La Locanda
del Duca** £
Italian **Road Map** D2
*26 Cornfield Terrace, East Sussex,
BN21 4NS*
Tel *01323 737177* **Closed** *25 &
26 Dec*
Sample a variety of classic Italian
dishes, including grilled *fegato*
(calves' liver), risotto and tiramisu,
and a great selection of wines. The
relaxed atmosphere makes this a
brilliant choice for family outings.

HASTINGS: Café Maroc £
Moroccan **Road Map** E2
37 High St, East Sussex, TN34 3ER
Tel *07500 774017* **Closed** *lunch;
Mon & Tue dinner*
Bring your own wine to this
small eatery offering authentic
Moroccan cuisine. From the short
menu, the melt-in-the-mouth
tagines and lemon-infused
chicken are the real standouts.

MARGATE: The Ambrette ££
Indian **Road Map** F1
44 King St, Kent, CT9 1QE
Tel *01843 231504*
This place serves adventurous
dishes, bursting with flavours
inspired by cuisines from France,
India and the rest of Asia. Local
ingredients include foraged seaweed, Kentish lamb and game.
The service is excellent.

Scrumptious roast chicken cassoulet at
the Royal Oak in Chichester, Sussex

MIDHURST: The Spread Eagle ££
Gastro-pub **Road Map** C2
South St, GU29 9NH
Tel *01730 816911*
Flavours of Sussex are the focus
at this 15th-century coaching
inn. There's a cozy beamed
dining room and a cool gin bar.

**PETWORTH: The Halfway
Bridge** ££
Gastro-pub **Road Map** C2
Lodsworth, West Sussex, GU28 9BP
Tel *01798 861281*
Superbly executed pub classics
and more sophisticated dishes
are served in an impeccably
restored pub. Try the open
sandwiches at lunchtime.

ROCHESTER: Topes ££
Modern British **Road Map** E1
60 High St, Kent, ME1 1JY
Tel *01634 845270* **Closed** *Tue*
Order first-rate food, made
with fresh seasonal produce,
from a variety of menus at this
charming restaurant housed in
a 15th-century building. Don't
miss the Sunday roasts.

**ROYAL TUNBRIDGE WELLS:
Thackeray's** £££
French **Road Map** D2
85 London Rd, Kent, TN1 1EA
Tel *01892 511921* **Closed** *Sun dinner*
A Michelin-starred restaurant
with an intelligent menu featuring
modern dishes that explode with
flavour. There are tables outside
on a pretty, canopied terrace.

RYE: The George Grill ££
Grill **Road Map** E2
98 High St, East Sussex, TN31 7JT
Tel *01797 222114*
This lively split-level restaurant
has an open kitchen with a
wood-charcoal grill. The seafood
is fresh from Rye Harbour, and
the local meat is expertly grilled.

WARTLING: The Lamb Inn ££
Gastro-pub **Road Map** D2
Hailsham, East Sussex, BN27 1RY
Tel *01323 832116* **Closed** *Sun dinner*
A lovely, intimate inn that's filled
with quirky antiques. The monthly
changing menus use local,
seasonal and organic produce.

WHITSTABLE: The Sportsman £££
Gastro-pub **Road Map** F1
Faversham Rd, Seasalter, Kent, CT5 4BP
Tel *01227 273370* **Closed** *Sun
dinner; Mon*
Try the Whitstable oysters,
served on a bed of sea shells,
or the daily tasting menu at this
Michelin-starred gastro-pub. It's
pricey but full of happy surprises.

Hampshire and
Salisbury Plain

AVEBURY: Circles Café £
Café **Road Map** A1
High St, Wiltshire, SN8 1RF
Tel *01672 539250*
A National Trust café, ideal for a
warming cup of tea and some
home-made cake after a trip to
the stones. Freshly prepared hot
dishes are also available. The café
also provides alfresco dining.

**BEMBRIDGE: The Pilot
Boat Inn** £
Pub **Road Map** B3
Station Rd, Isle of Wight, PO35 5NN
Tel *01983 872077*
Situated on the harbour's edge,
this inn resembles a boat, and
serves well-executed classic pub
fare. There's a log fire in winter
and two summer dining terraces.

**BRADFORD-ON-AVON:
Fat Fowl and the Roost** ££
Mediterranean **Road Map** F3
Silver St, Wiltshire, BA15 1JX
Tel *01225 863111* **Closed** *Sun dinner*
A friendly café by day and an
upmarket restaurant by night,
with pared-down neutral decor.

The tapas here are fantastic. There is also a special menu and a play area for kids.

CHIPPENHAM: Lucknam Park £££
Modern European   **Road Map** A1
Colerne, Wiltshire, SN14 8AZ
Tel *01225 742777*   **Closed** *Tue–Sat lunch*
Chef Hywel Jones serves diners outstanding Michelin-starred cuisine at this stunning 17th-century country-house hotel. If you prefer something less formal than the Park Restaurant, opt for the trendy Brasserie.

DK Choice

COWES: The Little Gloster £££
European   **Road Map** B2
31 Marsh Rd, Isle of Wight, PO31 8JQ
Tel *01983 298776*   **Closed** *Sun dinner; Mon; winter: Tue & Wed*
A family-run restaurant, the Little Gloster has spectacular views. The dining room is pared-back, contemporary and Scandinavian in style. The food is equally unfussy. Try the mouthwatering Nordic gravlax (raw salmon cured with salt, sugar and dill), served with crème fraîche, caviar and a shot of ice-cold Aquavit.

EMSWORTH: 36 on the Quay £££
Modern British   **Road Map** A1
47 South St, Hampshire, PO10 7EG
Tel *01243 375592*   **Closed** *Sun & Mon; two weeks Jan; one week May; one week Oct*
Overlooking the picturesque bay in the fishing village of Emsworth, this Michelin-starred restaurant serves fresh, healthy, creatively prepared food. The dining room has soothing decor, and the service is warm and professional.

LACOCK: The Bell £
Pub   **Road Map** A1
The Wharf, Bowden Hill, Wiltshire, SN15 2PJ
Tel *01249 730308*
An endearingly old-fashioned, award-winning pub on the outskirts of historic Lacock. The place specializes in British pub classics and comfort food, with a good selection of real ales.

LITTLE BEDWYN: The Harrow £££
Modern British   **Road Map** A1
Marlborough, Wiltshire, SN8 3JP
Tel *01672 870871*   **Closed** *Sun–Tue*
A sophisticated country restaurant, the Harrow is worthy of a detour. It is a paradise for oenophiles, with a 60-page wine list, and

for gourmets, with exceptional, Michelin-starred food. Set menus change daily to reflect the seasonal ingredients available.

LYMINGTON: The Mill at Gordleton £££
Modern British   **Road Map** B3
Silver St, Hordle, Hampshire, SO41 6DJ
Tel *01590 682219*
A superb restaurant set in a 400-year-old former water mill in the heart of the New Forest. You can eat in the riverside dining room or on the glorious wisteria-covered terrace. The set and children's menus are excellent.

LYNDHURST: Hartnett, Holder & Co. £££
Italian   **Road Map** B2
Beaulieu Rd, Hampshire, SO43 7FZ
Tel *02380 287177*
Expect remarkable, down-to-earth cooking from the partnership of celebrity chef Angela Hartnett and Lime Wood's *(see p176)* Luke Holder. The food is smoked in their own smokehouse, and served in a relaxed, stylish setting.

MALMESBURY: The Rectory ££
Modern British   **Road Map** A1
Crudwell, Wiltshire, SN16 9EP
Tel *01666 577194*   **Closed** *Mon–Sat lunch*
The Slow Food movement drives the menu at this refined restaurant. Eat in the beautiful panelled dining room or outside around a baptism pool once used by the church next door.

MALMESBURY: Whatley Manor £££
International   **Road Map** A1
Easton Grey, Wiltshire, SN16 0RB
Tel *01666 822888*   **Closed** *lunch; Mon & Tue dinner*
The two-Michelin-starred Dining Room is refreshingly devoid of ostentation. Six-course tasting menus are imaginative and seasonal. The informal brasserie, Le Mazot, has a pretty terrace.

MILFORD-ON-SEA: La Perle ££
Modern British   **Road Map** B3
60 High St, Hampshire, SO41 0QD
Tel *01590 643557*   **Closed** *Tue lunch & Sun dinner; Mon*
Rooted in the New Forest and its produce, La Perle's chef-patron, Sam Hughes, was a protégé of Raymond Blanc. His buzz words are "seasonal", "local" and "ethical". There's live jazz every Sunday.

PORTSMOUTH: Spice Merchants £
Indian   **Road Map** B2
44 Osborne Rd, Southsea, Hampshire, PO5 3LT
Tel *02392 828900*   **Closed** *lunch*
A small convivial restaurant featuring a menu of authentic recipes from all over India. Try one of the signature seafood dishes, such as Bengal prawns or monkfish in orange sauce. Eat in or take away.

PORTSMOUTH: Bistro Montparnasse £££
Modern European   **Road Map** B2
103 Palmerston Rd, Southsea, Hampshire, PO5 3PS
Tel *02392 816754*   **Closed** *lunch; Sun & Mon*
A good relationship with local suppliers lies at the heart of this bistro – one of Portsmouth's standout restaurants. Dine from a regularly changing menu in a relaxed, friendly environment.

SALISBURY: Hox Brasserie £
Indian   **Road Map** A2
155 Fisherton St, Wiltshire, SP2 7RP
Tel *01722 341600*
Set in an elegant dining room, Hox Brasserie specializes in South Indian cuisine. The restaurant also serves other traditional dishes such as tandoori chicken in fenugreek sauce, Rajasthani lamb curry braised with Kashmiri chilli and garlic, and tiger prawns cooked in a Goan sweet-and-sour sauce.

Inviting dining room at the Little Gloster in Cowes, Isle of Wight

For more information on types of restaurants *see pages 180–81*

SALISBURY: Charter 1227 ££
Modern British **Road Map** A2
6–7 Ox Row, The Market Pl, Wiltshire, SP1 1EU
Tel *01722 333118* **Closed** *Sun & Mon*
This stylish, top-rated restaurant overlooks Salisbury's vibrant marketplace and serves delicious, European-influenced British fare, such as pan-fried scallops with suckling pig, and pan-roasted lamb with ratatouille.

WINCHESTER: Chesil Rectory ££
Modern British **Road Map** B2
1 Chesil St, Hampshire, SO23 0HU
Tel *01962 851555*
Classic dishes are given a fresh, contemporary twist at Chesil Rectory. Housed in a charming 600-year-old building, the restaurant has glossy oak beams, ancient doorways and open fireplaces.

WINCHESTER: Kyoto Kitchen ££
Japanese **Road Map** B2
70 Parchment St, Hampshire, SO23 8AT
Tel *01962 890895*
Specializing in sushi and sashimi, this restaurant provides a great introduction to beautifully presented Japanese cuisine. Try the Winchester Roll, which substitutes wasabi leaf for seaweed. The service is good.

WINCHESTER: Old Vine ££
Pub **Road Map** B2
8 Great Minster St, Hampshire, SO23 9HA
Tel *01962 854616*
Conveniently placed if you're visiting Winchester Cathedral, this 18th-century inn is airy by day and cozy by night. Specialities range from hearty pub fare to tasty bistro classics, all made with fresh, local produce.

Log fires in the dining area at Chesil Rectory in Winchester, Hampshire

Dorset and Somerset

BATH: Acorn Vegetarian Kitchen ££
Vegetarian **Road Map** F3
2 North Parade Passage, Somerset, BA1 1NX
Tel *01225 446059*
All ingredients come from local suppliers and are prepared with skill at this lovely restaurant. Try the innovative lunchtime tasting plates, the popular Sunday roasts or the fruity cocktails.

BATH: The Circus ££
Modern European **Road Map** F3
34 Brock St, Somerset, BA1 2LN
Tel *01225 466020* **Closed** *Sun*
A stunning Georgian building houses this lively café-restaurant. The original menu includes wild boar meatballs, goat curry and "Whim Wham" Regency trifle.

BATH: Clayton's Kitchen ££
Modern British **Road Map** F3
The Porter, 15A George St, Somerset, BA1 2EN
Tel *01225 585100*
A low-key, split-level restaurant serving excellent, well-presented food. Staff are accommodating and welcome children.

BOURNEMOUTH: Chez Fred £
Seafood **Road Map** A3
10 Seamoor Rd, Westbourne, Hampshire, BH4 9AN
Tel *01202 761023* **Closed** *Sun lunch*
The fish and chips served here are considered to be the best in the country. High-quality, sustainably sourced fish is fried in a special-recipe batter and served with proper thick-cut chips. Eat in the restaurant or take away.

BOURNEMOUTH: Plates & Co. ££
Modern British **Road Map** A3
16 Landseer Rd, Hampshire, BH4 9EH
Tel *01202 765696*
Set in a beautiful 18th-century church, with vast stained-glass windows and oak panelling, this restaurant serves innovative reinterpretations of British classics as well as good roasts.

BRIDPORT: Hive Beach Café ££
Seafood **Road Map** E5
Beach Rd, Burton Bradstock, Dorset, DT6 4RF
Tel *01308 897070* **Closed** *Sun & Mon dinner; winter: dinner*
A popular, breezy café with scenic views of the Jurassic Coast and Lyme Bay. The simple, delicious food ranges from a modest crab sandwich to the signature seafood platter, with excellent West Country ice cream to finish.

BRISTOL: Maitreya Social £
Vegetarian **Road Map** F3
89 St Mark's Rd, Easton, BS5 6HY
Tel *01179 510100* **Closed** *Tue–Thu lunch; Sun & Mon*
In Bristol's buzzing east side, this modest, cheerful café showcases local art and live music. The inviting menu includes seasonal organic vegetarian dishes; daily specials are listed on the blackboard.

BRISTOL: Riverstation ££
Modern European **Road Map** F3
The Grove, BS1 4RB
Tel *01179 144434* **Closed** *Sun dinner*
Located on the first floor of a hangar-like building overlooking the harbour, Riverstation uses local and seasonal produce to create dishes full of flavour.

BRUTON: At the Chapel ££
Pizzeria **Road Map** F4
28 High St, Somerset, BA10 0AE
Tel *01749 814070*
Enjoy delicious pizzas (cooked in a wood-fired oven) and seasonal salads at this happening restaurant set in a former chapel with soaring ecclesiastical windows. There's an artisan bakery and wine store on site.

BRUTON: Roth Bar & Grill ££
Grill **Road Map** F4
Durslade Farm, Dropping Lane, Somerset, BA10 0NL
Tel *01749 814700* **Closed** *Sun–Thu dinner; Mon*
This terrific on-site restaurant at the Hauser & Wirth Somerset art gallery uses vegetables and herbs from its own kitchen garden. It also has a salt room for dry-ageing meat. There's live music on Friday evenings.

CHRISTCHURCH: The Paddle £
Café **Road Map** A3
397 Waterford Rd, Highcliffe, Dorset, BH23 5JN
Tel *01425 275148* **Closed** *Sun dinner*
A soothing modern café that turns into a proper restaurant on Thursday, Friday and Saturday evenings. Choose between superb wood-fired pizzas and home-made local dishes, such as smoked mackerel fishcakes.

CHRISTCHURCH: The Jetty ££
Seafood **Road Map** A3
95 Mudeford, Dorset, BH23 3NT
Tel *01202 400950*
Set in a dramatic contemporary building perched on the water's edge, the Jetty has sweeping sea views. The fish is caught just metres away, and cooked meticulously by respected chef Alex Aitken and his team.

CHRISTCHURCH: Lord Bute ££
Modern European **Road Map** A3
*181–185 Lymington Rd, Dorset,
BH23 4JS*
Tel *01425 278884* **Closed** *Sat lunch
& Sun dinner; Mon*
A reassuringly traditional hotel
dining room, where the service
is second to none and the food,
from set and à la carte menus, is
impressive. There are great jazz
and cabaret nights.

GLASTONBURY: Rainbow's End £
Vegetarian **Road Map** E4
17B High St, Somerset, BA6 9DP
Tel *01458 833896*
Glastonbury's original vegetarian
café serves home-made meals
and cakes. There's also a salad bar,
as well as a good selection of
vegan and wheat-free dishes.

**LYME REGIS: HIX Oyster &
Fish House** ££
Seafood **Road Map** E5
Cobb Rd, Dorset, DT7 3JP
Tel *01297 446910*
An uninterrupted view of the
famous Cobb is displayed through
a wall of windows at Mark Hix's
cool, contemporary, white-and-
wood restaurant. All dishes on the
menu are made with local and
market-fresh ingredients.

POOLE: Rick Stein ££
Seafood **Road Map** A3
*10–14 Banks Rd, Sandbanks, Dorset,
BH13 7QB*
Tel *01202 283000*
Rick Stein's Sandbanks outpost
is a stunning space, with pale
wood interiors and and picture
windows overlooking the bay
area. The menu features classic
dishes such as simple crab salads
and fabulous *fruits de mer*.

**STUDLAND: The Pig on
the Beach** ££
Modern British **Road Map** A3
*Manor House, Manor Rd, Dorset,
BH19 3AU*
Tel *01929 450288*
Vegetables, herbs and fruit grown
in the walled kitchen garden, plus
locally sourced fish and meat, are
all served in a lovely conservatory
at this hotel *(see p177)*. The restaurant dishes up tasty flatbreads
from the wood-fired oven.

WEYMOUTH: Crab House Café ££
Café **Road Map** F5
*Ferrymans Way, Portland Rd, Wyke
Regis, Dorset, DT4 9YU*
Tel *01305 788867* **Closed** *Mon & Tue*
Set in a rustic hut, the Crab House
overlooks Chesil Beach. The café
serves fresh crabs and oysters
from the nearby beds, and the
menu changes twice daily.

Bright, timbered interior of the Rockfish in Dartmouth, Devon

DK Choice

**WRINGTON:
The Ethicurean** ££
Modern British **Road Map** E3
*Barley Wood Walled Garden,
Long Lane, Somerset, BS40 5SA*
Tel *01934 863713* **Closed** *Mon*
This outstanding café-restaurant
overlooks the Mendip Hills.
Dynamic and experimental
organic food is served in a
rustic conservatory and is worth
the trek, especially in autumn.
Try a fabulous five-course vege-
tarian feast and don't miss the
sticky-toffee apple cake.

YEOVIL: Little Barwick House £££
European **Road Map** F4
Barwick, Somerset, BA22 9TD
Tel *01935 423902* **Closed** *Tue lunch;
Sun & Mon*
Come to this superb restaurant
for Tim Ford's grounded cooking,
accompanied by an excellent
wine list. The restaurant's setting
is truly enchanting.

Devon

**AXMINSTER: River Cottage
Canteen** ££
Modern British **Road Map** E5
Trinity Sq, EX13 5AN
Tel *01297 631715* **Closed** *Sun &
Mon dinner*
Hugh Fearnley-Whittingstall's
original restaurant and deli
showcases the very best produce
the South West has to offer in an
attractive industrial-style space.
There's also regular live music.

BARNSTAPLE: Terra Madre ££
Mediterranean **Road Map** C4
*Broomhill Art Hotel, Muddiford Rd,
EX31 4EX*
Tel *01271 850262* **Closed** *Sun dinner;
Mon & Tue*
A fantastic Slow Food restaurant
in a sculpture garden. The menu
includes freshly baked sourdough

bread and artisan salami, as well
as organic produce from the
coast and neighbouring farms.

**BIGBURY-ON-SEA:
The Oyster Shack** £
Seafood **Road Map** D6
*Milburn Orchard Farm Stakes Hill,
TQ7 4BE*
Tel *01548 810878*
A friendly, seaside-themed
restaurant, the Oyster Shack
serves great local seafood with a
Mediterranean twist. The oysters
and crab are reasonably priced.

DK Choice

**BUCKFASTLEIGH: Riverford
Field Kitchen** ££
Café **Road Map** D5
Wash Barn, TQ11 0JU
Tel *01803 762074*
Get a taste of the South West
at this wonderful family-friendly
restaurant. It serves simple meals
and indulgent feasts, all made
with organic ingredients straight
from the farm. Try the tender
blade of beef with butter beans
or charred corn and tomato
salad. Booking is essential.

CHAGFORD: Gidleigh Park £££
European **Road Map** D5
Gidleigh Park Hotel, TQ13 8HH
Tel *01647 432367*
The head chef at Gidleigh's *(see
p178)* two-Michelin-starred restau-
rant is the supremely talented
Michael Wignall. His cooking is
complex and carefully crafted
and the dishes are delightful.

DARTMOUTH: The Rockfish £
Seafood **Road Map** D6
8 South Embankment, TQ6 9BH
Tel *01803 832800*
This Mitch Tonks-run takeaway
and restaurant serves award-
winning local fish and seafood,
including sublime South Devon
crab. Gluten-free options are
available, plus great craft
beers and a kids' menu.

DARTMOUTH:
The Seahorse £££
Seafood **Road Map** D6
5 South Embankment, TQ6 9BH
Tel *01803 835147* **Closed** *Sun
(except public hol weekends) & Mon*
This elegant, upmarket restaurant
is another success from Mitch
Tonks. The emphasis is on
charcoal-roasted local fish and
seafood, including cuttlefish,
squid, turbot and sole. There's
also an extensive wine list.

EXETER: Jack in the Green ££
Gastro-pub **Road Map** D5
Rockbeare, London Rd, EX5 2EE
Tel *01404 822240*
A cheerful pub, Jack in the Green
serves delicious, beautifully
presented food made using
seasonal local Devon produce.

EXMOUTH: River Exe Café ££
Gastro-café **Road Map** D5
Taxis from Exmouth Marina, EX8 1XA
Tel *07761 116103* **Closed** *Oct–Mar*
Book a water taxi to reach this
unique floating restaurant on
the Exe estuary. The specials
menu changes daily, and features
locally caught and well-prepared
fish and seafood. The café also
serves burgers and pizzas.

ILFRACOMBE: The Quay ££
Modern British **Road Map** C4
11 The Quay, EX34 9EQ
Tel *01271 868090*
Choose to eat in the casual
café-bar or in one of two more
refined dining rooms at this chic
Damien Hirst-owned restaurant.
Freshly caught sea bass and
"Lundy" lobster number among
the many specialities here.

KINGSBRIDGE: Millbrook Inn ££
Gastro-pub **Road Map** D6
South Pool, TQ7 2RW
Tel *01548 531581*
A small, award-winning traditional
pub renowned for serving
remarkably good, wholesome
food. The menu focuses on
nose-to-tail eating and features
a mixture of British and European
influences. The pub also hosts
regular live-music nights.

OKEHAMPTON:
Lewtrenchard Manor £££
Modern British **Road Map** C5
Lewdown, EX20 4PN
Tel *01566 783222*
Dating from the early 1600s, this
Jacobean manor on Dartmoor
is now a country-house hotel. It
has an exquisite dining room
decorated with beautiful portraits
and chandeliers. The restaurant
serves top-quality local produce
cooked in exciting, novel ways.

PLYMOUTH: Barbican Kitchen ££
Modern British **Road Map** C6
*Plymouth Gin Distillery, 60 Southside
St, PL1 2LQ*
Tel *01752 604448* **Closed** *Sun*
The aim of this brasserie in
Plymouth's famous gin distillery
(see 145) is to deliver fresh local
food at a realistic price. The menu
takes full advantage of the West
Country's superb natural larder.

SALCOMBE: Captain Flint's £
Pizzeria **Road Map** D6
82 Fore St, TQ8 8BY
Tel *01548 842357* **Closed** *lunch*
Located in the town centre,
Captain Flint's has been a family
favourite for 25 years. The menu
features a wide selection of
home-made pizzas, pasta, burgers
and salads. Arrive early for a table
as advance booking isn't available.

SALCOMBE: Victoria Inn £
Pub **Road Map** D6
Fore St, TQ8 8BU
Tel *01548 842604*
A cozy, traditional pub with
low-beamed ceilings, a stone
fireplace and a secluded beer
garden. It's the perfect place for
a crab sandwich, a ploughman's
or a more substantial pub meal.

SOUTH MILTON: Beachhouse ££
Seafood **Road Map** D6
Kingsbridge, TQ7 3JY
Tel *01548 561144* **Closed** *Sun–Thu
dinner (except school hols)*
Try soup with crusty bread,
Exmouth mussels, Start Bay
scallops or the formidable
seafood platter for two at this
humble, salt-crusted beach
shack. A local institution, the
Beachhouse is not to be missed.

TOPSHAM: Darts Farm £
Café **Road Map** D5
Darts Farm Bridge Hill, EX3 0QH
Tel *01392 878200* **Closed** *dinner*
Showcasing the finest of Devon's
artisan produce, Darts Farm Shop
supplies the ingredients for this
seductive café-restaurant. Stop
off for all-day breakfast, a proper
meal or an indulgent smoothie.
The restaurant also has a mouthwatering selection of cakes.

TORQUAY: The Elephant £££
Modern British **Road Map** D5
3–4 Beacon Hill, TQ1 2BH
Tel *01803 200044* **Closed** *Sun & Mon*
This sophisticated-looking
Michelin-starred restaurant
and its accompanying low-key
brasserie are set in an elegant
two-storey Georgian townhouse.
There's a carefully planned
and delicious tasting menu.
Reservations are essential.

Herb-crusted lamb striploin served at
the Beach Restaurant in Bude, Cornwall

Cornwall

BUDE: The Beach Restaurant ££
Modern British **Road Map** C5
Summerleaze Crescent, EX23 8HJ
Tel *01288 389800*
Well-prepared fish dishes are
the highlight of this chic, modern
restaurant, where menus are
based around fresh local ingredients. There's a lovely terrace
with panoramic views and a
great selection of bar food.

FALMOUTH:
The Wheel House ££
Seafood **Road Map** B6
Upton Slip, TR11 3DQ
Tel *01326 318050* **Closed** *Wed–Sat
lunch; Sun–Tue; mid-Dec–Jan*
This unique crab and oyster bar
has no menu and serves just four
dishes, but the seafood will be
the best and freshest you'll ever
eat. A word-of-mouth gem.
Bookings are essential.

FOWEY: Sam's on the Beach ££
European **Road Map** B6
14 Polkerris, Par, PL24 2TL
Tel *01726 812255*
Part of a Cornish mini-chain,
this branch of Sam's is located in
the old lifeboat station. It serves
tasty wood-fired pizzas, lobster
and a delicious fusion of Cornish
and Mediterranean food.

FOWEY: Q Restaurant £££
Bistro **Road Map** B6
*The Old Quay House, 28 Fore St,
PL23 1AQ*
Tel *01726 833302* **Closed** *Mon & Tue*
An upmarket, relaxed restaurant
in a hotel with fabulous estuary
views *(see p179)*. Come here
for Fowey River oysters, local
scallops, Cornish cheeses and
West Country meat, including
the signature Kilhallon beef fillet.

HELSTON: Croust House £
Café **Road Map** B6
Roskilly's Farm, St Keverne, TR12 6NX
Tel *01326 280479* **Closed** *Christmas*
Enjoy delicious home-made food
from Roskilly's Farm, served
indoors by a roaring fire or out in
the old farmyard. The menu also
includes soups, wood-fired pizzas,
pasties, salads and ice cream.

HELSTON: Kota ££
Asian Fusion **Road Map** B6
Harbour Head, Porthleven, TR13 9JA
Tel *01326 562407* **Closed** *Sun–Tue*
In a harbourside setting, Kota
serves delicious Asian fusion food.
The restaurant is owned by New
Zealand chef Jude Kereama, who
took part in the BBC's *Great British
Menu* series in 2015 and 2016.

LOOE: Squid Ink ££
Seafood **Road Map** C6
Lower Chapel St, PL13 1AT
Tel *01503 262674* **Closed** *Tue*
A warm, laid-back and friendly
seafood restaurant hiding amid
Looe's narrow medieval streets.
It serves freshly caught fish and
all produce is sourced locally.

NEWQUAY: Fifteen Cornwall £££
Seafood **Road Map** B5
Watergate Bay, TR8 4AA
Tel *01637 861000*
Celebrity chef Jamie Oliver's large,
modern brasserie is perched on
the cliffs above the beach, with
eye-catching views through
wraparound windows. Fantastic
seafood with rich Mediterranean
flavours is on offer.

PADSTOW: Rafferty's ££
Wine Bar **Road Map** B5
St Merryn, PL28 8NF
Tel *01841 521561* **Closed** *lunch*
A welcoming wine bar and
restaurant, Rafferty's is particularly
well suited to families and groups.
The menu ranges from tapas and
sharing plates to hearty stews
and chargrilled steaks. There are
good Sunday roasts and there's
also a kids' menu.

PADSTOW: St Petroc's Bistro ££
Bistro **Road Map** B5
New St, PL28 8EA
Tel *01841 532700*
This Rick Stein-owned bistro has
a charming country-style dining
room, a pretty garden courtyard
and a cozy bar. Carnivores will
love the Devon Red Ruby steaks
cooked over a charcoal grill.

**PADSTOW: Paul Ainsworth
at No. 6** £££
Modern British **Road Map** B5
6 Middle St, PL28 8AP
Tel *01841 532093* **Closed** *Sun & Mon*
A Michelin-starred restaurant in a
handsome Georgian townhouse.
Chef Paul Ainsworth's seductive
cooking has its roots in the
region – in both the land and
sea. There are tempting vegetarian dishes and kids' menus.

DK Choice

**PADSTOW: The Seafood
Restaurant** £££
Seafood **Road Map** B5
Riverside, PL28 8BY
Tel *01841 532700*
Rick Stein opened his stunning
flagship restaurant in 1975,
and since then it has gained
an international reputation for
serving fresh seafood, simply
but exquisitely cooked. It's fun
to sit at the central bar and
order sashimi or oysters. Menus
change daily, according to what's
available, and there are rooms
upstairs too *(see p179).* No admit-
tance to children under three.

PENZANCE: The Victoria Inn ££
Gastro-pub **Road Map** A6
Perranuthnoe, TR20 9NP
Tel *01736 710309* **Closed** *Sun dinner*
Perfectly placed for a pit stop
if you're walking the South West
Coast Path, this 12th-century
inn serves well-prepared food,
fine wine, cider and Cornish
lager. The pub is family-friendly,
and dogs are allowed in.

**PORT ISAAC: Restaurant
Nathan Outlaw** £££
Seafood **Road Map** B5
6 New Rd, PL29 3SB
Tel *01208 880896* **Closed** *Wed &
Thu lunch; Sun–Tue*
Sample outstanding seafood
and (if booked ahead) vegetarian
tasting menus at this glossy two-
Michelin-starred restaurant.

ST IVES: Halsetown Inn ££
Gastro-pub **Road Map** A6
B3311, Halsetown, TR26 3NA
Tel *01736 795583* **Closed** *Sun dinner*
Set in the glorious countryside,
this genial pub serves modern,
boldly flavoured interpretations
of classic dishes. There's a good
selection of real ales and a
special menu for kids.

**ST IVES: Porthminster
Beach Café** ££
Café **Road Map** A6
Porthminster Beach, TR26 2EB
Tel *01736 795352* **Closed** *Nov–late
Mar: Tue, Wed & Sun dinner; Mon*
A multi-award-winning beach
café, Porthminster has spectacular
views across the bay to Godrevy
Lighthouse. Mediterranean- and
Asian-inspired seafood is served
in a convivial atmosphere.

ST MAWES: Tresanton £££
Seafood **Road Map** B6
27 Lower Castle Rd, TR2 5DR
Tel *01326 270055*
A striking, all-white restaurant
with a mosaic-tiled floor, tongue-
and-groove walls and a gorgeous
terrace with sea views. The
menu focuses on fish, simply
and perfectly cooked.

ZENNOR: The Gurnard's Head ££
Pub **Road Map** A6
Treen, TR26 3DE
Tel *01736 796928* **Closed** *24 &
25 Dec*
People come from far and wide
to eat at this cozy pub set in a
wild landscape. The menu is short
but inspired, driven by what
arrives daily at the back door.

Sam's on the Beach, a seaside restaurant in Fowey, Cornwall

For more information on types of restaurants *see pages 180–81*

SHOPS AND MARKETS

Although London's West End is the most famous place to shop in southern England, shopping in the regions can be more relaxed and equally pleasurable. Moreover, regional shopping tends to be less expensive and remarkably varied, with a wide range of quirky, independent shops. The South Coast is particularly rich in shops and emporia selling local art, antiques and second-hand vintage artifacts. Even small towns brim over with artisan craft studios. There are also plenty of farm shops, historic shopping areas, street markets and factory outlets, which will appeal to dedicated bargain-hunters.

Shopping Hours

Most shops are open Monday to Saturday from 9am or 10am, and close around 5:30pm. London's West End remains open till 9pm. Some stores are open late once a week, usually on a Thursday, while village shops sometimes close at lunchtime or for one afternoon a week. Larger shops have limited opening hours on Sundays, though most are open between noon and 4pm.

Westfield Stratford City shopping centre, one of the largest malls in Europe

How to Pay

Most shops, with the exception of markets and small outlets, accept debit and credit cards. Charge cards, such as American Express or Diners Club, are also widely accepted. "Contactless" cards allow you to pay up to £30 without the need for a signature or personal identification number (PIN), but not all shops have terminals equipped for them. Cash is still a popular way to pay for small purchases.

Rights and Refunds

If what you buy is defective, you are entitled to a refund provided you have your receipt as proof of purchase and return the goods in the same condition in which you bought them. This

Shoppers at the Christmas sales on Oxford Street, London

may not apply to sale goods marked as seconds, imperfect or shop-soiled. You do not have to accept a credit note in place of a cash refund.

Sales

Sales take place in January, June and July, when most shops cut prices to dispose of old stock. But you may find special offers throughout the year. Winter sales usually begin just before Christmas. Department stores and fashion houses, in particular, offer excellent bargains.

VAT and Tax-Free Shopping

In England, Value Added Tax (VAT) is charged on most goods and services and is included in the advertised price. At present, visitors from outside the EU who stay less than 3 months may claim this tax back. Take your passport with you when you go shopping. You must complete a form when you buy goods and give a copy to the customs authorities when you leave the country. You may have to show your goods as proof of purchase. If you

arrange to have goods shipped from the store, VAT should be deducted before you pay.

Historic Shopping Areas

Many of the region's bigger cities have historic shopping areas. Those with real charm and independent shops include **The Lanes** in Brighton, **The Pantiles** in Royal Tunbridge Wells and **The Square** in Winchester.

Shopping Centres

There are large shopping malls outside many towns and cities in southern England, which have the advantages of easy car access and cheap parking. Most are accessible by public transport too. Among the most popular are **Bluewater** in Greenhithe, Kent, **Cabot Circus** in Bristol, and the two **Westfield** centres in London.

Designer Outlets

These retail centres have stores selling luxury items at reduced prices. They include **Gunwharf Quays** in Portsmouth Harbour and **Kilver Court Designer Village** in Shepton Mallet.

Department Stores

Some department stores, such as **Harrods** and **Liberty**, are only found in London, but others, such as **John Lewis**, **Marks & Spencer**, **Debenhams** and **House of Fraser**, have branches throughout southern England. All these stores sell clothing, accessories and household items.

Clothes Shops

Large cities, such as London and Bristol, offer the widest range of clothes, but towns popular with tourists, such as Bath, Winchester and Brighton, have independently owned shops where you are likely to find unusual clothes and receive a personal service. You can also visit high street stores, such as **Jigsaw**, **Next** or **Hobbs**, for chic outfits. **Primark**, **H&M**, and **Topshop** offer younger, cheaper fashions, and **Crew Clothing** has yachting-style casual wear.

Supermarkets and Food Shops

The variety and quality of supermarket food is usually excellent. Several large chains compete for market share, which

Waitrose supermarkets offer fresh, quality produce in stores across the country

tends to keep prices lower than in smaller shops. **Sainsbury's**, **Tesco**, **Asda** and **Waitrose** are some of the national names. Groceries can be ordered online through all of them. Independent bakeries, delicatessens, greengrocers and farm shops usually offer a more interesting choice of regional produce.

Souvenir and Gift Shops

In every town there are shops selling attractive, well-made souvenirs and presents. For more unusual items, look in museum and gallery shops or at the gifts available in National Trust and English Heritage shops (see p202).

Antique Shops

Most towns have at least one shop selling antiques, second-hand vintage items or bric-a-brac. Towns such as Brighton, Honiton in Devon and Lostwithiel in Cornwall have many such shops. Out-of-town emporia, full of antiques, are also worth a visit.

Markets

Cities usually have a covered market with stalls selling a wide variety of goods, from food to household items. Bristol's **St Nicholas Market** (see p126) is a splendid example. Small towns often have a weekly open market in the main square. On weekends, farmers' markets offer fresh, organic produce.

The best markets in London include **Borough** in Southwark for fresh produce, **Columbia Road** in Tower Hamlets for plants and cut flowers, and **Camden Lock** for crafts, vintage clothing, books and records. You can also visit **Portobello Road** for jewellery and antiques (see p63); **Old Spitalfields** for crafts, clothes, food and vintage items; and **Covent Garden**'s Jubilee and Apple Markets (see p53) for crafts and clothes.

DIRECTORY

Historic Shopping Areas	**Kilver Court Designer Village**	**H&M**	**Markets**
The Lanes	w kilvercourt.com	w hm.com	**Borough**
w visitbrighton.com/ shopping/the-lanes	**Department Stores**	**Hobbs**	w boroughmarket. org.uk
The Pantiles		w hobbs.co.uk	**Camden Lock**
w thepantiles.com	**Debenhams**	**Jigsaw**	w camdenlock market.com
The Square	w debenhams.com	w jigsaw-online.com	**Columbia Road**
w visitwinchester.co. uk/square-market-lane	**Harrods**	**Next**	w columbiaroad.info
	w harrods.com	w next.co.uk	**Covent Garden**
Shopping Centres	**House of Fraser**	**Primark**	w coventgarden. london/markets
Bluewater	w houseoffraser.co.uk	w primark.com	**Old Spitalfields**
w bluewater.co.uk	**John Lewis**	**Topshop**	w oldspitalfields market.com
Cabot Circus	w johnlewis.com	w topshop.com	**Portobello Road**
w cabotcircus.com	**Liberty**	**Supermarkets and Food Shops**	w portobelloroad. co.uk
Westfield	w liberty.co.uk		**St Nicholas Market**
w uk.westfield.com	**Marks & Spencer**	**Asda**	w stnicholasmarket bristol.co.uk
	w marksandspencer. com	w asda.com	
Designer Outlets		**Sainsbury's**	
	Clothes Shops	w sainsburys.co.uk	
Gunwharf Quays		**Tesco**	
w gunwharf-quays.com	**Crew Clothing**	w tesco.com	
	w crewclothing.co.uk	**Waitrose**	
		w waitrose.com	

ENTERTAINMENT

London is unrivalled for the diversity and quality of its entertainment, with countless shows, films and concerts to choose from, but programmes at regional theatres, opera houses and concert halls should not be overlooked. Bristol, Brighton, Bath and Chichester have a lively arts scene and the coast buzzes with interesting things to do and experience in the summer months. There are arts festivals in Bath, Brighton and Ramsgate, among other locations, as well as classical music, pop and rock festivals. Ticket prices can vary substantially but are usually much cheaper outside the capital and when booked well in advance.

Open-air performance at the clifftop Minack Theatre in Cornwall

Sources of Information

To find out what's on at the theatre in London and the rest of southern England, check the websites of **WhatsOnStage** and **London Theatre Guide**.

London's free newspapers, *Metro* and *Evening Standard* (available Mon–Fri), and listings magazine *Time Out* (available Tue), give an overview of the capital's cultural programme. The arts sections of the broadsheet newspapers *(see p207)* publish comprehensive reviews and listings of countrywide events. The specialist magazine *NME* gives up-to-date news of the pop music scene.

For information on LGBT events, check the monthly *GT* and the online **Pink News**.

Theatre and Dance

England's theatrical tradition dates back before Shakespeare to the medieval Mystery Plays. There are more than 60 West End and fringe theatres in London, not including the many pubs that regularly host drama. The theatres range from sumptuous Georgian to bold Modernist buildings. Bristol also has a long dramatic tradition: its Theatre Royal *(see p126)*, home to the **Bristol Old Vic** company, is Britain's oldest working theatre. Some of the best productions are shown at **Chichester Festival Theatre**, where the National Theatre company was founded. Cities such as Bath and Brighton also have a reputation for good drama. Open-air performances include productions at Cornwall's dramatic clifftop amphitheatre, the **Minack Theatre**.

Ticket availability varies from show to show. For a midweek matinée, you may be able to buy a ticket on the day, but for a West End show tickets have to be booked well in advance. Beware of tickets sold by touts as these may be counterfeit.

For dance-lovers, London offers outstanding ballet productions at the **Royal Opera House**, **London Coliseum** and **Sadler's Wells**. The English National Ballet performs at the **Mayflower Theatre**, Southampton.

The contemporary dance company **Rambert** takes exciting new works by many choreographers to numerous locations, including Brighton, Bath, Plymouth and Truro.

Cinemas

Major cities usually have a more varied range of films, including foreign-language productions, often shown in arts or repertory cinemas. Mainstream English-language films are shown by the big chains such as **ODEON** and **Cineworld**. Ticket prices vary; look out for family discounts. Book in advance for new releases.

Pop-up outdoor cinemas are popular in the summer, notably at London's Somerset House and in Brighton. **Luna Cinema** has screenings in Leeds Castle *(see p70)*, Rochester Castle *(see p68)* and on Hastings Pier *(see p195)*.

Music

The south of England has a diverse musical repertoire across a variety of venues. Church choral music is an English tradition, and many churches host concerts, including Winchester, Salisbury and Exeter cathedrals. London, Bristol and Bournemouth all have their own excellent orchestras, and there is a highly regarded annual opera festival at **Glyndebourne** *(see p28)*.

The South is the heartland of the English festival scene, with

Performance of Mozart's 18th-century opera *La finta giardiniera*, at Glyndebourne

Glastonbury *(see p125)* and **Bestival** *(see p29)* among the most famous. Annual rock, jazz, folk and country concerts are staged throughout the region.

Clubs

London enjoys a lively nightlife with clubs such as **XOYO**, **Queen of Hoxton** (with its rooftop wig-wam) and **Ministry of Sound** (set in a former bus depot). Away from the capital, popular venues include **Volks** in Brighton, and **Motion** in Bristol. London's gay life is centred around Soho. The most popular clubs here are **Heaven** and **G-A-Y**. Outside London, cutting-edge LGBT clubs include **Legends** in Brighton and **Queen Shilling** in Bristol.

Children's Activities

London is a gold mine of fun for children of all ages. For more information on family-friendly sights check the **Visit London**

Children enjoy watching the sharks at the National Marine Aquarium in Plymouth

website. Along the South Coast, child-friendly activities range from petting farms, such as Devon's **Pennywell Farm**, to water parks, such as the **South Coast Wakepark** in Portsmouth.

For younger children there's the **Eastbourne Miniature Steam Railway**, the **Monkey Haven** rescue centre on the Isle of Wight and the zoo farm at **Woodlands** family theme park in Devon. Of the area's other theme parks, **Dreamland** in Margate has a retro look. Educational days out

can include a trip to the superb **Eden Project** *(see pp160–61)* or the **Newquay Zoo** in Cornwall, which is set in lakeside gardens.

Piers

Pleasure piers were built in the 19th century and many feature amusement arcades. The most famous one is **Brighton**; others include **Eastbourne**, **Weston-super-Mare** and **Hastings**. In 2016, the first "vertical pier", the i360 *(see p82)*, opened in Brighton.

DIRECTORY

Sources of Information

Evening Standard
w standard.co.uk

GT
w gaytimes.co.uk

London Theatre Guide
w londontheatre.co.uk

Metro
w metro.co.uk

NME
w nme.com

Pink News
w pinknews.co.uk

Time Out
w timeout.com

WhatsOnStage
w whatsonstage.com

Theatre and Dance

Bristol Old Vic
w bristololdvic.org.uk

Chichester Festival Theatre
w cft.org.uk

London Coliseum
w eno.org

Mayflower Theatre
w mayflower.org.uk

Minack Theatre
w minack.com

Rambert
w rambert.org.uk

Royal Opera House
w roh.org.uk

Sadler's Wells
w sadlerswells.com

Cinemas

Cineworld
w cineworld.co.uk

Luna Cinema
w thelunacinema.com

ODEON
w odeon.co.uk

Music

Bestival
w bestival.net

Glastonbury
w glastonburyfestivals.co.uk

Glyndebourne
w glyndebourne.com

Clubs

G-A-Y
w g-a-y.co.uk

Heaven
w heavennightclub-london.com

Legends
w legendsbrighton.com

Ministry of Sound
w ministryofsound.com

Motion
w motionbristol.com

Queen of Hoxton
w queenofhoxton.com

Queen Shilling
w queenshilling.com

Volks
w volksclub.co.uk

XOYO
w xoyo.co.uk

Children's Activities

Dreamland
w dreamland.co.uk

Eastbourne Miniature Steam Railway
w emsr.co.uk

Monkey Haven
w monkeyhaven.org

Newquay Zoo
w newquayzoo.org.uk

Pennywell Farm
w pennywellfarm.co.uk

South Coast Wakepark
w southcoast wakepark.co.uk

Visit London
w visitlondon.com

Woodlands
w woodlandspark.com

Piers

Brighton
w brightonpier.co.uk

Eastbourne
w eastbournepier.com

Hastings
w hastingspier.org.uk

Weston-super-Mare
w grandpier.co.uk

SPORTS AND OUTDOOR ACTIVITIES

Numerous sports and outdoor activities are on offer in southern England. With its miles of coastline, water sports are a major feature of the area. There is also a wide range of courses available to help you learn a new sport or practise an activity. If you prefer less-structured activities, there are a huge number of possibilities, from walking on the South Downs to surfing in Cornwall. For those who prefer to watch rather than participate, there is a variety of spectator sports, including football, cricket and horse racing.

Walking

With a network of long-distance footpaths and shorter routes crisscrossing southern England, walking is an excellent way to see the glorious countryside. Highlights include England's longest National Trail, the **South West Coast Path**, Dartmoor *(see pp142–3)*, **Exmoor** *(see pp122–3)*, the **South Downs** *(see pp86–7)*, and the **New Forest** *(see p97)*.

The **Ramblers** is England's main walking organization, and its website provides information on most routes and walking areas, and lists suitable hotels, B&Bs and hostels. The **National Trust** website *(see p202)* also recommends walks, including buggy- and wheelchair-friendly routes. **Ramblers' Worldwide Holidays** offer guided group walks through lovely landscapes, and **Sherpa Expeditions** organize self-led walks.

All walks are rated easy to moderate. Travel companies will advise on the level of fitness required and any essential clothing and footwear.

If you are planning to walk on your own, especially in remote areas, it is essential to be well equipped and to leave details of your route with someone.

Cycling

The region's bridleways, tranquil lanes and designated tracks are perfect for cyclists. **HFH Cycling Holidays** offer group holidays on the Isle of Wight (one geared to families), guided by an experienced leader. Self-led tours are offered by **Compass Holidays** in Cornwall, and **Headwater** in Dorset. The operators provide bike hire, accommodation, route maps

Mountain biking along the coast of the spectacular Isle of Wight

and luggage transport. If you are organizing your own cycling holiday, contact **Cycling UK**, England's main recreational cycling body, and **Sustrans**, the organization responsible for the National Cycle Network. Both provide important information on cycling and rules of the road.

Horse Riding and Pony Trekking

The most outstanding locations for riding are the New Forest and the South Downs. Dartmoor, Exmoor and Cornwall offer pony trekking, an activity popular with novice riders and children, since the ponies are well trained and rarely go faster than a canter. Pony-trekking holidays usually include basic training, a guide,

meals and accommodation. The **British Horse Society** has information on where to ride and a list of approved training schools. For riding in the national parks, check the websites of Dartmoor, Exmoor and the New Forest.

Golf

Many of southern England's golf courses are welcoming; other, more high-profile clubs only admit players above a certain handicap. Green fees and facilities vary greatly. Some clubs require a valid handicap certificate, although a letter of introduction from a home club may suffice. Specialist operators such as **Golf Vacations UK** arrange packages, including temporary club membership. If you wish to go at it alone, the **Golf Club Great Britain** has information on where to play.

Boating and Sailing

The pleasure crafts that fill South Coast marinas are testament to how enthusiastic the English are about boating and sailing. The **Royal Yachting Association** has a list of approved schools. One of the most trusted is Cornwall's **Falmouth School of Sailing**, which offers a range of sailing

Horse riding on the wild, grassy moorland of Dartmoor National Park in Devon

The English and Welsh national rugby teams at Twickenham Stadium in London

and powerboat courses in the Fal Estuary. For the more adventurous, sea kayaking is offered by **Sea Kayak Devon**.

Surfing

The best surfing is in the West Country. Tuition is available in many resorts, and equipment can be hired. Devon-based **Surfing Great Britain** has accredited surf schools with

professional coaching catering to a range of abilities, from novices to advanced surfers.

Fishing

One of England's most popular participatory sports is sea and river fishing. Regulations, though, are strict. Check for restrictions at the **Angling Trust**. Southern England has good game fishing (trout, seatrout and salmon). For

Hampshire chalk streams rich in freshwater fish, try **The Rod Box** outside Winchester. For fishing holidays in Devon get in touch with **Anglers Paradise**.

Spectator Sports

The football (soccer) season runs from August to May. The top clubs belong to the Premier League, run by the **Football Association**. Rugby, administered by the **Rugby Football Union**, also has a loyal following. Cricket, the national game, is played at different levels in all counties. Top-level test cricket is played at **Lord's**, the **Ageas Bowl** and at **Kia Oval**. The main tennis event, Wimbledon, is held in July at the **All England Lawn Tennis Club (AELTC)**. Horse racing is very popular too. Of the South Coast's many racecourses, **Goodwood** is the best known. It hosts several days of flat racing in July known as Glorious Goodwood (see p87).

DIRECTORY

Walking

The Ramblers
Camelford House, 87–90 Albert Embankment, London, SE1 7TW.
w ramblers.org.uk

Ramblers' Worldwide Holidays
w ramblers holidays.co.uk

Sherpa Expeditions
1B Osiers Rd, London, SW18 1NL. w sherpa expeditions.co.uk

South West Coast Path
w southwestcoastpath. org.uk

Cycling

Compass Holidays
w compass-holidays. com

Cycling UK
w cyclinguk.org

Headwater
w headwater.com

HFH Cycling Holidays
w hfhcycling.co.uk

Sustrans
w sustrans.org.uk

Horse Riding and Pony Trekking

British Horse Society
w bhs.org.uk

Golf

Golf Club Great Britain
w golfclubgb.co.uk

Golf Vacations UK
w golfvacationsuk.com

Boating and Sailing

Falmouth School of Sailing
Grove Place Boat Park, Falmouth, Cornwall, TR11 4AU. w falmouth-school-of-sailing.co.uk

Royal Yachting Association
RYA House, Ensign Way, Hamble, Hampshire, SO31 4YA. w rya.org.uk

Sea Kayak Devon
16B Duke St, Dartmouth, Devon, TQ6 9PZ.
w seakayakdevon.co.uk

Surfing

Surfing Great Britain
The Yard, Caen St, Braunton, Devon, EX33 1AA.
w surfinggb.com

Fishing

Anglers Paradise
The Gables, Winsford Lane, Beaworthy, Devon, EX21 5XT.
w anglers-paradise. co.uk

Angling Trust
w anglingtrust.net

The Rod Box
London Rd, Kings Worthy, Winchester, Hampshire, SO23 7QN.
w rodbox.com

Spectator Sports

Ageas Bowl
Hampshire County Cricket Ground, Botley Rd, West End, Southampton, SO30 3XH.
w ageasbowl.com

All England Lawn Tennis Club (AELTC)
Church Rd, Wimbledon, London, SW19 5AE.
w wimbledon.com

Football Association
Wembley Stadium, PO Box 1966, London, SW1P 9EQ. w thefa.com

Goodwood
Goodwood, Chichester, West Sussex, PO18 0PS.
w goodwood.com

Kia Oval
Surrey County Cricket Ground, Kennington, London, SE11 5SS.
w kiaoval.com

Lord's
Marylebone Cricket Club, St John's Wood, London, NW8 8QN.
w lords.org

Rugby Football Union
200 Whitton Rd, Twickenham, Middlesex, TW2 7BA.
w englandrugby.com

SURVIVAL GUIDE

PRACTICAL INFORMATION

The beautiful cliffs, castles, churches, coves and beaches of the South Coast of England have attracted summer visitors in droves since the railway boom of the 1850s. Visitor numbers usually peak during school summer holidays (July and August) and a little planning can help avoid the most crowded areas. London, not surprisingly, is the most expensive city but, as you go further afield, your budget may stretch further. This effect is even more exaggerated in low season, when you will also find you have to compete less to do what you want, when you want. This section provides helpful practical advice on a range of important issues, including passport and visa formalities, travel safety, personal security, banking, communications and how to find useful local facilities.

Sheltered Porthgwidden Beach, popular with families, in St Ives, Cornwall

When to Go

England's South Coast enjoys a temperate climate, warmer than the North and with few temperature extremes. However, constantly shifting patterns mean the weather can change quickly and vary widely in places only a short distance apart. Summer days can be hot and sunny, with refreshing sea breezes. Since it can be difficult to predict rain or shine reliably, it is advisable to pack a mix of warm and cool weather clothes and an umbrella, irrespective of when you visit.

The South Coast is an all-year destination, but many attractions are only open between Easter and October. The main school holiday months, July and August, are always busy and the most accessible beaches can become packed with people. Spring and autumn offer a good compromise, with reasonably good weather and fewer crowds.

Passports and Visas

Visitors with a valid passport or national identity card issued by any European Economic Area (EEA) or European Union (EU) country or Switzerland do not need a visa to enter Britain. Neither do visitors from the US, Canada, Australia and New Zealand who are staying for less than 6 months. Britain's decision to leave the EU could affect regulations, so visit the **UK Visas and Immigration** website for the most up-to-date information. Most countries have consular representation in London, including the **US**, **Canada**, **Australia** and **New Zealand**.

Travel Safety Advice

Visitors can get up-to-date travel safety information from the **UK Foreign and Commonwealth Office**, the **US Department of State** and the **Australian Department of Foreign Affairs and Trade** websites.

Customs Information

Incoming travellers have to pass through customs channels: green if you have nothing to declare, red if you have goods to declare, and blue if you are arriving from an EU country and have already cleared customs there. Random checks are made to detect prohibited goods, particularly drugs, indecent material and weapons. Never, under any circumstances, carry anything through customs for someone else.

Britain is free of rabies, and pet dogs and cats cannot be imported without a passport or veterinary certificate. For more information visit the government **Pet Passport** website.

Health Insurance

It is sensible to take out travel insurance to cover cancellation or curtailment of your holiday, theft or loss of money and possessions, and the cost of any medical treatment, which may include hospitalization, repatriation and specialists' fees. Emergency treatment in a British NHS casualty ward is free for all visitors, but only those with a European Health Insurance Card (EHIC) are entitled to free additional treatment under the NHS. At present, this applies to visitors from EU and EEA countries, as well as some Commonwealth countries, such as Australia and New Zealand. Be aware, though, that certain benefits covered by medical insurance will not be included.

Visitor Information

VisitBritain is the official tourist organization for Great Britain and its website includes destination guides, maps and an accommodation booking service.

Tourist information is available in almost all towns. Look out for the tourist information symbol,

◀ Fishing boats in Penberth Cove on the Land's End peninsula in Cornwall

Tourist information centre on Digby Road in Sherborne, Dorset

which can indicate everything from a major tourist bureau to a simple kiosk. They can help you with anything ranging from local attractions and guided walks to hotels and B&Bs. It is wise to book accommodation well in advance, particularly if you're planning to arrive in high season.

Heritage Organizations

English Heritage and the **National Trust** are two associations which preserve and protect Britain's national treasures, including historic castles, stately homes and gardens, and vast tracts of countryside and coastline. Entrance fees for these sights are often quite steep, so it may be worth taking out an annual membership if you are British, which allows free access to any of their properties for a calendar year. Visitors from overseas can buy an English Heritage Overseas Visitor Pass, which gives access to dozens of sights across southern England, and a National Trust Touring Pass, which also allows entry to numerous properties and gardens. Both passes are available online and offer reduced price entry to the organizations' many historic buildings and gardens. Be aware that many properties may be closed in winter.

Many of the National Trust's properties are "listed", meaning that they are recognized as having special architectural or historical interest and are therefore protected from alterations and demolition. This guide identifies English

Heritage and National Trust properties in the practical information section with the symbols EH and NT.

Admission Prices

Museums and sights have varied admission charges, ranging from under £10 to more than £25 for the most popular attractions. Reductions are often available for groups, senior citizens, families, children and students. Visitors should ensure that they have proof of eligibility with them when buying tickets. Many major national museums and some local authority museums and galleries are free, although donations are encouraged.

Opening Hours

Museums in London tend to open late one evening a week, while those outside the capital may have shorter hours and close one day a week. Opening times for other attractions vary widely: always check the details before you journey to a sight. Last admission to many attractions is 30 minutes before closing.

In most towns and cities, shops are open Monday to Saturday from 9am or 10am until 5:30pm. Shops in big city centres, particularly London, generally have longer opening hours *(see p192)*. Banks are usually open from 9am to 5pm on weekdays, and main branches are open on Saturday mornings as well *(see p204)*.

On public holidays, also known as bank holidays, banks, offices and some restaurants,

shops and attractions close, and transport networks may run limited services.

Travellers with Special Needs

Facilities for disabled visitors are steadily improving. New or renovated buildings and public spaces provide lifts and ramps for wheelchair access, plus grab rails and specially designed toilets. Buses are also increasingly accessible and transport staff will help disabled passengers if given advance notice. Although non-UK residents are not eligible for a **Disabled Persons Railcard**, they can book assistance on trains through the provider's website. **Transport for London (TfL)** *(see p213)* offers a turn-up-and-go assistance service on the Underground, publishes accessibility guides and maps, and produces a travel support card for people with communication problems, which can be downloaded from its website.

Many museums, theatres and banks provide aids for the visually impaired. Some also offer earphones for the hearing-impaired. Specialist tour operators, such as **Tourism for All**, cater for physically disabled visitors.

Several car hire firms offer hand-controlled vehicles, including **Avis** and **Budget** *(see p211)*, and wheelchair-accessible vehicles are available from specialist firms, including **Angel Vehicle Hire** and **Adapted Car Hire**. For general information on facilities for disabled travellers, contact **Disability Rights UK** or **Open Britain**.

TfL staff assisting a wheelchair user on the Underground

Interactive displays for children at the Science Museum in London

Travelling with Children

The South Coast offers a wealth of activities and fun days out for families. Local tourist office websites provide plenty of tips and useful information.

Peak holiday times – Easter, school half-terms, July, August and Christmas – have most to offer in terms of entertainment for children. Museum websites highlight child-orientated events, and organizations such as **Day Out With The Kids** and **Let's Go With The Children** provide information on child-friendly sights. Discounts for children or family tickets are available for travel, shows and other forms of entertainment.

You will find a good choice of child-friendly restaurants *(see p181)* on the South Coast, plus baby-changing facilities at most shopping centres and major museums. Stores such as **Mothercare** also deliver basic necessities if you order online.

Smoking and Alcohol

Smoking is forbidden in all public indoor spaces and the use of electronic cigarettes is also banned in many places. For information on smoking-related issues, visit the **ASH** (Action on Smoking and Health) website. It is illegal to buy cigarettes if you are under the age of 18.

Visitors should note that age restrictions also apply in pubs, where you must be over 18 to be served alcohol. Some bars cater to over-21s only, and customers may be asked for identification.

Time

During the winter months, Britain is on Greenwich Mean Time (GMT), which is 5 hours ahead of New York and 10 hours behind Sydney. From late March until late October, the clocks go forward 1 hour to British Summer Time (BST). At any time of year, you can check the correct time by dialling 123 for the Speaking Clock.

Electricity

The voltage in Britain is 220/240 AC, 50 Hz. Electrical plugs have three rectangular pins and take fuses of 3, 5 and 13 amps.

Rooms in most hotels will have regular plug sockets but the bathrooms will only have two-pronged European-style sockets for shavers. North American visitors will need both plug adaptors and voltage converters for appliances such as laptops, hairdryers and phone chargers, while most other visitors will need only plug adaptors.

DIRECTORY

Personal Security and Health

London and other major cities in southern England are densely populated, with their share of social problems. However, other towns and cities in the South are not dangerous for visitors and it's unlikely that you will come across any violence or crime. If you do encounter difficulties, contact the police immediately. The National Health Service can be relied upon for both emergency treatment, for which there is no charge, and routine treatment, for which you may have to pay if your country has no reciprocal arrangement with England.

A Hampshire Fire and Rescue Service fire engine

DIRECTORY

Police and Emergencies

Accident and Emergency (A&E) Departments
w nhs.uk (for your nearest unit)

Emergency Services
Tel 999 (24 hours)

Police Non-Emergency Service
Tel 101 (24 hours)

Outdoors

Royal National Lifeboat Institution (RLNI)
w rnli.org

Medical Treatment

British Dental Association (BDA)
w bda.org

NHS 111 Service
Tel 111 (24 hours)
w nhs.uk

Police and Emergencies

If you have been the victim of a robbery or an assault, contact the police; call the **Emergency Services** if the offender is still on the scene, or the **Police Non-Emergency Service** if the crime has already taken place. Calling the Emergency Services will also put you in touch with the fire, ambulance and – along the coast – the HM Coastguard rescue service. The NHS website lists the details of all **Accident and Emergency (A&E) Departments** in the UK.

Personal Property

Report lost or stolen property at the nearest police station or call the Police Non-Emergency Service. For a theft, ensure you get a crime reference number, which will be required to make a claim on your insurance. For lost or stolen passports, also contact your country's embassy or consulate. All of the main bus and railway stations have lost property offices.

Make sure your possessions are adequately insured before you travel, and never leave them unattended in public places or on display in your hotel room. Keep your valuables concealed, especially in crowded places. Stay away from deserted and unfamiliar places at night, and always use licensed taxis.

Outdoors

Be careful around the sea – it can be dangerous. Currents can suddenly sweep people, especially children, out to sea, and inflatables can drift easily in a breeze, so tie them securely on the shore. Never enter the water when a red warning flag is flying. If you see someone in trouble, dial 999 and ask for the coastguard. Not all beaches are supervised by a lifeguard. To find those that are, visit the **Royal National Lifeboat Institution (RNLI)** website.

If you are walking along clifftops, stay away from the edge, which can be slippery. There are ticks on wooded heathland – such as the New Forest (see p97) and Exmoor (see pp122–3) – which can carry Lyme disease, so wear long sleeves and trousers, tucked into socks, and use insect repellent when walking in these areas. If you pick up a tick on your skin, seek medical help. Unless you are experienced at identifying fungi, do not pick and eat mushrooms.

Pharmacy sign

Medical Treatment

A wide range of over-the-counter drugs are sold in England. Many medicines, however, are available only with a doctor's prescription. If you are likely to need medication, either bring it with you or ask your doctor to write out the generic name of the drug.

If you are entitled to an NHS prescription, you will be charged a standard rate; if not, you will be charged the full cost of the drug. Remember to ask for a receipt to support any subsequent insurance claim. Some pharmacies are open until midnight; contact your local hospital for a list. For non-emergency medical problems, call the **NHS 111 Service**, or consult a pharmacist.

If you see a dentist in England, you will have to pay. To find NHS and private dentists near you, visit the **British Dental Association (BDA)** website.

Banking and Currency

Although people now tend to buy most things with credit and debit cards, visitors will still find it useful to carry some cash. The high-street banks usually offer the best rates, commission-free, for currency exchange, and cash machines (ATMs) are readily available at banks and elsewhere. Before using one of the many privately owned bureaux de change found in major airports, railway stations and tourist areas, check commission, handling and minimum charges.

Visitors at the Travelex Currency Exchange counter near the Tower of London

Bureaux de Change

Private bureaux de change may be more conveniently located and have more flexible opening hours than banks, but rates of exchange vary and charges can be high. **Moneycorp** and **Travelex** all have branches across southern England and usually offer good exchange facilities, as do many main branches of the **Post Office** *(see p207)*.

Banks

Every large town and city in the south of England has a branch of at least one of these five banks: **Barclays**, **Lloyds**, **HSBC**, **NatWest** and **Royal Bank of Scotland (RBS)**. Banking hours vary but most are open 9am to 5pm Monday to Friday. Main branches open on Saturday mornings too. Banks close on public holidays, although **Metro Bank** offers longer opening times, including Saturday afternoons, Sundays and most public holidays.

If you run out of funds or need money quickly, family or friends can use their own credit or debit cards on the **Western Union** website to transfer up to £800 for collection at any one of their many agent locations.

ATMs

Most banks have an ATM, from which you can obtain money with a debit or credit card and your PIN *(see p192)*. Cash machines can also be found in some supermarkets, shopping centres and post offices, and in petrol, train and London Tube stations. Some ATMs may charge for cash withdrawals (typically £1.70 per transaction). **American Express** cards have a handling charge for each transaction of 3 per cent or £3 (whichever is greater). Be vigilant while using ATMs as there have been some incidences of card crime.

A typical ATM for HSBC, one of Britain's popular high-street banks

DIRECTORY

Bureaux de Change

Moneycorp
w moneycorp.com

Travelex
w travelex.co.uk

Banks

Barclays
w barclays.co.uk

HSBC
w hsbc.co.uk

Lloyds
w lloydsbank.com

Metro Bank
w metrobankonline.co.uk

NatWest
w personal.natwest.com

Royal Bank of Scotland (RBS)
w rbs.com

Western Union
w westernunion.com

ATMs

American Express
w americanexpress.com

Currency

FairFX Currency Card
w fairfx.com

Credit Cards

Throughout England credit cards are widely used. However, some small shops, guesthouses, markets and cafés may not accept them, so always check in advance of your purchase. Cards that are accepted are usually displayed on the windows of the establishment. England uses the "chip and PIN" system instead of a signature. A four-digit PIN is required, so check with your bank before you leave home. With a "contactless" card, you can pay for items costing £30 or less by placing your card on the terminal.

A credit card allows visitors to obtain cash advances up to the credit limit at any bank or ATM displaying the appropriate card sign. You will be charged the credit card company's interest rate for obtaining cash and may incur a currency exchange fee.

Currency

England's currency is the pound sterling (£), which is divided into 100 pence (p). Paper banknotes are gradually being replaced with ones made from polymer, a more durable material. The new £5 note was issued in September 2016. There are no exchange controls in England, so you may bring in and take out as much cash as you like. Many large stores in the UK accept payments in US dollars and Euros, but often at a poor exchange rate.

The safest alternative to carrying large amounts of cash is a pre-paid or stored value card, which is both economical and user friendly. Load the card before leaving home, then use it to buy goods or withdraw cash from an ATM when in England. You can cancel it if it is lost or stolen. Among those available are the Travelex Cash Passport and **FairFX Currency Card**.

Although safe, traveller's cheques are no longer popular – they incur hefty charges, are rarely accepted by retailers and have been superseded by cards.

Banknotes

English notes are produced in denominations of £50, £20, £10 and £5. Some shops may refuse the larger notes, so always try to get small denominations.

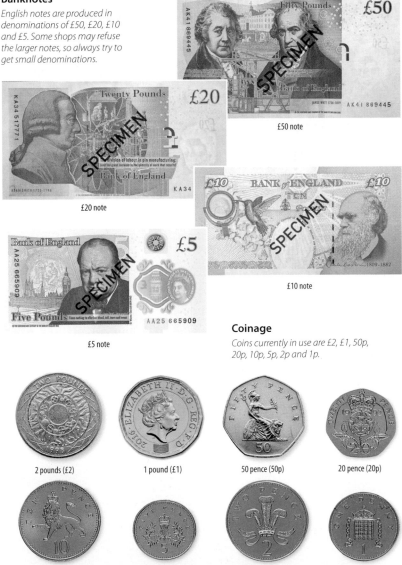

£50 note

£20 note

£10 note

£5 note

Coinage

Coins currently in use are £2, £1, 50p, 20p, 10p, 5p, 2p and 1p.

2 pounds (£2)

1 pound (£1)

50 pence (50p)

20 pence (20p)

10 pence (10p)

5 pence (5p)

2 pence (2p)

1 penny (1p)

Communications and Media

The UK has excellent communication systems. The landline network is efficient and modestly priced, although very cheap international calls can be made by using override providers, firms that give you an access number that you dial first. Keep in mind that hotels often charge more than the standard rate for all phone calls. For mobile devices with no pre-arranged plan, a UK SIM is often the answer. Visitors will find competitive SIM-only deals (including data-only for tablets) in most high-street phone shops. Alternatively, you can avoid expensive data roaming by using social media apps via the free Wi-Fi offered in many establishments. By arrangement, mail can be sent to you poste restante for collection from many UK post offices.

Public Telephones

With the increase in mobile phone ownership, there has been a decrease in the number of public telephones. You can usually find them in airports and railway stations. The minimum cost of a call is 60p and you can pay with coins, a credit or debit card, or a prepaid phonecard. Credit card calls are charged at a higher rate.

Mobile Phones

Mobile network coverage is widespread in England, and every high street has at least one mobile-phone shop. The most common brands are **Vodafone, O2, EE, Three** and **Carphone Warehouse**.

The UK networks use the 900 or 1800 GSM system, so visitors from the US (where the systems are 800 or 1900 MHz band) will need to ensure their phones are compatible or acquire a tri- or quad-band device through their service provider.

You may need to get your home network operator to enable your roaming capability before you travel. Keep in mind while abroad, you will be charged for the calls you receive as well as the calls you make; in addition, you have to pay a substantial premium for the international leg of the call. Unless you have a pre-arranged package, data-roaming charges can be very expensive, so it is advisable to disable this feature. A cheaper option is to purchase a SIM card locally and top it up with credit.

This will allow you to use a local mobile-phone network, as long as your handset is suitable and not locked to another network.

Available from post offices and mobile phone companies, prepaid phonecards can help to save money, particularly on international calls from mobiles and landlines. The cards (£5–20) are simple to use, with access and PIN codes, and expire after 30–90 days. Unlike some, the **Post Office Phonecard** has no hidden charges.

Override Providers

If you plan to make a small number of international calls on your trip, override providers can cut the cost of your calls. One of the cheapest services in the UK is **18185**. Before you travel, set up an account online. Then, before you make your call from the UK, remember to dial 18185 before entering the international number.

Internet

Smartphones and tablets have revolutionized Internet access for travellers and exchanges of emails and SMS messages are now sent as standard. Most social media apps now enable free messages and calls anywhere in the world. Most locally available SIMs include a data allowance, and free Wi-Fi is available in all kinds of different places, such as hotels, stores, restaurants, coffee shops, stations and airports. Free Internet access is usually available in libraries, though you may have to book a time slot.

Internet cafés usually charge by the minute and printing always costs extra. Most offer a VoiP (Voice over Internet Protocol) facility to those with their own accounts and many provide a headset if you do not have your own.

Postal Services

Stamps can be bought at many outlets, including supermarkets, petrol stations and stationery shops. When writing to a UK address, include the postcode, which can be obtained from **Royal Mail**. Within the UK, mail can be sent first or second class (the latter is cheaper and takes longer) or, for anything urgent or valuable, by Special Delivery (which guarantees the arrival time, has to be signed for on delivery and can be tracked online). The price of postage depends on the size and weight of your letter and package. For more information, visit the Royal Mail and **Post Office** websites.

Customers enjoying free Wi-Fi access at a coffee shop in London

A traditional post office with postcards for sale in Cornwall

Large urban post offices have a poste restante service, where letters can be collected. All correspondence should be addressed to the recipient at Poste Restante, followed by the address of the relevant post office branch. To collect your post, you will have to show your passport or another form of official identification. Overseas post is kept for one month.

Main post office branches offer various mail services, but there are also small branches in newsagents, grocery stores and general information centres. Post offices are usually open from 9am to 5:30pm Monday to Friday, and until 12:30pm on Saturday (sometimes longer).

Newspapers

British national newspapers generally fall into two categories: broadsheet papers, such as *The Times* and *The Guardian*; and tabloids, which are heavy on gossip, such as the *Daily Mail*, *The Sun* or the *Daily Mirror*. The weekend newspapers, more expensive than dailies, are packed with supplements on the arts, entertainment, travel, listings and reviews. Free newspapers, with an emphasis on celebrity gossip, are given away at railway and Tube stations in London. Local papers are available across the South Coast, including the

Dorset Echo and the *Cornish Guardian*. Many newspapers can now be read online.

Television and Radio

All television in the UK is now digital. The state-run **BBC** (British Broadcasting Corporation) has eight national TV channels, several regional channels (including many covering the South Coast) and a reputation for making some of the world's best television. Its commercial rivals include **ITV**, **Channel 4** and **Channel 5**. ITV is known for its soap operas and game shows; Channel 4 shows reality and chat shows; and Channel 5 relies on US imports and TV movies. There are more than 60 freeview TV channels, including high-definition ones (depending on area), and many hotels have hundreds of national and international channels via subscription services.

The BBC's radio stations range from pop music on **Radio 1** (97.6 FM) to current affairs and drama on **Radio 4** (92.5 FM). There are also many local commercial radio stations, such as the South Coast's **SAM FM** (106.6 MHz FM).

Full TV and radio schedules appear regularly in newspapers and listings magazines; you can also find them online.

The Times, one of England's national newspapers

TRAVEL INFORMATION

Visitors to the South Coast of England have a choice of options for travelling to the region. A wide selection of air carriers link the south of England to the rest of Europe, North and South America, Australasia and Asia. Coach travel is a cheap, if rather slow and uncomfortable, form of transport from Europe, while travelling by train has been transformed thanks to the Channel Tunnel. Travelling within southern England is also easy. There is an extensive network of roads linking all parts of the South Coast, and hiring a car is a convenient way of exploring. The railway network is efficient and far-reaching, especially from London. Coaches also cover most of the area and are the cheapest, but slowest, option.

Arriving by Air

There are a number of airports in southern England. The largest is **Heathrow**, west of London. Served by leading airlines and with direct flights to and from most major cities, it is one of the world's busiest international airports and a principal European hub. **Gatwick** in the south is the other international airport in the region. Heathrow has five terminals and Gatwick has two, so before you fly, check the terminal you need to get to. **London City** is in the heart of the capital and **Stansted** and **Luton** are located north of the city, with good transport to the centre. **Bristol** and **Southampton** are smaller regional airports with regular flights from Europe.

Most of England's largest airports have excellent facilities. Security is strict, so it may take time to get through passport control and customs. It is important never to leave your luggage unattended.

British Airways flies from most of the world's biggest cities. Other British international airlines include **Virgin Atlantic**, with routes from the USA and the Far East, and **Flybe**, which flies from Western Europe. American airlines offering scheduled services to Britain include **Delta**, **United Airlines** and **American Airlines**. From Canada, the main carrier is **Air Canada**. From Australasia, the national carriers **Qantas** and **Air New Zealand** vie with several Eastern rivals, including **Emirates**.

Passengers standing in a queue waiting to board a National Express airport coach

The no-frills budget airlines **easyJet** and **Ryanair** fly to England from Europe, Morocco and Israel, and offer exceptionally cheap flights, especially if you book well in advance. Check their restrictions though.

Transport from the Airport

London's international airports are well-connected and transport to and from them is efficient. The most convenient form of door-to-door travel is a taxi, but it is also the most expensive. Traffic congestion can slow down taxis, buses and coaches (although the latter two are much cheaper), but designated lanes mean they are not held up for long in London.

Visitors arriving at Heathrow can also take the Underground (see p212) or the **Heathrow Express** fast train to Paddington Station. Those arriving at Gatwick can take the **Gatwick Express** to London Victoria or local services, which are cheaper and can be almost as fast. There's also the reliable, fast **Stansted Express** to Liverpool Street.

National Express (see p211) coaches provide good direct connections from major airports to many British destinations, and run a regular service between Heathrow and Gatwick.

Arriving by Ferry

Ferries can be convenient and economical for those travelling by car or on foot. Services operate from several ports on the European mainland and have good link-ups with international coach companies. Car and passenger ferry services link six South Coast ports to those in Northern France and Spain. Fares vary according to season and route, but early booking means big savings.

Dover is the busiest port, with frequent services from France: **DFDS Seaways** run ferries from Dunkerque and Boulogne and **P&O Ferries** offer services from Calais. There are also ferry services from Spain: **Brittany Ferries** travel

Virgin Atlantic Airbus 320 at Heathrow Airport, London

to Plymouth and Portsmouth from Santander. Crossing times vary from 90 minutes on the Calais–Dover route to 24 hours on sailings from Spain. Cabins are available on overnight sailings.

Arriving by Train

The Channel Tunnel connects England to Europe via the **Eurostar** (for train passengers) and the **Eurotunnel/Le Shuttle** (for vehicles). Eurostar costs much the same as flying, but is more convenient (it takes less than 2 hours and 30 minutes from Paris to central London) and less environmentally damaging. Passengers on buses and in cars board a freight train run by Eurotunnel that takes 35 minutes to travel between Calais and Folkestone. For Eurostar rail travellers, there are several direct services from Brussels, Paris, Lille and Calais to Ashford, Ebbsfleet and St Pancras, and from Disneyland Paris, Lyon and the South of France to Ashford and St Pancras.

Information and bookings for connecting trains from other parts of Europe can be found on the **Voyages-sncf** website. If you plan to do a lot of train travel around Britain, it is worth buying a rail pass. **Rail Europe**

and **BritRail** (see p211) offer several options covering rail travel for just a few days or up to two weeks.

Arriving by Coach

If you have time and want to stop off en route, travelling by coach can be convenient. Your ticket will include the cost of the ferry or Channel Tunnel.

Green Travel

With big congestion problems, driving in British cities is not advisable. Instead, make use of the extensive public transport network. Most towns or cities are served by trains and/or buses, and services tend to be fairly regular. However, trains in Britain can be overcrowded at peak

times, and they are often expensive. Booking tickets in advance can bring the cost down. The **GroupSave** ticket scheme allows discounted rail travel for groups of three or four, and various other discounts are available with a travel card. The **National Trust** (see p202) offers some incentives, including discounted entry to those who use public transport when visiting some of their sites.

The National Cycle Network, created by **Sustrans**, provides more than 20,000 km (12,427 miles) of cycle paths across Britain. A bike can be taken on most off-peak trains, but you may have to book a spot for it. Check before you travel. For more information on environmentally friendly travel options, contact Sustrans.

Cyclists riding beside the Torridge Estuary in Appledore, North Devon

DIRECTORY

Arriving by Air

Air Canada
w aircanada.com

Air New Zealand
w airnewzealand.co.uk

American Airlines
w americanairlines.co.uk

Bristol
w bristolairport.co.uk

British Airways
w britishairways.com

Delta
w delta.com

easyJet
w easyjet.com

Emirates
w emirates.com/uk

Flybe
w flybe.com

Gatwick
w gatwickairport.com

Heathrow
w heathrow.com

London City
w londoncityairport.com

Luton
w london-luton.co.uk

Qantas
w qantas.com

Ryanair
w ryanair.com

Southampton
w southamptonairport.com

Stansted
w stanstedairport.com

United Airlines
w united.com

Virgin Atlantic
w virginatlantic.com

Transport from the Airport

Gatwick Express
w gatwickexpress.com

Heathrow Express
w heathrowexpress.com

Stansted Express
w stanstedexpress.com

Arriving by Ferry

Brittany Ferries
w brittany-ferries.co.uk

DFDS Seaways
w dfdsseaways.co.uk

P&O Ferries
w poferries.com

Arriving by Train

Eurostar
w eurostar.com

Eurotunnel/ Le Shuttle
w eurotunnel.com

Rail Europe
w raileurope.com

Voyages-sncf
w uk.voyages-sncf.com

Green Travel

GroupSave
w nationalrail.co.uk

Sustrans
w sustrans.org.uk

Getting Around England's South Coast

No other method of transport will give you as much flexibility to explore the South Coast as a car. A large network of toll-free motorways and trunk roads ensures that travelling around the region is easy and enjoyable. Trains are also useful if you are travelling to towns and cities. Mainline trains are fast and comfortable, but the popular routes tend to get booked during peak season, so it is advisable to reserve your seat in advance. The cheapest ways to get around are by coach and regional buses, though consider them only if you have time.

Winding roads in the picturesque countryside of Dartmoor, Devon

By Car

To drive here you need a current driving licence. You must also carry proof of ownership or a rental agreement and insurance documents in your vehicle. It is illegal to drive without third-party insurance; it is best to buy fully comprehensive insurance.

Cars in England drive on the left and distances are measured in miles. Speed limits are 50–65 kmph (20–40 mph) in built-up areas, 97 kmph (60 mph) on single carriageways and 110 kmph (70 mph) on motorways or dual carriageways.

Navigation

A good road map is a valuable resource, especially as GPS does not always work in rural areas. The AA (Automobile Association) and RAC (Royal Automobile Club) have excellent motoring atlases. The Ordnance Survey series is also a good option.

Motorways are marked with an "M" followed by their identifying number. "A" roads, sometimes dual carriageways, are main routes, while secondary "B" roads are often less congested

and more enjoyable. Rural areas are crisscrossed by a web of tiny lanes. Directional signs are colour-coded: blue for motorways, green for major routes and white for minor routes.

Rules of the Road

It is mandatory to wear seatbelts and illegal to use a mobile phone while driving unless it is hands-free. Do not drink and drive: the laws are strict and penalties are high. The Highway Code, available on the **Department for Transport** website, is a guide to current regulations, traffic signs and the legal alcohol limit.

Advisory or warning signs are usually red and white triangles, with easy-to-understand pictograms. Look out for electronic warning signs on motorways.

Parking

Pay and display and parking meters operate during working hours (usually 8am–6:30pm Mon–Sat). Most accept coins, but sometimes you need to pay over the phone or via an app. Cities often have "park and ride" schemes, where you take a bus from an out-of-city car park into the centre. Avoid double yellow or red lines at all times; single yellow lines mean you can park outside the hours of control. Illegally parked cars will be given a ticket, clamped or towed away. If in doubt, find a car park, usually signed by a blue "P". You should never leave valuables in your car.

Breakdown Services

England's main motoring organizations are the **AA** and the **RAC**. They provide 24-hour breakdown assistance for members and visitors belonging to overseas motoring organizations with reciprocal arrangements. The organizations can be contacted by mobile or from roadside SOS phones.

Car Hire and Ride-Sharing

Hiring a car in England can be expensive, and is usually cheaper if arranged from home. Details of car-hire companies at airports are on the **VisitBritain** website (see p202). Reputable car-hire companies include **Avis**, **Hertz**, **Europcar** and **Budget**.

Companies usually require a credit card number, and you will need your driving licence and passport to collect the car. Most companies will not hire cars to novice drivers, and may have age limits (normally 21–74). Most offer their own insurance cover, and their charges include 24-hour breakdown assistance.

An AA rescue truck transporting a car

Lift-sharing is now a common practice. **BlaBlaCar** is a reliable carpooling service.

By Rail

England's South Coast is covered by six main train operating companies: **Southern**, **South West Trains**, **Southeastern**, **CrossCountry**, **Thameslink** and **Great Western Railway (GWR)**, which runs the Night Riviera Sleeper to Cornwall. It is possible to travel across the region via train, but most journeys will involve changes and possibly travelling via London. The main stations serving the South in London are Paddington, Victoria, Waterloo, St Pancras and London Bridge.

Many rural tracks were made redundant in the mid-20th century. However, some short, picturesque sections have been restored by enthusiasts. Outstanding rides in the South are the **Bluebell Railway**, which operates steam trains between Sheffield Park and East Grinstead, and the **St Ives Bay Line**, linking St Erth and St Ives.

The railway is generally reliable, though it is best to check online before travelling. If you are disabled and need assistance, call the train operator in advance.

Paddington station in London, designed by Isambard Kingdom Brunel

Tickets and Rail Passes

Train tickets can be bought online, by phone and at railway stations. An advance ticket is usually cheaper than one bought on the day. You can buy tickets directly from the rail provider, **National Rail**, or third-party online portals, such as **Trainline** or **Raileasy**, which may offer discounted fares. Children aged 5 to 15 pay half fare; two children under the age of 5 travel free for every fare-paying adult. If you do not have a valid ticket, inspectors can levy on-the-spot fines.

If you plan to travel extensively by train, consider buying a rail pass. **BritRail** offers three passes covering the South – BritRail England, BritRail London Plus (including southeast England) and BritRail South West.

A **Network Railcard** is an economical option if you are making numerous trips. The railcard can be bought online or at a station within the area.

By Coach

The largest coach operator in England is **National Express**, which serves several hundred destinations in southern England and offers online discounts. It is advisable to book ahead for the more popular routes. **Megabus** also offers tickets to a number of South Coast destinations from as little as £1 (plus 50p booking fee).

For coach tours, from day trips to longer excursions including guided tours, contact the **Coach Tourism Council** or local tourist offices. You can also book directly from overseas through a specialist travel agent.

By Regional Buses

Buses are run either by private companies or local authorities, and there is usually just one operator – the driver – on board. Always check routes, schedules and fares at the local tourist office or bus station. Disabled visitors should note that not all buses are equipped for wheelchairs.

DIRECTORY

Rules of the Road	Europcar	Southeastern	National Rail
Department for Transport W gov.uk	W europcar.co.uk **Hertz** W hertz.co.uk	Tel 0345 3227021 W southeasternrailway. co.uk	W nationalrail.co.uk **Network Railcard** W network-railcard. co.uk
Breakdown Services	**By Rail**	**Southern** Tel 0345 1272920 W southernrailway. com	**Raileasy** W raileasy.co.uk
AA Tel 0800 887 766 W theaa.com	**Bluebell Railway** Tel 01825 720800 W bluebell-railway. co.uk	**South West Trains** Tel 0345 6000650 W southwesttrains. co.uk	**Trainline** W thetrainline.com
RAC Tel 0333 2000 999 W rac.co.uk	**CrossCountry** W crosscountrytrains. co.uk	**Thameslink** Tel 0345 0264700 W thameslinkrailway. com	**By Coach**
Car Hire	**Great Western Railway (GWR)** Tel 0345 7000125 W gwr.com		**Coach Tourism Council** W coachtourism association.co.uk
Avis W avis.co.uk		**Tickets and Rail Passes**	
Budget W budget.co.uk	**St Ives Bay Line** Tel 01752 584777 W greatscenicrailways. co.uk		**Megabus** W megabus.com
BlaBla Car W blablacar.co.uk		**BritRail** W britrail.com	**National Express** W nationalexpress.com

Getting Around London

Public transport in London is extensive, efficient and busy. The city and its suburbs are served by the Underground, buses and railway, all coordinated by Transport for London (TfL). There is a common ticketing system for all TfL transport in the form of the Oyster Card, which affords passengers reduced fares. Taxis are easily available on the street and at ranks in the centre. Among the best ways to see London are by bicycle and on foot, though try to avoid the rush hours from 8am to 9:30am and 5pm to 6:30pm. Downloading real-time apps such as Citymapper can help you navigate and plan your routes.

Underground and Train

The Underground network (also known as the Tube) is run by **TfL** and has six main fare zones with 270 stations, each marked with the London Underground logo. Trains run every day, except Christmas Day, from about 5:30am until just after midnight. With the launch of the Night Tube in 2016, some lines now run for 24 hours on Fridays and Saturdays. Fewer trains run on Sundays and public holidays.

An Oyster card

The 11 Underground lines, the Overground (a suburban rail network) and the Docklands Light Railway (DLR), the driverless train system linking the East End suburbs with the City, are colour-coded and full maps are posted at every station, while condensed maps are displayed in all trains.

Tickets and Travelcards can be bought at stations, but paper tickets are expensive and most travellers use a contactless debit or credit card, or an Oyster Card, a prepaid electronic card that can be topped up for use on all forms of TfL transport. Using an Oyster Card or one of the several mobile payment applications are the cheapest ways of travelling on Tubes and buses, but passengers must tap in and tap out at stations or they will be charged the maximum fare. Visitors should note that not all contactless payment cards issued outside the UK can be used; those that can include American Express, Visa, MasterCard and Maestro.

There is a dedicated Visitor Oyster Card that can be bought at Tube stations and some railway stations, and at Oyster Ticket Stops. It can also be bought online and from some outlets abroad.

If you are visiting for a day, opt for a paper ticket if you are just making one or two journeys, or a Travelcard if you only plan to use public transport a few times within a single day. If you use an Oyster Card or contactless card and make multiple journeys on the same day, TfL will automatically cap the cost of your journey when you have been charged a certain number of fares (paper tickets are not capped). Check the TfL website to see if a Travelcard or capped Oyster fares will be more cost effective for you.

Buses

Buses in London come in all shapes and sizes, with automatic doors and spacious interiors for wheelchairs and buggies. There are driver-operated double-deckers, sleek environmentally friendly New Routemaster buses and smaller single-deck buses that are able to weave in and out of traffic more easily. The iconic old Routemaster still exists in London, but only as a Heritage bus on route number 15, linking Trafalgar Square with Tower Hill.

Visitors should note that bus fares cannot be paid in cash. One-day passes can be bought from Oyster Ticket Stops. You can also use your TfL Travelcard, Oyster or contactless payment card. The standard pay-as-you-go fare of £1.50, using an Oyster or contactless payment card, applies to all buses displaying the red roundel. However you pay, touch your pass or card on the yellow card reader as you enter the bus. You do not need to touch out when you leave. If you need to changes buses you can make a second journey for free within an hour of touching in on the first bus.

Buses generally run from 5am until 12:30am, with night services available on many major routes from around midnight until 5am. Night buses are pre-fixed with the letter "N", and day passes are valid on these buses until 4:30am. Be careful when travelling alone late at night, when there may be few other passengers on board, and sit downstairs near the driver.

All main bus stops have illuminated signs displaying the number of the next buses that are due and their times. Destinations are shown on the front of buses. For routes and timetables, check TfL's website or the **Citymapper** app.

At bus stops, the driver will not halt unless you signal that you want to get on or off. If you

London's famous red double-decker buses in Parliament Square

want to board, raise your arm as the bus approaches; if you want to get off, ring the bell once before your stop.

London has bus lanes, intended to bypass traffic jams. These can be effective, but your journey could still take a long time. Schedules are hard to keep to, so regard timetables as advisory.

Driving

Driving in central London is discouraged, with a congestion charge in force. If you drive or park within the congestion zone from Monday to Friday (7am to 6pm), you will be charged £11.50, which is to be paid online or by text before midnight that day. Not paying the charge will lead to a heavy fine. See TfL's website for more information. Parking in central London is expensive and controlled to prevent congestion.

Taxis

London's famous black cabs are almost as much of an institution as its big red buses, though you will now see them in a variety of different colours or covered in advertising. They are the safest taxis to use in London since all the drivers are licensed and have undergone strict tests. All licensed cabs must display an orange "Taxi" sign, which is lit up whenever they are free. The newer cabs are equipped to carry wheelchairs. If a cab stops for you in London, it must by law take you anywhere within a radius of 10 km (6 miles) so long as it is within the Metropolitan Police District. This includes most of London and Heathrow Airport.

All licensed cabs have meters that start ticking as soon as the driver accepts your custom. Most drivers expect a tip of between 10 and 15 per cent of the fare. If you have a complaint, note the serial number found in the back of the cab.

Visitors are advised not to use unlicensed minicabs as they may be mechanically unsound or uninsured. Licensed minicabs will always display a TfL sticker. Never accept any offer of an unbooked minicab ride in the street.

A tour guide with cyclists beside the Royal Artillery Memorial

Guided Bus Tours

Weather permitting, a trip on an open-topped double-decker bus is a good way to see the city. **The Original Tour** and **Big Bus Tours** offer hop-on, hop-off services, with tickets valid for 24 or 48 hours.

River Buses

Regular River Bus services are operated by **MBNA Thames Clippers** on five routes from 20 piers between Putney and Woolwich. You can use a contactless card or Oyster card to pay.

Cycling

Cycling is one of the greenest ways of getting around London. Santander Cycles is a public bicycle-sharing scheme, with distinctive red bikes available for hire at docking stations across the capital (check the TfL website). **London Bicycle Tour Company** rents out bikes and organizes bicycle tours.

Traffic in London is not very cyclist-friendly, and is definitely not for beginners or the out-of-practice cyclist. Keep to the cycle lanes, where available, never leave your bike unlocked, and always wear a helmet.

Walking

Although it is large, London can be enjoyably explored on foot. Remember that traffic drives on the left, and do take care crossing the road. There are two types of pedestrian crossing: striped zebra crossings and push-button crossings at traffic lights. At a zebra crossing, traffic should stop for you, but at push-button crossings, cars will not stop until the green man lights up.

The TfL website features seven suggested city walking routes, and you can book a range of walking tours through **VisitLondon** (see p195). Blue Badge tour guides can also be booked for special tours through **Guide London**.

(see p195)

DIRECTORY

Underground

TfL
Tel 0343 222 1234
W tfl.gov.uk

Buses

Citymapper
W citymapper.com

Guided Bus Tours

Big Bus Tours
W eng.bigbustours.com

The Original Tour
Tel 020 8877 1722
W theoriginaltour.com

River Buses

MBNA Thames Clippers
Tel 020 7001 2200
W thamesclippers.com

Cycling

London Bicycle Tour Company
Tel 020 7928 6838
W londonbicycle.com

Walking

Guide London
Tel 020 7611 2545
W guidelondon.org.uk

General Index

Acknowledgments

Dorling Kindersley would like to thank the following people whose help and assistance contributed to the preparation of this book.

Main Contributors
Ros Belford, Leonie Glass, Matthew Hancock, Nick Rider, Joe Staines, Amanda Tomlin

Fact Checker
Kate Hughes

Proofreader
Christine Stroyan

Indexer
Hilary Bird

Design and Editorial
Publishing Director Georgina Dee
Publisher Vivien Antwi
Managing Editor Sally Schafer
Managing Art Editors Sunita Gahir, Marisa Renzullo
Executive Editors Ankita Awasthi Tröger, Michelle Crane
Project Editor Sophie Adam
Senior Executive Cartographic Editor Casper Morris
Executive DTP Designer Jason Little
Jacket Designer Richard Czapnik
Production Controller Poppy Werder-Harris

Picture Credits
a = above; b = below/bottom; c = centre; f = far; l = left; r = right; t = top

The publisher would like to thank the following individuals, organizations, companies and picture libraries for their kind permission to reproduce their photographs:

123RF.com: Helen Hotson 105bc

Alamy Stock Photo: A-plus Image Bank 149bc; Per Andersen 109cb; Marie-Louise Avery 30c; Avpics 47tc; Simon Balson 126cl; Banana Pancake 65cb; Luise Berg-Ehlers 138bc; James Boardman 30cla; Ian Bottle 113br; Chris Brignell 143tl; Kevin Britland 165bc, 183cb; Adam Burton 144bc; Ian M Butterfield (Sussex) 78br; Paul Carstairs 54bl; Paul Chambers 100clb; David Cheshire 127cr; Carolyn Clarke 44cla; Ashley Cooper pics 134clb; Rob Cousins 182cla; David Crausby 48bl; Tim Cuff 137bc; Ian Dagnall 18tl, 76tl, 135br, 172br; Ian Dagnall Commercial Collection 11br, 13cb; Dbphots 95br; Kathy deWitt 204cla; Stephen Dorey 21tc; Michael Dutton 122cla; Patrick Eden 5cr, 187br, 196ca; eye35 10br; eye35.pix 54cla, 126br; Fotomaton 66bl; Tony French 170–171; Darren Galpin 145br; Gapper/Creative 28c; Kevin Gatrell 150cr; David Gee 93cl; Lisa Geoghegan 26tr; Dave Gibbeson 150tl; Paul Glendell 116cr, 139bl; David Gowans 136br; Tim Graham 19tc, 70bl; Stan Green 96tl, 105tc, 113tc; Paul Grover 31cla; Simon Hadley 149tl; Andrew Harker 106tl; Chris Harris 38–39; Andrew Hasson 12br; Nick Hawkes 160tr; Paul Heinrich 24tr; Hemis 53br, 58c, 207tl; Heritage Image Partnership Ltd 84ca; Marc Hill © Tim Shaw. All rights reserved/© DACS 2016 152, 210cla; Jim Holden 71crb; Angelo Hornak 59br, 84br; Peter Horree 63cra; Scott Hortop News 30br; Helen Hotson 117clb, 159cra, 159bc, 198–199; Michael Hudson 100cr, 101crb; Yanice Idir 192bl; ImageBROKER 89cb; Incamerastock 104tr, 207clb; International Photobank 97bc; Eric James 107bl; John James 203crb; Carolyn Jenkins 150bl, 201tl; Tim Jones 166cr, Justin Kase z12z 210br; John Keates 24cl; Lenscap 82clb; David Lichtneker 117cra; Loop Images Ltd 2–3; Paul Martin 159cl; Terry Mathews 151br; Neil McAllister 125tl; Shaun McCaughan 143cr; Malcolm McDougall Photography 29bc; Malcolm McHugh 87c, 115bc; John McKellar 157bl; Paul Melling Barbara Hepworth Museum, St Ives 168crb; MH Coast 209cr; Stephen Miller 26clb; Beata Moore 97cr; Robert Murray 161clb; The National Trust Photolibrary 25crb, 69bc, 71tr, 106br, 107tl, 107ca, 107br, 118tl, 169cra, 183bc; newsphoto 47cr; Christopher Nicholson 123bl, 148tc; NobleIMAGES 92tr, 146–147, 163clb; NorthScape 117cla; Anne-Marie Palmer 95clb; David Pearson 193tc; Ian Pilbeam 101tl; Simon Reddy 169br, 182br, 183bl, 183br; Matthew Richardson 150clb; Chris Robbins 163cla; Robertharding 59cra, 88, 148bc, 153bc, 154cla, 163br; Grant Rooney 206br; Grant Rooney Premium 83bl; Alec Scaresbrook 196br; Peter Scholey 52tl, 55br, 57tr; Sheree Sedgbeer 143br; Alex Segre 55cra, 181br; Neil Setchfield 181cr; SFL Travel 128bc; Felix Shoughi 19c; Steve Speller 119tl; Kumar Sriskandan 125br; Slawek Staszczuk 83cra; Derek Stone 122cb; Rick Strange 77br; CountryCollection - Homer Sykes 165tc; Steve Taylor ARPS 123cra; Mark Thomas 82cla; Transport for London 201br; travelbild.com 41crb; travelibUK 25tl; Urbanbuzz 120br; Colin Varndell 22tr; Ivan Vdovin 74–75; VDWI Aviation 208bl; Vibrant Pictures 29cra; Bax Walker 81tr; Mike Walker 97tr; Tony Watson 71bc; Richard Wayman 126tr; Robin Weaver 96br; Westmacott 145cl; Kevin Wheal 121cr; Rob Wilkinson 20bl; funkyfood London - Paul Williams 98–99, 102cla, 125clb; Phil Wills 208cra; Ian Woolcock 135tr; Peter Worth 145tr; Justin Kase zninez 45bl; Justin Kase zsixz 213tr

AWL Images: Nature in Stock 41bl

The Beach at Bude: David Griffen Photography 190tr

Belle Tout Lighthouse: Rob Wassell 175tl

Bridgeman Images: The Wife of Bath, detail from The Canterbury Tales by Geoffrey Chaucer (c.1342–1400) Ellesmere Manuscript, facsimile edition, 1911, English

School, (15th century) (after)/Private Collection 73tc; Margate, c.1822 (w/c on paper), Turner, Joseph Mallord William (1775–1851)/Yale Center for British Art, Paul Mellon Collection, USA 76br; St Ives Harbour: February 1948, Heron, Patrick (1920–99)/Private Collection/ Photo © Peter Nahum at The Leicester Galleries, London/ © The Estate of Patrick Heron. All rights reserved/© DACS 2016 168br; Cornish smuggling scene, English School, (20th century)/ Private Collection/© Look and Learn 167tr; Royal Dipping, 1789 (coloured engraving), Nixon, John (1760–1818)/ Photo © Historic Royal Palaces/Claire Collins 114crb; The landing of the Romans in Britain, 54 BC (colour litho), Skelton, Joseph Ratcliffe (fl.1888–1916)/Private Collection/© Look and Learn 32

British Airways i360: 41br

Canterbury Cathedral: 72br

Chesil Rectory: 188bl

© DACS 2016: © The Estate of Patrick Heron. All rights reserved 168br; The Rites of Dionysus/© Tim Shaw. All rights reserved 152

Dean and Chapter of Westminster: 50clb; Jim Dyson/ Westminster Abbey 50cla, 51tl

Dorling Kindersley: Geoff Dann/Science Museum, London 62cra; Tim Draper/Rough Guides 142br, 164bc; Frank Greenaway 27cr, 27bl; Frank Greenaway/ Natural History Museum, London 26cra; Paul Hams 23fbr; Nigel Hicks/Prideaux Place 157tc; Dave King 27cl, 27cb, 27crb; Stephen Oliver 48tr, 48cl, 50tr, 51ca, 57crb; Rob Reichenfeld 23cr, 23ftr, 23fcra, 23fcrb, 72tl; Kim Sayer 27br; Tony Souter 121bl, 129cr; Matthew Ward 27tr

Dreamstime.com: Acceleratorhams 40cla, 90bl; Alanjeffery 79br; Alexirina27000 91br, 93tc, 111br, 166tl; Allouphoto 108; Altezza 48cla; Annacurnow 40crb; Arenaphotouk 111cra; Arndale 81bl; Anthony Baggett 35bc; Bargotiphotography 80tl; Gordon Bell 67tr; Rafael Ben-ari 60br; Arun Bhargava 94tl; Philip Bird 12cl, 73ca, 86ca, 87tc; boboling 129br; Martin Brayley 203cla; Dan Breckwoldt 49bl; Anthony Brown 125cra, 130tr, 131bc; Chris148 158bc; Claudiodivizia 49c; Mike Clegg 46cla; Paladuta Cornelia 63tl, 202tl; Cpphotoimages 22crb; Kristof Degreef 54br; Songquan Deng 41tr; Dennis Dolkens 20tr; Chris Dorney 61tr; Sarah Dowson 116tl, 120tl; Thomas Dutour 37bl; Mark Eaton 197tl; Andrew Emptage 131cr; Exflow 63bc; Alexey Fedorenko 64, 83cr; Filip Fuxa 77ca; Gavran333 182bl; Hel080808 101bc; Helen Hotson 10cla, 28cla, 78tr, 91tl, 142cl, 164tl; Wei Huang 45tr; Tadeusz Ibrom 87bc; Savo Ilic 116br; Irishka777

43bc, 54tr, 55crb; Irstone 55bl; Clare Jackson 16; Valerijs Jegorovs 67br, 68tc, 103br; Jjfarq 129cla, 130bl; Johnhill118 200cla; Aagje De Jong 156tl; Jorisvo 79tl, 80bc; Lali Kacharava 47br; Fenlio Kao 4tc; Denis Kelly 37c, 141bc; Patryk Kosmider 60tl, 114tl, 115ca; Kozlik5 117cr; Wendy Leber 31clb; Amanda Lewis 94c, 101c; Lymey 40tr, 137tl, 167c; Madrabothair 211tc; Maisna 61cr; Marbo 1c; Martinmates 55tr; Giuseppe Masci 212br; Mglyde 102bc; Micaelasanna 124tl; Mikocreative67 169bl; Nadia Mikushova 192cra; Ml12nan 61clb; David Morton 11tl; Luciano Mortula 59tc; Mrsacf 86bl; Nigel Nudds 106cla; Nui7711 62bc; Ohmaymay 72c; Dalina Rahman 58cla; Ian Redding 104bl; Michael Retallick 169cla; Guy Richards 33crb; Simonprbenson 17bc; Ludmila Smite 51bl; Christopher Smith 151crb; James Talbot 46bl; TasFoto 78clb; Tea 204br; Theclarkester 122br; Jennifer Thompson 26cla, 139cr; Peter Titmuss 95cla; Vicki Vale 194cla; Desislava Vasileva 212cla; Vlue 124bl; Vvoevale 31br; Shao-chun Wang 41tl; Keith Wheatley 70tr; Ian Woolcock 4crb, 5clb, 21cb, 40bl, 110bl, 112tc, 114bl, 116clb, 119br, 128cl, 129tc, 133bc, 136tl, 142bc, 154tr, 168tc; Bahadir Yeniceri 142tr

Driftwood Hotel: 179br

The Eden Project: 160cla, 160br, 161tl, 161cra

FLPA: Bill Broadhurst 121ca; Robert Canis 27tl; Erica Olsen 26bl

Getty Images: Stefano Baldini 34bl; Martin Barraud 69ca; Bettmann 35tr; Stefano Bianchetti 34crb; Adam Burton 121cl; Ashley Cooper 123tl; Culture Club 35crb, 68bl; DEA/A. DAGLI ORTI 156bl; Design Pics 59bc; Stephen Dorey 112br; W. & D. Downey 118bc; Epics 144tc; Leonardo da Vinci (Italian, 1452–1519), Virgin of the Rocks, 1495–1508, oil on panel, 189.5 x 120 cm (74.6 x 47.2 in), National Gallery, London./Fine Art 52br; Heritage Images 36tc, 85cla, 85cra; Hulton Archive 25cra; Robbie Jack - Corbis 18br, 28br, 194br; Bob Krist 158tl; Portrait of Queen Elizabeth I of England (The Ditchley portrait). Painting by Marcus Gheeraerts (Gerards or Geerards) the Younger (1561–1635) Circa 1592. 2,41 x1,52 m. National Portrait Gallery, London/ Leemage 53tc; Pawel Libera 42; Peter Macdiarmid 51cr; Jon Philpott Photography 140tr; 'Hastings', 19th century (1910). Artist: J M W Turner/Print Collector 8–9, 50bc, 85tc, 131tc, 140cb; Oli Scarff 182tr; Stock Montage 92bc; David C Tomlinson 71cra; Peter Unger 80cr; Universal Images Group 36bl; Ivan Vdovin 73bl

The Goods Shed: 183tl, 185tr

The Goring Hotel, London: 172ca, 174bc

J Sheekey Atlantic Bar: 184bl

Image courtesy of the Leach Pottery: Matthew Tyas 168c

Mary Evans Picture Library: 73cr

National Trust Images: John Bethell 167br

Ottolenghi, Islington: Keiko Oikawa 180cla

Pecorama: 136cl

The Pig Hotels: The Pig at Combe 178tr; The Pig on the Beach 173cr; The Pig, Brockenhurst 176tl

Robert Harding Picture Library: Adam Burton 13tl, 122tr, 132; Dan Burton 195tr; Craig Easton 141ca; Adam Woolfitt 33c

Rockfish, Dartmouth: 189tr

The Royal Crescent: 177br, 180crb

The Royal Mint: 205clb

The Royal Oak: 186tc

Royal Pavilion & Museums, Brighton & Hove: 82cr, 84tr

SuperStock: 34tc; Christopher L. Smith/age fotostock 151ca

Totnes Elizabethan Museum: WR Photography 138tr

The Trustees of the British Museum: 56cla, 57tl, 57c; Christy Graham 56tr; Peter Hayman 57bc; Nick Nicholls 56cl

Visit Cornwall: Dune Dreams Photography 155br; Paul Watts 162tl

Weald & Downland Open Air Museum: 86br

Winchester Cathedral: 93cr

Front Endpapers
Alamy Stock Photo: Marc Hill (fcla); Robertharding (tr). Dreamstime.com: Allouphoto (tl); Alexey Fedorenko (br). Robert Harding Picture Library: Adam Burton (bl)

Cover Picture Credits
Front Cover & Spine: Alamy Stock Photo: Chris Harris
Back Cover: Dreamstime.com: Justin Black (tc)

All other images © Dorling Kindersley
For further information see: www.dkimages.com

Special Editions of DK Travel Guides
DK Travel Guides can be purchased in bulk quantities at discounted prices for use in promotions or as premiums. We are also able to offer special editions and personalized jackets, corporate imprints, and excerpts from all of our books, tailored specifically to meet your own needs.

To find out more, please contact:
in the US **specialsales@dk.com**
in the UK **travelguides@uk.dk.com**
in Canada **specialmarkets@dk.com**
in Australia **penguincorporatesales@ penguinrandomhouse.com.au**

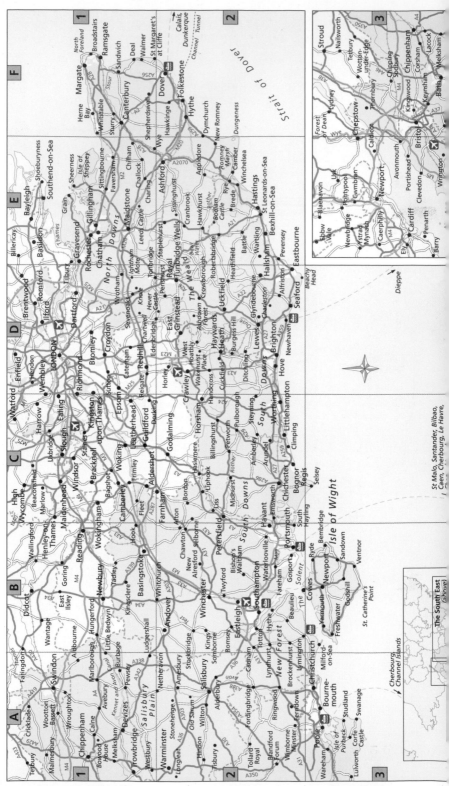